Patriotism and the Cross

Patriotism and the Cross

A Theology of Nationalism

Glen M. E. Duerr

RESOURCE *Publications* · Eugene, Oregon

PATRIOTISM AND THE CROSS
A Theology of Nationalism

Resource Publications
An Imprint of Wipf and Stock Publishers
199 W. 8th Ave., Suite 3
Eugene, OR 97401

www.wipfandstock.com

PAPERBACK ISBN: 978-1-5326-9187-4
HARDCOVER ISBN: 978-1-5326-9188-1
EBOOK ISBN: 978-1-5326-9189-8

This book is dedicated to my wife, Rebecca, and our children, Declan, Harper, and Camille.

Contents

Tables

Acknowledgments

The ACKNOWLEDGEMENTS SECTION OF a book is always a difficult task, somewhat akin to wedding or birthday invitations. There are multitudes of people that contribute to the life of a couple/person, but who gets an invite is often a question of memory—it certainly has shortcomings. That said, there are two people in particular that deserve special recognition. First, I would like to thank my department chair, Mark Caleb Smith at Cedarville University, for his encouragement to write this manuscript. Every faculty member at Cedarville is required or encouraged (depending on tenure status) to write an "integration paper" assessing how one's field or discipline of study can be integrated with Scripture. Mark first provoked my interest to write this book as a continuation of my integration paper but also as a contribution to the study of nationalism as seen through the lens of the Bible. Second, I would like to thank Pastor Tony Chester for his encouragement to give our "first fruits" to God in our respective vocations. Even though my academic work thus far has focused on nationalism, secession, and Supranationalism in great detail, I had scantly published on the topic of integrating these subjects to Scripture. One of the central goals of this point is to change that, for me to give the first fruits in my academic work to God. Let me start by thanking Resource Publications and Wipf and Stock for the opportunity to present these ideas to a wider community. In particular, I would like to thank Matthew Wimer for the invitation to publish, Calvin Jaffarian for his commitment to excellence throughout the editing process, Mike Surber for the front and back cover designs, and George Callihan and Caleb Shupe for their help along the way.

Additionally, I am very thankful to be part of a rich and vibrant academic community in the Department of History and Government. In particular, Kyung-Hwa (Christine) Kim and Frank Jenista have been wonderful colleagues and extremely valuable in their thinking about the issue of faith in the international arena. Numerous other colleagues in the department have also helped to encourage me through the years including J. Murray Murdoch, Bob Parr, Patrick Oliver, Marc Clauson, Dave Rich, Kevin Sims, Robert Vaughn, John Hart, Emily Ferkaluk, Jewerl Maxwell, Justin Lyons, Robert Clark, and Steve Meacham. Many friends throughout the wider faculty, at various points, also encouraged my work. I would like to single out Mark Owens for special gratitude here given his encouragement of this project.

Next, I would like to thank a number of very talented Research Assistants, then undergraduate students at Cedarville University: Kelly Parliament, Spencer Woody, Marcus Waterman, and Lauren Payne. Each one of them worked hard finding new and different definitions that are key factors in the start of each chapter. Two other Research Assistants, Sarah Schopps Rea and Jacob Mach were very helpful in their suggested edits for the first few chapters of this manuscript.

A special note is also due for five students who participated in the Washington D.C. semester in the fall of 2017, and agreed to read sections of this manuscript, and then debate the contours of my argument. They are Molly Bolender, Mae Dewhurst, Sarah Schopps Rea, Esther Holm, and Amanda Kwak. All well-traveled and bright thinkers, their in-depth debates over my arguments were extremely informative.

Generically, I would also like to thank students from numerous classes. In particular, my students from International Relations and Comparative Politics have been very helpful in crafting some of these ideas. For example, Rachel Rowland gave me the idea of describing this work as a "theology of nationalism." In other classes, History and Politics of Western Europe, History and Politics of Russia and Eastern Europe, and the History and Politics of the British Isles and Canada, some other ideas came to fruition. It is hard to say exactly where I gained the impetus from every idea, but I would like to cast a broad net of thanks to my thousands of students over the years that have encouraged and enriched my thinking on these subjects.

Over the last two decades, I have been blessed to sit under several Godly pastors who have engaged in expository preaching of the Bible. In no particular order, I have benefitted from sermons from a range of different preachers. They include: Cole Tawney, Brian Bales, Lon Snyder, Jonny Norman, Greg Graham, Tony Chester, Chris Williams, Chris Voltz, Andy Hahn, Jeff Bogue, Ryan Rodeman, Brian Childs, Paul Sartarelli, Knute Larson, Aaron Tredway, Jonathan Ortlip, Jason Wing, Phil Wing, Shane Hawkins, Jeremy Kimble, Scott Dixon, Mark Dever, and Bobby Jamieson.

Moreover, at Cedarville University, I have been abundantly blessed by hundreds of chapel speakers over the course of my eight years at the institution. Again, it is hard to pinpoint exactly when a point was learned or gleaned, but the faithful teaching of Scripture contributed towards this work. Of note here, Cedarville University administrators, Thomas White, Bill Brown, Tom Mach, and General Loren Reno deserve particular recognition.

One of the particular joys I have in serving as a professor at a Christian university is that I am often asked to speak about political and international issues on faith-based radio stations. Several, very talented radio show hosts have asked thousands of terrific questions that have likewise honed my thinking on matters of faith as connected to international political issues and the wider Body of Christ. Moody Radio has been a terrific source of inspiration for me. In particular, in Cleveland, Brian Dahlen and Jannelle Nevels on WCRF have been long-time friends, and I have also been blessed to appear occasionally on the Indianapolis, Chicago, and Quad Cities stations; my good friend, and former on-air TV partner, Mark Zimmerman who is now with Heartfelt Radio, WKJA in northeast Ohio; Bob Burney of WRFD in Columbus (Ohio); Ken Kettering of WFCJ in Dayton (Ohio); and Mark Elfstrand, formerly on WYLL in Chicago. I have also had the blessing of appearing on the Janet Mefferd show, as well as World Magazine's podcast and K-LOVE. All of these outlets have tested my ability to respond to world events, and to think Christianly about them.

Of course, even with the wealth of help and information from numerous sources, there are shortcomings in this book. For these limitations, it is natural that I alone incur all of the responsibilities for any shortcoming. No book is perfect, and all commentaries are subject to oversights in terms of time, place, and culture. This limitation weighs heavy on me when discussing Scripture, especially across time, place, and culture. Nevertheless, I offer this book as a "first fruit" replete with its limitations.

Finally, but certainly not least, the biggest debt is owed to family. My wife, Rebecca, has been an ongoing encourager of my academic work often selflessly finding time so that I can write or study. Our children, Declan, Harper, and Camille, have been a constant source of joy—and, at times, a much needed distraction. In many ways, it is thinking through the world that the next generation of Christians will inherit, that makes a work like this one, I pray, important.

SDG

Glen M.E. Duerr

Cedarville, Ohio, USA

March 12, 2020

About the Author

GLEN DUERR IS ASSOCIATE Professor International Studies at Cedarville University. He was born and raised in the UK, lived in Canada for a decade, and now resides in the USA where he completed his Ph.D. in Political Science from Kent State University. The author of two other books, Dr. Duerr has conducted extensive research in several more countries. He is a frequently sought after media interviewee, and has been featured on Moody Radio, CBN News, WORLD, and numerous local, regional, international, Christian, and secular outlets such as FoxNews.com, CTV News (Canada), and La Rázon (Spain). He and his wife, Rebecca, have three children, and live in Beavercreek, Ohio, USA, where Glen serves as a City Council Member.

Chapter 1

Introduction: Patriotism and the Cross

> Jesus said to him, "I am the way, and the truth, and the life; no one comes to the Father but through me. If you had known Me, you would have known My Father also; from now on you know Him, and have seen Him."
>
> —JOHN 14:6–7

IMAGINE, FOR A MINUTE, a conversation between Peter, Mary Magdalene, Augustine of Hippo, Thomas Aquinas, Martin and Katharina Luther, Billy and Ruth Graham, and twenty-first century church leaders in Brazil, Nigeria, and South Korea,[1] on Scripture and questions of God. The conversation, one could imagine would be rich in theological depth, but also fascinating in terms of the comparison of traversing time and space wherein, for example, a first century friend of Jesus (Peter or Mary) interacts with a sixteenth century pastor (Martin Luther). How did Christians, for example, at a specific point in time publicly identify their Christianity with one another?[2]

It would be instructive to ask personal questions of Peter about Jesus's ministry, peering in to the Sea of Galilee from a beach on its shores to look at multicolored fish, or watching the myriad birds flying behind Christ as he delivered the Sermon on the Mount. Likewise, to hear a personal account from Martin Luther on the Holy Roman Empire (HRE) and its reach across

---

1. Commenting on contemporary leaders, in any area of society, has its drawbacks since scholars are not able to see the full historical context of their leadership. In this case, imagine prominent church and theological leaders from these societies.

2. Schaeffer, *The Mark of the Christian*, 13.

1

much of Western and Central Europe, as connected to small parishes like Eiselben (Luther's hometown). Hearing the reaction of some of the early church leaders to an update on life and society, especially technology, from the twenty-first century would also be fascinating, especially for Augustine to hear of the Bible being translated into thousands of languages and disseminated to people all around the world—far beyond the extents of the known world in the fourth century. Yet, his insightful dichotomy of the differences between earthly and heavenly cities remain apropos for Christians almost 1600 years after its publication in 426.[3]

Such a conversation would allow the viewer/listener to see and hear issues within the church over time and to compare controversies of theology. An added component of this hypothetical conversation, though, would also have to include geography and issues of nationality. Peter, originally from Bethsaida (John 1:44) or Capernaum (Matthew 8:14), talking with Augustine from Numidia (modern day Algeria), speaking with Aquinas from Italy communicating with Martin and Katharina Luther from Germany. Throughout the timeline of the church, nationality and place are factors in the sharing and movement of the Christian faith. In the twenty-first century, the gospel has been spread throughout the world, to the ends of the earth, and translated into hundreds of languages. Rather than being a potential stumbling block between Christians, or a Christian sharing the gospel with someone, issues of nationality should be discussed.

What does the Bible teach about issues of nationality, nationalism, and patriotism? The question matters because even though all humans are unified as descendants of Adam, the world is divided into numerous nations, states, and ethnic groups.[4] The above is a perplexing, multifaceted question. In general, most people have a sense of what these terms—nationality, nationalism, and patriotism—connote, but the application is often narrow, and the application of these concepts are used to fit their own lives in a general, non-encompassing way. One of the central goals of this work is to avoid asserting positions without defining what is meant, or narrowly applying them to one's own circumstance but not others. This is an impossible task, but the final goal is to write a book that is accessible to as many people as possible in a variety of differing circumstances. This work extends field of nationalism to also encapsulate concepts such as multiple national identities, Supranationalism, secession, and transnationalism, which increasingly affect the lives of Christians in the twenty-first century.

---

3. Augustine, *City of God*.
4. MacArthur and Mayhew, *Biblical Doctrine*, 439.

As an example, this book examines supranational organizations (also known as multilateral free trade blocs) such as the European Union (EU) or Mercosur in South America (in English, known as the Southern Common Market) increasingly dictate how people live, including Christians, in member states in Europe and South America respectively. These supranational trade blocs add a layer of governance that exists in addition to national and local governments. Organizations like the EU have power over the food people eat and the air they breathe through regulations; a Belgian chocolatier is equally at the mercy of bureaucrats in Brussels who provide technical guidelines on her list of ingredients as she is to tourists from New York or Lagos or Beijing who buy her chocolates. These supranational organizations also contribute to new ways of thinking about land and space. For example, the average Christian in Germany may be concurrently connected to the southeastern Länder (the equivalent of a state/region/province) of Bavaria, the country of Germany, and Europe through the EU. Each layer of government (region, Country, and EU) may entice a person to form a strong layer of geographic attachment gluing the person to specific parts of the land.

Another component of this book involves Christians who find themselves living in regions with active secessionist movements, such as, for example, Flanders in northern Belgium, or West Papua in Indonesia. This situation raises an important question: at what point should a Christian rebel—in the case of secessionism, against the government? Or should he follow specific New Testament guidelines in Romans 13, 1 Peter 2, and 1 Timothy 2 on honoring and respecting the government? Is there a third option to do a mix of both actions—rebel in some areas and submit to the governing authorities in others? For people living in Catalonia in the northeast of Spain, or part of the Southern Cameroons/English-speaking movement in Cameroon, these are arduous, possibly sweat inducing political decisions concerning those who are focused on heavenly issues.

Finally, this book also examines what Scripture teaches regarding transnationalism, or the inherent global linkages between believers in Christ. As expressed in John 14:6–7 at the start of the chapter, the goal of the follower of Christ should be to know God. But, beyond this primary task, how should Christ followers approach and respond to issues of nationality whilst on earth? This work then end with sixteen conclusions on how Christians should live in light of nationality issues in the twenty-first century.

Overall, the aim of this book is to add a layer of complexity to the discussion on nationality, and to start a dialogue as to how Christians should approach the issue of their national identity with all of its idiosyncrasies and nuances. Living at the present time may be complex if a person is connected simultaneously to national, supranational, and secessionist discussions, as is the case for a Christian in the aforementioned case of Catalonia. How should a pastor lead his church when the Estelada (Catalan independence flag) is ubiquitous throughout Barcelona, but members of the congregation also have allegiance to Spain, and feel to some degree European?

This book is also written specifically for followers of Jesus Christ, or for those interested in the subject matter, who may live in a heterogeneous, multiethnic city, region, or country, or whose family is heterogeneous in terms of national identity or origins. The design of this work is to provide overarching biblical principles to provide answers to the main assertion outlined in the subtitle of the book: a theology of nationalism. Each aspect of nationalism is debated with Scripture to see what the Bible teaches on the issue. For instance, the split of the Kingdom of Israel in 1 Kings 12 is an early, historical case of secession. Nevertheless, just because it happened and is recorded in Scripture, should Christians follow this example? Under what circumstances can a Christian rebel against his government?

Finally, this book is written to inspire Christians to better engage with their new immigrant neighbors; to think about their new, pluri-national families; and to facilitate missions work, often conducted by missionaries who represent a veritable "United Nations" of different national backgrounds—for example, missionary work in Papua New Guinea is often conducted by the local/indigenous population, but also by missionaries from North America, Europe, Latin America, and Asia, all working together and living in close proximity.[5] People from a range of different backgrounds are interacting with increased frequency. How should the average Christ follower respond? Even if a Christ-follower in Sweden can trace her ancestry back for centuries all within the same town, literally observing the grave markers of her family members in the local cemetery, how should she respond to the Eritrean migrant or the Syrian refugee in her midst? What about the Rwandan Christian who is confronted with the well-intentioned young American trying to provide help in the aftermath of the fissiparous 1994 genocide[6] that tore his homeland apart in a brutal span of 100 days wherein around 800,000 people were murdered? Should a Christian couple adopt a child from their own neighborhood, or from a country on the other side of the world? These are pertinent questions, related to nationality, that confront believers in the modern era. Not all answers can be provided concretely because there are myriads of specific situations, but general principles of what can be done will be discussed throughout this book.

5. There are an estimated 420,000 missionaries dedicated full-time to sharing the gospel throughout the world (Escobar, *The New Global Mission*, 28).

6. Dallaire, *Shake Hands with the Devil*; Chua, *World on Fire*, 169

Primarily, the approach taken in this book is to instruct the "born-again" Christian who has personally entrusted Jesus Christ to atone as the propitiation for their sins (John 3:7). Since all human beings are fallen and sinful (Genesis 3), humanity is in need of a savior in order to bridge the gap between human beings and God. In the life of Jesus Christ, through the fulfillment of Old Testament Scriptures, the Messiah came to earth, lived a perfect, sinless life, and died on the cross as an atonement for the sins of human beings. Whoever places their trust in Jesus will be saved (Romans 10:9).

Of course, Christianity is a broad religion, and a broad subject. Believers may be drawn from a range of different denominational backgrounds including a wide range of Protestant positions, the Orthodox Christian faith, and the Roman Catholic Church. The path to salvation, however, is through the aforementioned route, and can be claimed alike by any believer in Christ if individuals trust Jesus as their Lord and Savior. This book is, therefore, written with the intention of instructing and discussing issues of nationalism and national identity with all followers of Christ who have a personal relationship with Christ.

A Personal Story

Part of the motivation for writing this book is personal. As a citizen of three countries—the United Kingdom, the United States, and Canada—how do these countries impact my walk as a follower of Christ? Does it matter as to the country in which I reside? Should I pay a greater allegiance to one country, or another? Does it depend on circumstance? Should I pay respectful homage to my grandparents, who, among other things, helped to win World War II, or look excitedly at the lives of my future grandchildren? Or, should I think solely of my relationship with Christ above all other earthly matters including my wife and our three children? After all, I possess a heavenly citizenship in addition to three on earth.

Like many other stories, there are further complexities. For example, my father is from the United States, but left the country in his early to mid-twenties. So, while granted citizenship at birth (through my father), I am simultaneously a first generation American, a fourth generation American, and a sixth generation American—depending on the ancestor, different relatives immigrated to the United States at varying points in history. Like most Americans, my father is a mix of many different nationalities. Of my great-grandparents, one emigrated directly from Germany at the end of the nineteenth century; one from Slovakia then part of the Austro-Hungarian Empire on the eve of World War I; another was born in the United States but traced her roots to emigration from Ireland (then still part of the UK) and the Potato Famine of the 1850s; and the other was also born stateside but whose ancestors moved from Slovakia at an earlier time. Tangentially, but also noteworthy, my Slovak great-grandparents are interesting because they frequently referred to themselves as Slovak, despite the fact that an independent Slovakia had never existed prior to 1993.

My mother is from the United Kingdom, from the southern English county of Sussex, with a long line of people with the surname, Cook (my grandmother's maiden name). But, even my English side is not so homogenous. Although this might not sound like an enormous issue to some readers, my grandmother is from Sussex in the south, and my grandfather from the northern county of Yorkshire—historically this north/south divide presented an issue in marriage. Moreover, outside of this inter-England divide, my maternal line traces people from across the UK (Scotland and Wales), Ireland, Germany, and France, in just a few generations. My bloodline is a mix of different historic national groups.

Furthermore, my lineage is hardly the most complex in the modern world.[7] Very few people have three citizenships, mainly because many countries still forbid dual citizenship, but the bloodlines of many people encompass virtually all major geographic regions of the world. One of my brothers-in-law was born in Canada, but his family had just moved to Hong Kong. Thus, two of my nephews, who have all the same ancestral diversity as me because of my sister, also have half their bloodline through Hong Kong and China. The world has become increasingly complex for many people, so providing biblically-based answers to these questions will not only be self-edifying, but hopefully will also edify the body of Christ.

The Changing Face of Global Christianity

The face of global Christianity in the twenty-first century is not what it was in 1900.[8] To cite a few examples: Tanzanian missionaries rent the iconic, bright red iconic double decker busses in London to evangelize the population by sharing the gospel via megaphones. The stunning growth of the church throughout the twentieth and twenty-first centuries in South Korea now makes up over one-third of the population[9] and contributes significant money and people to missions.[10] And, at least one million people—in

7. Escobar, *The New Global Mission*, 11.
8. Jenkins, *The New Faces of Christianity.*
9. Jenkins, *The New Faces of Christianity*, 84.
10. Grudem, *Politics according to the Bible*, 46.

a carnival like atmosphere—march annually to support Jesus on the main thoroughfare streets of Brazil; the 27th annual event in Sao Paolo was attended by an estimated 3 million Christians.[11] From these three quick examples alone, it is evident that Christianity is no longer bounded to Europe or North America. The church is global in the twenty-first century, and, as a result, needs to be aware of issues pertaining to nationality, and relationships between people of different national backgrounds.

In his trilogy on the growth of Christianity across the world, the American historian Philip Jenkins examines the idea of global Christianity,[12] fervent belief in the Bible in the Global South,[13] and the state of Christianity as compared to Islam in Europe.[14] The books describe a picture of how the church has changed, especially from 1900 to 2000, to more closely reflect the picture of Revelation 7: "After these things I looked, and behold, a great multitude which no one could count, from every nation and all tribes and peoples and tongues, standing before the throne and before the Lamb, clothed in white robes, and palm branches were in their hands; and they cry out with a loud voice saying: 'Salvation to our God who sits on the throne, and to the Lamb'" (Revelation 7:9–11).

At the height of globalization in the early decades of the twenty-first century, Christians are confronted, but not necessarily well-equipped with issues of nationality, nationalism, and patriotism. Frequently, Christians move across national borders, conduct regular business deals around the world, marry across borderlines, and serve in missions in new and unexpected fields. Take, for example, the "father" of modern missions, an Englishman, William Carey, who traveled to India to share the gospel in 1793, his national identity might have remained English, but his desire in life was to make disciples in India.[15] Moreover, Carey's "Englishness" did not help him as colonial authorities took issue with his presence, so he had to move to an area of India under Danish rule to start his mission.[16]

In light of these changes pertaining to borders, this book aims to provide answers to one, central question, as noted earlier: What does the Bible teach about issues of nationality, nationalism, and patriotism? Obviously, from the question, there are undulations that come with a study of nationalism. Linked in the question are issues of nationality and patriotism.

11. Parke, *3 million evangelicals march in Brazil.*

12. Jenkins, *The Next Christendom.*

13. Jenkins, *The New Faces of Christianity.*

14. Jenkins, *God's Continent.*

15. Piper, *Let the Nations be glad!,* 20.

16. Escobar, *The New Global Mission,* 49.

Moreover, in the above quote from Revelation 7:9, the text notes people from every nation and all tribes and peoples and tongues. Stunning diversity, but oneness in Christ.[17] The implication here is that human beings from different nations, tribes, and people groups, as well as groups of people who speak different tongues, will one day stand before the throne praising God.[18] Digging deeper into the implication is to examine countries, regions of countries, people groups, and linguistic groups who identify as different from one another. There is a considerable complexity to the peoples of many countries in the world with a cacophony of different voices purporting historic identities, languages, and cultures.

In some respects, many people look at the world as a collection of 193 (at least according to the United Nations) recognized member states, typically referred to as countries.[19] Other organizations differ; for example, FIFA, the world governing body of soccer, has 211 national associations in 2020.[20] Yet, when one delves deeper, there are thousands of people groups that exist across the 193 recognized countries of the world. People often speak different, mutually unintelligible languages, and even though they may reside within the same country as millions of other people, their national, people, or linguistic group may be viewed—or they view themselves—as different. And, thus, are treated very differently in economic, political, and social matters of the country.

Within this complexity, the gospel of Jesus Christ has spread to most parts of the world such that believers can be found in the vast majority of all countries, nations, tribes, and tongues across the world. Many paradoxes exist in the twenty-first century global church. The largest number of Christians ever currently resides in the world, yet more Christians are persecuted and killed for their faith than at any previous point in history. At the same time, so-called "Mega" churches abound—especially in the western world—yet there are still numerous unreached people groups in the world today.[21]

Taken as a whole, Christians now number over two billion people in a world (as of mid-2016) of an estimated 7.6 billion (2020 population figure).[22] Yet, Christians are also harassed in over 100 countries across the world at any given time.[23] The number of Christians killed for their faith, or simply

---

17. Ham and Ware, *One Race, One Blood.*

18. Piper, *Let the Nations Be Glad!*, 234.

19. UN.

20. FIFA.

21. Piper, *Let the Nations be glad!*, 92–95.

22. Pew Forum, "*Global Christianity.*"

23. Pew Forum, "*Arab Spring Adds to Global Restrictions on Religion.*"

for being Christian, is, at least according to scholars David Barrett and Todd Johnson, reportedly the highest ever. It is argued, for example, that in the twentieth century there were more martyrs than the previous nineteen centuries combined—approximately 45 million between 1900 and 2000 compared to 35 million between Christ's ministry and 1900.[24] Martyrdom (in this case, the killing of Christians by the government) is often connected to the issue of nationalism in that the motive behind the killing of Christians is to preserve the status quo for the government, be it a dictatorship and/or supported by a non-Christian religious or ideological majority. This point—that non-Christians fear the growth of Christianity as a mechanism to topple their governing structures—is frequently underemphasized in discussions on martyrdom and persecution. Rapid declines in the number of Christians in the Middle East provides some evidence as to how these policies have been implemented, and what "success" they have had.[25]

As noted earlier, this book wrestles with issues at the intersection between the Christian faith and the topic of nationalism. Biblically, under God's sovereignty, every human being is placed on the earth in a particular place—we each have an earthly citizenship, or, sometimes, multiple citizenships. In addition to an earthly citizenship, according to Philippians 3:20, every believer in Jesus Christ is also described as a "citizen of heaven." For the believer in Christ, there is a coterminous allegiance both in heaven and on earth.

With globalization, migration has increased across the world. Take, for example, the number of immigrants who come to the United States each year. According to the U.S. Department of Homeland Security, almost 10 million people received their green card in the 1990s—an all-time high.[26] Or, within the EU, the Schengen Zone allows for travel across a borderless continent albeit with some, fairly limited controls for work migration.[27] As another example, across the sugarcane fields of the Dominican Republic in the Caribbean there are thousands of Haitian migrants daily hacking away at the sweet chambers of sugar readying it for export; some moved to make money, others to flee the stinging aftermath of hurricanes and earthquakes. Migration may be voluminous and controlled, or sporadic based on economic, security, or environmental matters.[28]

24. Barrett and Johnson, *World Christian Trends*.

25. The journalist, Mindy Belz, has extensively documented the martyrdom of Christians in the Middle East over the course of the last 20 years, see Belz, *They say we are infidels*, 139–155.

26. Department of Homeland Security, "*2018 Yearbook of Immigration Statistics*," 5.

27. Gattrell, *The Unsettling of Europe*.

28. Gattrell, *The Unsettling of Europe*.

In response to migration, both legal and undocumented, there has been a backlash across a number of different countries. There are genuine and perceived fears on the part of people that they may lose their job, be denied an opportunity, or lose a sense of culture in the migrant fluctuation. Sometimes, political violence is an outcome of tension over migration as was the case in the 1960s when thousands of Salvadorans moved to Honduras.[29] The question, then, is how should followers of Christ balance faith in the midst of this tension? How does belief in Christ meld with the concepts of nationalism and citizenship?

Preliminary Definitions

An important component part of this work is to define terms. People familiar with definitions pertaining to nationalism could certainly skip this section, and move to the next. To start, basic definitions of nation and state are the most important. To the American ear at least, the distinction between the terms nation and state is particularly important because a "global" definition of these terms differs dramatically from what is taught in American schools and discussed in everyday parlance. Put succinctly, a nation can be better described as a people group with territorial boundaries, whereas, a state is a country with a form of government.

A nation—according to the Merriam-Webster dictionary, is "a large area of land that is controlled by its own government," as opposed to "*the* nation," which is defined as "the people who live in a nation." Historian and nationalism scholar Anthony D. Smith describes a nation as "a named human population sharing a historic territory, common myths and historical memories, a mass, public culture, a common economy, and common legal rights and duties for all members."[30] Smith continues by noting that a nation "signifies a cultural and political bond, uniting a single political community all who share an historic culture and homeland."[31] According to the political scientist, Cathal Nolan, there are two main meanings for "nation," the first being "a self-conscious, imagined[32] (but nonetheless real) political community composed of those who share ethnicity, language, and possibly also a

29. Durham, *Scarcity and survival in Central America*.

30. Smith, *National Identity*, 14.

31. Smith, *National Identity*, 14–15.

32. The "imagined" component of this definition comes from Benedict Anderson's book on nationalism, *Imagined Communities*, arguing that citizens will never know, meet, or hear of many of their fellow citizens; thus, some level imagination is required to form national identity (Anderson, *Imagined Communities*, 6).

common religion and/or culture, but may or may not possess a legally sovereign state."[33] In further discussing a nation, Nolan adds to his definition to include the point that a nation is a "political community that need not share common race, language, or culture but has a recognized and defined territory and government derived from historical circumstance, which it defends with a display of some degree of common purpose."[34] The description continues to include that "such nations may contain one or more regional identities or sub-nationalities, which, under different circumstances, could themselves constitute nations."[35] The definition from another political scientist is quite simple: "a group of people who share a common ethnic, religious, territorial, and historical background."[36] All of these definitions have their subtleties, but there are common themes. Very few scholars have sought to define nation from the standpoint of the Bible. The Israeli scholar, Yoram Hazony is an exception. He defines nation as "a number of tribes with a common language or religion, and a past history of acting as a body for the common defense and other large-scale enterprises.[37]

All of these academic definitions can be quite confusing. Therefore, it is helpful to more simply define a nation as a people group who share ethnic, linguistic, cultural, and/or religious beliefs, and mobilize for self-government. The above definitions each add a useful layer of complexity. Smith, for example, discusses historical memory; Nolan, conscious belonging; Barrett et al., historical background; and Hazony, defense and large-scale enterprises. The goal in listing these academic definitions is to provide nuance to the definition listed at the start of this paragraph to show the contours of a discussion.

As an additional note, it is, in many regards, quite strange to a reader from the United States to think about a definition of a nation because ethnicity is not a provision in the American constitution. This is a great asset to Americans because citizenship is based on the constitution, not on ethnic or racial measures, as is the case with many other countries in other parts of the world. The American nation, based on citizenship alone under the constitution, is naturally aligned with statehood. But for the average Nigerian reader, the term nation is more obvious in that Yoruba, Igbo, and Hausa-Fulani (three of the largest ethnic groups among many) all reside in one state. For the Nigerian, this distinction amongst the three major ethnic

---

33. Nolan, *The Greenwood Encyclopedia of International Relations*, Nation.

34. Nolan, *The Greenwood Encyclopedia of International Relations*, Nation.

35. Nolan, *The Greenwood Encyclopedia of International Relations*, Nation.

36. Donovan et al., *People, Power, and Politics*, 286.

37. Hazony, *The Virtue of Nationalism*, 18.

groups only serves as a very rudimentary introduction as to the complexities of nationality in the West African state.

When accessing the Bible, theologian Wayne Grudem argues that the definition of a nation in Scripture is "not different in any substantial way from what we mean by a nation today."[38] Grudem's definition of a nation overlaps with that of a state as presented herein, but without drawing too fine of a line here, the central assessment if that states that existed in the Old Testament still fit the pattern of states today.

In contrast to a nation, a state—according to the Merriam-Webster dictionary, is "a politically organized body of people usually occupying a definite territory," particularly "one that is sovereign." It can also refer to "the political organization of such a body of people" or "a government or politically organized society having a particular character" (i.e. "police state" or "welfare state"). Again, the political scientist, Cathal Nolan, notes that a state is "political entity which occupies a defined territory, has a permanent population, and enjoys independence and sovereignty."[39] A third definition of a state is offered here: "a legally formalized entity having accepted jurisdiction over a territory and a population and the capacity, within that territory, to make rules binding on the whole population and to enforce those rules through generally accepted legal procedures and applications of force;" "the state is an entity in which sovereignty—the authoritative capacity to govern within a country—rests."[40] Finally, to return to Hazony, he argues that "members of a nation should regard one another as brothers, and Mosaic law offered the Israelites a constitution that would bring them together in what today would be called a national state."[41]

Put simply, a state is a country. There is more to the definition as noted in the above paragraph, but simplicity is helpful. Furthermore, statehood also connotes other elements like a form of government, a physical territory, recognition by other states, internal control by said government, and a set of rules, among other potential additions.

Although dense, definitions of nation and state are important in order to proceed. By decoupling nation from state, the reader can more easily see the complexities of living in a multinational state, that is, a country with multiple different groups of nations. For example, a Christ follower who happens to be an immigrant from Chile living in the city of Montreal faces several issues of national contention. On the one hand, she has a personal

38. Grudem, *Politics according to the Bible*, 110.

39. Nolan, *The Greenwood Encyclopedia of International Relations*, State.

40. Donovan et al., *People, Power, and Politics*, 19.

41. Hazony, *The Virtue of Nationalism*, 18.

and ancestral tie to Chile where her parents still might reside. She lives in a country, Canada, but also has an added layer of living in a multinational state wherein some members of her community support the idea of an independent Quebec, which, some of her friends might argue, should be separate from Canada. Moreover, her career in business, which has her discussing purchasing orders from clients in the United States and Mexico, means that she deals with the nuances of the United States, Mexico, Canada Agreement (USMCA), formerly known as the North American Free Trade Agreement (NAFTA). Although not a potent force in the life of the average Canadian, American, or Mexican, USMCA/NAFTA does set the rules for her conduct of business, and connects the people of the three countries, albeit in a fairly limited way right now.

The Argument in Brief

What does the Bible teach about issues of nationality, nationalism, and patriotism? The central argument in this book is that a coterminous—in this case, one of heaven and one of earth—view of nationality is the optimal way forward, that is, a Christ follower must be aware of the transnational nature of the faith, which links believers across national lines, whilst also affirming God's sovereignty in placing people in specific situations to make a difference for the cause of Christ in their own country. Philippians 3:20, for example, notes that the believer in Christ is a citizen of heaven. The apostle Paul, on numerous occasions, exhorts the brethren to love another across all types of social, economic, and *national* lines. Yet, as human beings, each one has a national identity. This allegiance to nationality is important. In Acts 10, for example, the Roman centurion Cornelius is confronted with the gospel. He accepts Jesus as savior, but is not required to revoke his Roman citizenship, or stop being a centurion. Similarly, in the Book of Esther, God has a clear plan to save the Jews from the schemes of Haman. Esther, with the assistance of her uncle, Mordecai, rises to become queen to Ahasuerus (also known as Xerxes). Esther is not forced to renounce her role, despite being in a country that is not an ethnically Jewish homeland. While the story weaves in unexpected ways, Esther is positioned to petition Ahasuerus in order to protect her people from destruction.

If applied to national identity, a case can be made for rendering to God what is God's, and then rendering to Caesar what is Caesar's, as in Luke 20:25. Put simply, Christians must render to God, but they also have an earthly obligation to work and to be good citizens—to render to Caesar as well, with the caveat that God's Word trumps any earthly Caesar. In Scripture, everything belongs to God, but human beings also have to interact and live in a given context on earth. The psalmist writes "Blessed is the nation whose God is the Lord" (Psalms 33:12). Since the world is divided into states/countries, Scripture teaches that some of these countries are blessed if God is the Lord of that country. Obviously, a definition of what exactly is meant by blessing is important, but it is an assumed good.

If God is sovereign and has a plan and purpose for each life (Psalms 135:6; Proverbs 19:21), then the Christ follower has to accept what God has for them at that particular moment. For many people, this involves being an influencer in a specific country. However, for many people who may move from one country to another (and maybe several more), there are also some additional considerations. On the one hand, due respect must be given to the governmental authority under which one presently lives (Romans 13:1–7; 1 Peter 2:13–14; 1 Timothy 2:2). But, of course, if the government forcibly requires a follower of Christ to not follow Christ, then the allegiance is to God first and foremost.

A central component to this work is thinking through the dangers, from both a biblical and an historical perspective. If one clings too tightly to national identity, or, most worryingly, if nationalism is promoted too strongly by political leaders, it can become rampant, and then violent. Many, well-meaning Christians have been caught in the intoxicating web of protecting the church via the state only to see volumes of human rights abuses carried out by the same government punishing people made in the image of God.

The reverse issue is also a challenge, that is, some followers of Christ view national identity as unimportant. First, this can lead to division. Second, this view can also lead to a lack of vision for the Christ-followers of that country to have an impact in the time and place that God has placed them. In each country, within their language and culture, there are redeemable qualities that can "naturally" point people to the gospel.

Table 1.1 below examines the many different options that people have in the world when it comes to their national identity. Some facets are more historic, but there are a wide range of topics. These options also come with risks and challenges. One of these risks is violence. If a follower of Christ, for example, living in the German city of Cologne in the 1930s votes for and supports the policy platforms of Adolf Hitler and the National Socialist Party, there are major negative implications for the world. Support for these positions resulted in significant political violence; some of these positions should have been clear.

Table 1.1: A Continuum of nationalism[42]

Globalism (Post-nationalism)	Regionalism	Patriotism	Nationalism	Colonialism	Hyper-nationalism
Very weak sense of national identity	Sense of regional identity	Sense of national identity	Strong sense of national identity	Very strong sense of national identity	Extraordinary sense of national identity
Unknown	Unknown	Low likelihood of political violence	Fairly low likelihood of political violence	Fairly high likelihood of political violence	High likelihood of political violence

Table 1.1 above notes six, major different options for the Christ-follower. Ranging from globalism, wherein a person effectively values the world over any given national identity; to regionalism, which articulates a desire to be part of a continental bloc; to patriotism and nationalism, which are more benign in terms of national belonging; to colonialism and hyper-nationalism, which seek to dominate other nations and states. All of the above are options for national allegiance. In this book, I argue that the average follower of Christ, and this depends on the situation, should align most closely between the positions of patriotism and nationalism, with a strong leaning towards patriotism. Patriotism "reinforces a shared sense of national identity and purpose."[43] This is a position similar to that of the professor John Eidsmoe, who advocates that Christians should be patriots.[44] The rejoinder here is that nationalism is one of the "most potent political forces in the world," which can turn negative very quickly.[45] Thus, nationalism should be very closely bounded.

Neither term—nationalism or patriotism—has been fully defined yet, but the biblical balance between Philippians 3:20, that followers of Christ have a heavenly citizenship, with the admonition of Romans 13/1 Peter 2/1 Timothy 2,[46] that followers of Christ live under a government, best leads to the conclusion that national allegiance between patriotism and nationalism is most optimal. The question, here, is whether the actions of the state "can be

42. This continuum seeks to examine national identity rationally. However, a useful caveat is that national identity is often emotional, as well as rational. A flag, for example, has meaning because of the emotion it inspires (Marshall, *A Flag worth Dying For*, 1).

43. Grudem and Asmus, *The Poverty of Nations*, 359.

44. Eidsmoe, *God and Caesar*, 39.

45. Hechter, *Containing Nationalism*, 3.

46. Eidsmoe, *God and Caesar*, 40.

justified as legitimate actions"?[47] This is a useful question to ask so as to bound the power of the state from engaging in unethical policies.

Of course, there may be situations wherein some deviation from the optimal line between nationalism and patriotism for the follower of Christ may be necessary. Some, limited application of globalism is a better choice for a Christ follower. For example, a South Korean missionary who has spent his life in Paraguay whilst raising support in North America and Western Europe, is transferred to the Ivory Coast for a second major stint in the mission field. Although this scenario is unlikely, there are people whose lives have been characterized by this type of movement across borders. National identity means very little to the missionary; although, recalling the discussion earlier in this chapter, some rendering to Caesar is necessary in Ivory Coast, and in South Korea where he may still pay taxes and ultimately receive retirement benefits one day.

Patriotism and nationalism, although different, connote an attachment to the country, but not to the detriment of other countries. Perhaps a sense of cultural superiority is present, but this rarely overshadows relationships with other countries. On the other hand, adherents of colonialism, and also hyper-nationalism tend to view people of other countries and cultures with a level of inferiority, and even disdain. The Berlin Conference in 1884–85 allowed European powers to effectively divide Africa among themselves as they saw fit without answering to anyone.[48] Violence was rife in this time period.

Moreover, colonialism and hyper-nationalism, for example, spawned the chattel[49] Slave Trade presenting assumptions that black people were inferior to others leading to one of the most colossal human rights abuses in history. After years of sinful ethnic-based slavery spurred by colonialism, a Christian member of the British parliament, William Wilberforce, led the campaign to end the heinous practice. Bolstered by the Evangelical Revival in the UK in the late 18th and early 19th centuries, missionaries, laypersons, and political leaders sought to support the rights of slaves.[50] In 1808, the British parliament ended the slave trade; it took until 1833 to outlaw slavery in the British Empire.[51] Colonialism did not end, however, even with the conclusion of chattel slavery.

---

47. Metaxas, *Bonhoeffer*, 153.

48. Mutibwa, *Uganda since independence*, 3.

49. "A system in which one person, theoretically, legally owns another" (Martin, *Prevailing Worldviews*, 136).

50. Evans, *Pursuit of Power*, 267.

51. Metaxas, *7 Men*, 55; Metaxas, *Amazing Grace*, 215, 274.

The sense of national identity is very strong, and often perpetuates myths of national superiority over others. These categories should be avoided, wherever possible, by followers of Christ. The Dutch theologian and Prime Minister, Abraham Kuyper, for example, flatly rejects notions of colonialism when considering the actions of the Dutch government in the late nineteenth century.[52] At most, Kuyper argues, the "only sound, lawful, and honorable system for us as a Christian nation is a system of trusteeship."[53] Yet, during Kuyper's tenure as prime minister of the Netherlands from August 1901-August 1905, he inherited the longstanding Aceh War (in modern day Indonesia), which resulted in 1904 in a full Dutch victory.[54] Moreover, Kuyper, at times, made some pejorative statements about Africans connoting a sense of cultural superiority.[55] It would be unfair to Kuyper to leave his statements here as he did much to emphasize the sovereignty of God over all of creation. His governance of a country also shows the practical difficulties of implementing philosophical positions based on Scripture. In essence, talking is easy, governing justly and with fidelity is much more difficult.

For many, the idea of trusteeship is still too much and encourages one group to rule over another. In the twenty-first century, this concept is difficult given that some smaller islands belonging to the British, French, or Dutch, among others, may not have the ability to sustain themselves alone given the history of colonialism in their "national" context.

The second row/line of Table 1.1 also outlines whether or not each viewpoint is likely to lead to political violence. Although a category like globalism is unproven, regionalism has not spawned much political violence since this category grew in popularity since the end of World War II, yet still unproven because of a lack of real power. Patriotism and nationalism generally tend to have fairly low levels of violence. Colonialism, and especially hyper-nationalism, have been shown, in contrast, to result in high levels of political violence.[56] When one views other nations and states as inferior, the likelihood of conflict is higher by virtue of the political stance taken. Major, global wars like the Napoleonic Wars, World War I, and World War II, all resulted, in significant measure, on the basis of colonialism hypernationalism. If Christ followers are called to be peacemakers (Matthew 5:9),

52. Kuyper et al. *Our Program*; Joustra, "Abraham Kuyper among the Nations."

53. Kuyper et al. *Our Program*; Joustra, "Abraham Kuyper's Overseas Manifesto."

54. Joustra, *"Abraham Kuyper among the Nations."*

55. Kuyper, *Wisdom & Wonder*, 28.

56. Mutibwa, *Uganda since Independence*, 6–10.

then purporting situations where violence is less likely, is the most optimal to bring glory to the Father.

Plan of the Book

The first major component of this book is to unpack the argument in greater detail. In order to effectively accomplish this task, it will require an examination of the undulations of the subjects of nationalism and national identity. This is not an easy task, nor is it easy to accomplish in any obvious sense of direction. Nonetheless, this work will start by focusing internally of issues of national identity specific to one country, before moving into issues like Supranationalism, or some form of pooled sovereignty; issues of secessionism and rebellion wherein one (or more) regions of a country seek their own independence; and, finally, a discussion of transnationalism wherein the linkages between all Christ-followers across the world will be discussed. Given this context, the book will be divided into the following chapters:

Chapter 2 investigates the distinction between nationalism and patriotism. Often conflated, these two terms are similar, but, when taken at their core, connote two very different policy positions. This chapter also examines ethnic versus civic types of nationalism on a continuum, and how a given polity interacts towards either one of these two poles. Finally, this chapter ends with a discussion of more heightened elements of nationalism such as colonialism, and then hyper-nationalism, also known as ultra-nationalism—ultimately, this is the worst and most dangerous form of nationalism. And, hyper-/ultra-nationalism is typically the most violence prone.

Chapter 3 analyzes how Christians, especially those who have lived in two or more countries, and may possess two or more passports, should try to live in the contemporary world. What Biblical examples are available to guide these types of situations? The story of Joseph in Genesis 37–50 is very useful, as is the story of Ruth in the Book of Ruth. Several other examples are drawn from the Old and New testaments to show how the average Christian can leverage her position in the world in several communities and countries for the glory of God.

Chapter 4 investigates the issue of Supranationalism and free trade amongst different countries. There are many cases of economic interactions in the Bible, but perhaps most interesting is the relationship between Solomon and Hiram in 1 Kings 5. The intent here is not to utilize the Bible as a prescriptive text on what all countries and leaders should do. Rather, this case is descriptive such that the account provides an example of the type of options available to countries and leaders. In 1 Kings 5, the two kings create a pact, which ultimately helps the Kingdom of Israel to rebuild its temple. In many respects, open, fair, and free trade between countries can be very beneficial to both if the agreement is implemented well. Supranationalism, however, is another matter altogether. It connotes a reduction of sovereignty in exchange not only for economic trade, but also political, legal, and social integration. A definition of Supranationalism is essentially an entity "above" states.[57] It "involves states working with one another in a manner that does not allow them to retain complete control over developments."[58] Put simply, Supranationalism is an entity that combines countries into one larger organization. In practice, it is not this clean; national governments still maintain some level of power, even if they cede some areas to the supranational government, or pool certain areas of policy with other national governments.

Chapter 5 examines the interrelated issues of rebellion and secession. Rebellion, through the fall of humanity in Genesis 3, is at the core of the human experience. Some scholars argue that human nature is currently going through a major improvement such that war[59] and societal violence[60] are decreasing significantly. The evidence here is, at best, mixed, given that a range of factors could be responsible for the lull in war deaths. Moreover, both books gloss over the number of civil wars around the world, some of which started decades ago.[61]

Both books were published in 2011, and note that the progress could reverse. This has proven correct with the start of internationalized civil wars in Syria, Yemen, South Sudan, and Libya, as well as the rekindling of conflicts in Iraq, and ongoing violence in Afghanistan and Myanmar. Arguably, there was even intermittent violence in other countries like Somalia, Pakistan, as well.[62] In Genesis 3, all human beings are sinful and prone to negative behaviors, even if wider systemic features have temporarily decreased the likelihood of global conflagration. At a larger societal level, rebellion is related to secession in that a region of the country seeks to rebel from the national government. The causes of rebellion are complex. Yet, usually, there is some level of relative deprivation—a sense that Group A is gaining an advantage over Group B such that Group B's expectations are not met, thus culminating in rebellion.[63]

---

57. Slaughter, *A New World Order*, 145.

58. Nugent, *The Government and Politics of the European Union*, 558.

59. Goldstein, *Winning the War on War*, 4.

60. Pinker, *The Better Angels of our Nature*.

61. Hinronaka, *Neverending Wars*, 38.

62. Jeremiah, *The Coming Economic Armageddon*, 39.

63. Gurr, *Why Men Rebel*.

Before moving further, two definitions are useful. Secession is defined as the "formal withdrawal from an established, internationally recognized state by a constituent unit to create a new, sovereign state,"[64] or,
similarly, by another scholar, "a demand for formal withdrawal from a central political authority by a member unit or units on the basis of a claim to
independent sovereign status."[65] Relatedly, irredentism can be defined to:
"assume a more general usage concerning demands by any ethnic group
for acquisition of territory claimed to be part of a historic homeland or
populated by ethnic kin."[66] In the midst of these situations, how should a
Christ-follower respond? What options are available? What does Scripture
say about these topics?

Chapter 6 engages in a discussion over transnationalism. How should
Christians work with other believers who were born, or may hold citizenship, in another country? There are several parts to this chapter. First, a
definition is necessary. Transnationalism can be defined as follows: "transnational" relationships are described as international relationships "those
not involving activities between governments only."[67] Likewise, "transnational interactions" can defined as "covering the movement of tangible or
intangible items across state boundaries when at least one actor is not an
agent of government or an international organization."[68] A "transnational
organization" is formed when "such relationships between more than
two participants become institutionalized by agreement into a formal,
continuous structure in order to pursue the common interests of the participants, one of which is not an agent of government or an international
organization."[69] As such, transnationalism connotes the idea of interaction
between actors, people. These formal definitions provide more information
on relationships across countries, but what does it mean pragmatically for
followers of Christ? Second, the issues of movement, migration, and im-
migration/emigration are discussed. At what point should a Christ follower
who has moved from one country to another become a citizen? How long
can a person retain ancestral identity?

Chapter 7 concludes the book with a discussion of the different types
of nationalism. Obviously, scenarios and circumstances differ based on the
country in question, but all questions come back to their anchor in the Bible.

64. Bartkus, *The Dynamic of Secession*, 3.

65. Wood, "Secession," 110.

66. Nolan, *The Greenwood Encyclopedia of International Relations*, Irredentism.

67. Archer, *International Organizations*, 1

68. Archer, *International Organizations*, 38

69. Keohane and Nye, *Transnational Relations and World Politics*, xii

Sixteen conclusion are proffered as a means to answer the central question of this work on nationality, nationalism, and patriotism.

Patriotism is often preferred to nationalism, but, depending on the situation could be reversed. Secession and Supranationalism are two very different situations, and invariably shape the life of the Christian. What can the believer in Christ do if they find themselves in this position by birth, or marriage, or circumstances beyond their control?

Chapter 2

Nationalism vs. Patriotism

You have established all the boundaries of the earth.

— Psalm 74:17a

We Christians must never forget that we have more in common with a Chinese Christian, an African sister, and a brother in South America than a next-door neighbor who does not know Christ.[1]

ALTHOUGH IT IS SOMETIMES difficult to decipher between academic definitions of nationalism and patriotism, the difference can be monumental. Most politicians and policymakers want to drape themselves in the veil of patriotism, but, in some cases, this simply betrays the evidence—a given leader may be a nationalist in practice. Nationalism, with its notably sharper edges and connotation, can also snowball into policies exerting colonial and, eventually, hyper-national, outcomes. For example, people with some introduction to the Bible have carried out some of the greatest atrocities of the twentieth century by fighting within Hitler's army during World War II to participating in the atrocious bloodletting genocide in Rwanda in 1994. Well-meaning Christians, on occasion, are caught up in nationalist fervor disbanding their core tenets to show the love of Christ; this is one of the reasons why the twentieth-century French pastor, Jean Lasserre asserts that

1. Akin, *Exalting Jesus in 1, 2, 3 John*, 9.

one cannot be a Christian and a nationalist simultaneously.[2] The reason is that a sense of national allegiance is wrapped in the same kinds of threads as devotion for God: in essence, to be a good Christian is to be a good citizen of the state, thus, a Christian must carry out the will of the state. These actions are unbiblical, but it is easier to see why the Christian made these choices; as the political scientist, David Koyzis, notes, "some (Christians) have so closely tied their faith to nationalism that the two have become almost indistinguishable in their minds."[3] In many different contexts across time and space, this interrelationship between church and state had some good outputs, such as pointing people towards God; in other scenarios, like the aforementioned Nazi Germany example, disastrous. This debate over the connections between church and state have been ongoing almost since the time of Christ—Tertullian,[4] a second century Christian, famously asked, "What does Athens have to do with Jerusalem?"[5] For these reasons, wading through the academic definitional "weeds" of patriotism and nationalism may make all the difference in the real world application.

It is, of course, easier to critique the definitions of others, rather than to defend one's own definition. Thus, given the importance of definitions to this work, here is my own definition of nationalism: "The collective sentiment on behalf of a nation, or national group—whether civic or ethnic—that purports policies exerting control over a territory coterminous with a state, and utilizes military action, where it is deemed necessary, to defeat enemy states/entities."

My definition starts with a collective sentiment on behalf of a nation, or national group. Sentiment connotes a shared history and core set of political beliefs that intertwine with the definition of a nation in chapter 1. More broadly, this definition can also fit national groups, extending to the definition of a state, also noted in chapter 1. The national group can be either civic or ethnic, but is more likely to be defined by ethnic characteristics. Policy is also an important component of the definition as the policies exerted by said nation or national group are coterminous with the state, that is, the nation or the national group seeks to dominate politics within the state. An historical example of this idea is Germany. If one examines Germany in the in the aftermath of World War II, most people living in Germany

2. Metaxas, *Bonhoeffer*, 111; Lasserre, *War and the Gospel*.

3. Koyzis, *Political Visions and Illusions*, 119

4. Tertullian's question here is layered. While part of the question pertains to church and state relations, an aspect of this question also engages the relationship between faith and reason. I would like to acknowledge my colleague, Mark Owens, for his help on this point.

5. Smith et al. *Rendering to God and Caesar*, 244.

were ethnic Germans. Rather than creating an open form of collective senti-ment, ethnic Germans sought to dominate politics within the country, and implemented policies that subjugated non-ethnic Germans. Germany, in the aftermath of its unification in 1871, is historically viewed as possessing an archetypal example of ethnic nationalism.[6] The next component within the definition—policies also exert military action where it is demonstrably necessary. These policies are, in general, for self-defense. The overarching goal of these policies is to defeat the opposing state or non-state actor (a non-state actors includes ISIS, for example).

Before going further, it is useful to take a step back to draw greater con-text as to the term, nationalism. Another, simplified, 30,000-foot definition of nationalism—akin to a person flying over the world from an aircraft—is simply that the world should be divided into different countries with clear boundary outlines. Wayne Grudem argues that "the existence of many in-dependent nations on the earth should be considered a blessing from God."[7]

The 30,000-foot definition may sound like a simple definition, but the world has not always been made up of countries. Human beings orga-nized themselves into tribes, city-states, and empires at different points in history.[8] Take the New Testament, for example, Jesus's entire ministry took place under the powerful, expansive, and polyglot Roman Empire, all bow-ing to a centralized Caesar in Rome. In many respects, the organization of people into countries began in earnest at the conclusion of the Thirty Years' War (1618–1648) with the signing of the Peace of Westphalia.[9] This treaty cemented the idea that countries should be predominant and that empires should were no longer useful as a primary form of identification. Obvi-ously, numerous empires continued after 1648 such as the Holy Roman Empire, the Ottoman Empire, and the Habsburg/Austrian Empire (known as the Austro-Hungarian Empire post 1867), but all of these monolithic structures ended with the conclusion of World War I (1914–1918). Con-ceptually, the idea that people should be granted national identity with religious freedom grew in popularity over the idea that people should be subjects of a ruling emperor (or other monarch). National identity usually brought accompanying characteristics like a shared language and culture. It brought personal autonomy, civil liberties, religious freedom, and a growing ability to take responsibility for one's own life. Sometimes devious elements such as ethnicity became the hallmark of national identity, but, in

6. Renan, "Qu'est-ce qu'une nation?"

7. Grudem, Politics according to the Bible, 110.

8. Hazony, The Virtue of Nationalism, 90.

9. Wilson, The Thirty Years War, 751.

general, the advance of national identity over subjection within an empire grew in popularity after 1648.

Another definition of nationalism is that "it is the process that leads to national identity in the first place."[10] This definition helps to simply define the process of what is happening in nationalism, and takes away value judgments of policy. Moving into the political sphere, another definition that helps to introduce the subject is from renowned French nationalism scholar, Ernest Gellner: "nationalism is primarily a political principle that holds that the political and the national unit should be congruent."[11] In this case, there is more of a value judgment to nationalism in that it is an inherently political principle that is mobilized to assimilate the nationality of every citizen of the state. The American sociologist, Michael Hechter, largely concurs with this definition, but adds the importance of the boundaries of the nation and congruent with the governing unit.[12] This last point on boundaries is an important one because any discussion of national identity pertains to who can govern where, there is a spacial and geographic component to nationalism. Thus, standing on the shoulders of these academic "giants" I have proffered my own definitions of patriotism and nationalism.

Patriotism

A definition of nationalism has its own merit, but given the similar term, patriotism, the definition of the former is useful in defining the latter. My definition of patriotism has some overlap with my earlier definition of nationalism, but is distinct in several different ways. I define patriotism as follows: "The collective sentiment on behalf of a national group, under a constitution, which exhibits a moderate level of pride in the state, but not a jingoistic national identity, such that immigrants can gain membership in the society in a relatively easy manner by adopting core constitutional principles."

This definition of patriotism coincides with that of nationalism in that a similar collective sentiment exists across the national group. Note that the word, nation, has been removed. In this definition, there is a prohibition on the ability for an ethnic group to mobilize or dominate the state under a definition of patriotism. Beyond this initial comparison of collective sentiment, the definitions of nationalism and patriotism diverge.

Thus, this definition of patriotism contrasts with that of nationalism in that there is no territorial component, only a collective sentiment that denotes

10. Anderson, *Chosen Nation*, xiii.

11. Gellner, *Nations and Nationalism*, 1.

12. Hechter, *Containing Nationalism*, 7.

a moderate level pride in the state.[13] Patriotism avoids the jingoistic national identity of nationalism, but still provides adequate room for a sensible level of pride in one's state and national attachment. In real life, ascertaining what is "sensible" or not is difficult, but examples are presented throughout the latter part of this chapter. Patriotism is inherently supportive of a civic community within the state wherein peoples of different ethnic backgrounds can rightly work and live without the prejudice of an ethnic-driven constitution. This is not to ignore group differences or to assume color-blindness, since there are shortcomings to glossing over groups of people,[14] but to say that ethnicity does not play a leading role in the Constitution. The constitution, instead, provides protections for all people regardless of the color of their skin, or their ethnic background. The American Constitution, albeit with some historical flaws, is a great, modern example of protecting all peoples with equality under the law to build lives, businesses, and families. Given the ethnic diversity of the United States, this model makes sense with large minority populations and numerous smaller ethnic identities.[15] However, the American Constitution is merely a model, with application possible to many other countries in the world, which similarly feature various different ethnic communities all residing within one state.

The civic constitution is evident especially concerning immigrants. If someone who may have been born elsewhere can become a member of the society through citizenship, then this action provides tangible evidence of patriotism. If the country has a jingoistic sense of national identity such that newcomers cannot join, then the country is better defined as nationalistic— probably as a form of ethnic nationalism.

Of course, immigration is a complex subject. The number and origin of immigrants may affect definitions of patriotism. If, for example, a small country of approximately 500,000 people (similar to Luxembourg in Western Europe, or Suriname in South America, or Cabo Verde off the west coast of Africa) readily accepts some immigrants, perhaps 1,000–5,000 per year, it falls under a definition of patriotism. However, said country would have a very difficult time accepting an additional 500,000 people—in essence, doubling the existing population—the addition is simply impractical if Luxembourg, Suriname, or Cabo Verde, are to retain some semblance of heritage and history, let alone linguistic or cultural connections.

13. Answering this question in practical terms is difficult. The case of the Spanish-American War in 1898 is an interesting case study since the United States as a rising world power sought to push out the Spanish from the Western Hemisphere. At what point is this nationalism justified? (McCullough, *Cross of War*).

14. Chua, *Political Tribes*, 17.

15. Anderson, *Gracism*, 31–32.

Nevertheless, under a definition of patriotism, some immigrants should be able to gain membership in another country, especially if there is a natural disaster in a neighboring country where people need temporary assistance. The rulers and the people of the country should decide together as to the number of immigrants allowed into the country. A small percentage (of the country's total population) of people should be able to enter the country for a range of different reasons: family, work, asylum, among others. This number should be sufficiently small so as to not change the collective sentiment of the national group, but welcoming such that people can enter if the circumstances are appropriate.

Throughout Scripture, there are admonitions to love the foreigner or stranger (Leviticus 9:34) and the sojourner in the land (Deuteronomy 10:19). This admonition must be balanced with other admonitions in Scripture: 1) to love one's neighbors (Mark 12:31), and 2) avoid becoming indebted (Proverbs 22:7). In sum, accepting some immigration is very good, but not a biblical requirement if the economic situation is problematic. Loving one's neighbors means having appropriate resources to take of said neighbors, especially if they have refugee or asylum status, so the country must be appropriately prepared and able to take care of the strangers and sojourners in the land. Indebtedness is likewise problematic for the "debtor is the slave to the lender." Without adequately assessing the national resources, the difficulty is passing along debt to future generations. This does not mean that immigration should be halted if a country holds some national debt— merely, the equation of taking care of strangers and sojourners in the land must be balanced with the ability to properly care for these newcomers, and to have available resources, which means not being indebted.

On origins, the place of origin, or birth, or background, should be of little to no concern if the Christian admonition of, all people being made in the image of God, is followed. Skin color should be of no concern for Christians as God is the creator of all people.[16] Origin can become a concern if all the immigrants come from a singular country. Take the same hypothetical country of 500,000 people in the earlier example; if all immigrants to said country have the same national origin, then their acceptance could serve to replace the existing national identity. As an example, imagine that people from one country in another region of the world all move to Luxembourg. This act will immediately water down Luxembourgish national identity, and may even completely change the governing structures of the country. In sum, a country (especially a small country) might lose its national culture if immigrants from only one country concurrently immigrate to the same destination. Patriotism

16. Ham and Ware, *One Nation, One Blood.*

does not mean giving up one's national identity. However, if immigrants come from a range of different origins, then a patriotic country can accept immigrants from various different countries if the newcomers to the society adopt core constitutional principles and in good faith accept the protections and norms of their new country. Modern-day Luxembourg includes peoples of various different backgrounds that have been accepted by the government. In the same breath, the Luxembourgish language remains steadfast in the country even with a polyglot background of other official languages like French and German, but also other immigrants and tourists who speak English, Portuguese, Serbo-Croatian, and Arabic.

From another perspective, some countries have extensive out-migration. More people emigrate from the host country to other countries than immigrate into a particular country. In this scenario, a government can still make a distinction between patriotism and nationalism by its treatment of minority groups. As an example, take the neighboring Central American countries of El Salvador and Honduras, both of which have greater out-migration, especially to Mexico and the United States. In the late-nineteenth to mid-twentieth century, thousands of Salvadorans moved to Honduras in search of land and opportunities.[17] At times, this movement of Salvadorans to Honduras contributed to the significant hostilities between governments including the brief "soccer war" in 1969.

Virtually every country in the world—with the exception of a very few that are ethnically and linguistically homogenous—has minority groups that can be treated with respect. The Honduran government can act with grace towards Salvadorans residing within its borders, with the aforementioned caveats on acceptance by citizens, and relative debt levels. To cite another scenario, even in Japan where the people are very ethnically and linguistically homogenous, over 99 percent, still can treat ethnic Korean and Ainu populations with dignity. Migration—in and out—is commonplace all over the world. Governments differ on what policies to implement, and much depends on the situation. But, some guidelines based on Scripture have been provided here.

In sum, the line between nationalism and patriotism is very nebulous at times. Nonetheless, there is a clear distinction in tone that a government can purport, which should then be disseminated and adopted by the people. If a country has a strong and shared collective sentiment, but concurrently hold to a loose and welcoming national identity, then a definition of patriotism applies. Most political leaders will try to frame themselves as patriots, as opposed to nationalists, but this is where specific definitions can be important.

---

17. Durham, *Scarcity and Survival in Central America*, 55.

Where a political leader fails to adopt the core tenets of patriotism, the label of nationalism is better suited. In a biblical sense, a definition of patriotism better recognizes the humanity of people, rather than dehumanizing people as an "other." This is not to argue that immigrants or refugees must be allowed into a country; political leaders have every right to control borders, but the general tone towards people must be one of dignity and respect, that all people are image of bearers of God.

Examples of Nationalism and Patriotism

In chapter 1, a continuum was presented as way of showing a range of possible identities that people could hold ranging from globalism, regionalism, patriotism, nationalism, colonialism, to hypernationalism. The two categories on the left of the continuum are discussed in great detail in chapters 6 on transnationalism (globalism) and 4 on Supranationalism (regionalism) respectively. The two categories most closely connected to amassing territory—colonialism and hypernationalism—serve more to satiate human greed rather than reaching people with the gospel of Jesus Christ. Both subjects will be discussed in passing in this chapter. To introduce the terms, colonialism was prominent in previous centuries, especially amongst European powers from the fifteenth century until the end of World War II. Missionaries were sometimes tangential to the expansion of territory. In particular, Catholic missionaries often accompanied French and Spanish settlers and colonists. Colonialism served to exploit local populations, and subjugate them. The negatives far outweigh the positives, and no real line of biblical inference can be applied to support colonialism. Some historic figures tried to utilize a "biblically defensible" line for colonialism is Genesis 1:28 on having dominion over the earth, but this does not give one group of people a divine right on dominion, nor does it connote domination and subjugation over people. So, in my view, colonialism does not have any biblical authority. In general, colonialism was very negative, but some "positive" aspects are noteworthy: democratic tenets, rule of law, mass printing, and literacy. This is not to argue that colonialism was positive, rather, the infiltration of a Christian worldview against colonialism helped to push towards some positive outcomes within a deeply negative institution. Therefore, nearly all of these "positive" aspects are heavily correlated with the presence of conversionary protestant missionaries.[18] These missionaries also served in the aftermath of colonial expansion, and had more limited connections to those in power. Where conversionary protestant missionaries were not welcome or present

18. Woodberry, "*The Missionary Roots of Liberal Democracy*," 244.

in colonized areas, few of these positive elements took hold.[19] These regions remain undemocratic, authoritarian, and more illiterate than all other regions of the world. Hypernationalism (also called ultra-nationalism) should be viewed as a vitriolic extension of colonialism, which seeks to violently subjugate people based on unbiblical views of superiority and inferiority, mainly adjudicated along racial and ethnic metrics. Hypernationalism, in my view, has no biblical pretext or support.

Given that the two positions on the left of the continuum (globalism and regionalism) are dealt with elsewhere, and that the two position on the right of the continuum (colonialism and hypernationalism) are discussed in specific places, this chapter will focus on the categories in the middle of the continuum: patriotism and nationalism. Both colonialism and hypernationalism are tangential to a discussion of nationalism and will be discussed in places in this chapter. But, given that colonialism is much less prominent today, the subject does not warrant its own chapter. Similarly, hypernationalism is much less prominent today. Nazi Germany and Imperial Japan in the 1930s and 1940s provide the most recent examples. Iraq's conquering of Kuwait in 1990 and the subsequent Gulf War in January 1991 to restore Kuwaiti sovereignty,[20] as well as Russia's military incursions in Georgia in 2008 and Ukraine in 2014[21] may provide exceptions, which makes a discussion of hypernationalism still relevant today as in it is not extinct.[22] Hypernationalism, then, fits in within a broader discussion of nationalism. Nevertheless, since there is no biblical imperative for hypernationalism with the exception of particular God warranted situations like conquering the Promised Land in the book of Joshua, there is no separate chapter on the subject. Modern hypernationalism (based on national identity), though, is very different from destroying the Canaanites (based on very specific religious identity) as the command was to remove pagan influence in the Promised Land.

The pastor and author, David Jeremiah, notes that God only created three human institutions. First, in Genesis 1–3, God created the family; second, in Genesis 9, God created civil/human government; finally, in Acts, God created the church. In one reading of Genesis 11, which features the toppling of the Tower of Babel, the country is one institution that God did not explicitly create. However, on the other hand, God did create civil government.[23] It makes sense that this civil government is contained within a

19. Woodberry, "*The Missionary Roots of Liberal Democracy*," 260.

20. Fazal, *State Death*, 3.

21. Gatrell, *The Unsettling of Europe*, 378.

22. Kasparov, *Winter is Coming*.

23. Jeremiah, *The Coming Economic Armageddon*, 42.

physical territory or land. In addition, since the languages were separated in Genesis 11, tangentially it could be argued that countries were formed since linguistic separateness is often a modern reason for independent countries to be created. If nothing else, a sense of territorial identity was purported, but usually under a monarch or emperor of some sort. There is no explicit case, then, that God created countries, but He did institute human governance in Genesis 9, and scattered language groups in Genesis 11—a position that is close to the foundation of modern countries. In this book, I argue that patriotism is the most acceptable form of national belonging according to the Bible; I also argue that under very specific circumstances, nationalism is acceptable. I do not view any of the other four points along the continuum to be biblical; although, Christians can certainly interact with these layers of government in specific places. The question then is what is the biblical basis for my view on the biblical acceptability of patriotism, but also nationalism?

First, the Old Testament is largely juxtaposed on the idea that national units are important. Numerous countries from Edom to Phoenicia to Aram to Ammon amongst many others all vie for contention with Israel, and often go to battle. In the modern era, only Israel and Egypt still remain from the time, and are now members of the United Nations with full recognition in the twenty-first century.[24] But, the central idea is that national units have existed throughout recorded history, and these national units have fallen into the categories of patriotism and nationalism, even if some countries are no longer in existence.

In the New Testament, the concept of statehood changed. Instead of the warring countries in the Middle East, the predominant entity is the Roman Empire (discussed further in chapter 4). Nonetheless, the provinces of the Roman Empire are still signified as different, and territorial boundaries are discussed as reference points throughout the New Testament. Both testaments highlight the idea of the 30,000-foot version of the definition of nationalism, which separates land into countries—various states that are separate from one another, and autonomous.

To provide an argument as to why patriotism and nationalism are acceptable forms of national attachment according to the Bible, I will examine numerous sections of Scripture. I will start in the Old Testament, and then move to the New Testament. After creating humanity, God then creates civil government in Genesis 9. In Genesis 11, countries are concretely defined. Genesis 11:1–9 reads:

> "1 Now the whole earth used the same language and the same
> words. 2 It came about as they journeyed east, that they found a

24. UN, *The United Nations Today.*

plain in the land of Shinar and settled there. 3 They said to one another, "Come, let us make bricks and burn them thoroughly." And they used brick for stone, and they used tar for mortar. 4 They said, "Come, let us build for ourselves a city, and a tower whose top will reach into heaven, and let us make for ourselves a name, otherwise we will be scattered abroad over the face of the whole earth." 5 The Lord came down to see the city and the tower which the sons of men had built. 6 The Lord said, "Behold, they are one people, and they all have the same language. And this is what they began to do, and now nothing which they purpose to do will be impossible for them. 7 Come, let Us go down and there confuse their language, so that they will not understand one another's speech." 8 So the Lord scattered them abroad from there over the face of the whole earth; and they stopped building the city. 9 Therefore its name was called Babel, because there the Lord confused the language of the whole earth; and from there the Lord scattered them abroad over the face of the whole earth."

Genesis 11 begins in the context of the Tower of Babel. In verse 4, there is a description of building a collective, global city that reaches to the heavens. The idea being that arrogant human beings can somehow compete with the majesty of God and instead create a worldwide government.[25] In verse 6, the languages of the world revolve around one single language as a means of again decreasing the power of God and elevating human beings. As noted in verse 9, the Lord scatters the people over the face of the earth. Coupled with verse 7, languages are confused, and people no longer have one centralized mode of communication. This section of Scripture highlights the 30,000-foot definition provided earlier in the chapter—that human beings are separated into national units. Obviously, this distinction has been different at alternate points in time, but, in general, biblical accounts, as well as human experiences, show that countries are the most common way for human beings to group.

In numerous different sections of psalms, the authors note the importance of Israel, and of national belonging. Sometimes even, the verbiage is more general. For example, the writer of Psalm 33 extols: "Blessed is the nation whose God is the Lord" (Psalm 33:12). In many regards, this verse notes the importance of having a country, and influencing that country towards God from the inside. The connotation here is that there is a national blessing if the God of Israel is worshipped across the country. Sometimes, the connotation in psalms is simply that God should be worshipped in general: Psalms 68:32a, "Sing to God, O kingdoms of the earth." People in every

25. Jeremiah, *Agents of Babylon*, vii.

country should worship God. But, the verse does separate out people into their different national units. National belonging can also have a challenging element, especially if one's country loses a battle. A good example of this point can be found in Psalm 79.

Psalm 79:1–4:

> "1 O God, the nations have invaded Your inheritance; They have defiled Your holy temple; They have laid Jerusalem in ruins. 2 They have given the dead bodies of Your servants for food to the birds of the heavens, The flesh of Your godly ones to the beasts of the earth. 3 They have poured out their blood like water round about Jerusalem; And there was no one to bury them. 4 We have become a reproach to our neighbors, A scoffing and derision to those around us."

In Psalm 79, the psalmist (Asaph) is lamenting the invasion and conquering of Jerusalem—presumably by the Babylonians—and noting that enemy nations have divided the kingdom, and brought down Jerusalem. The central idea here is that there are two different, opposing nations who are doing battle over Jerusalem. Countries, with positions of patriotism or nationalism, are central to the themes in psalms.

Elsewhere in the Old Testament, similar sentiments are commonplace across the 39 books. Here are a few examples. The book of Obadiah, verses 15 and 16 provide a dire warning to some nations.

> 15 "For the day of the Lord draws near on all the nations. As you have done, it will be done to you. Your dealings will return on your own head. 16 "Because just as you drank on My holy mountain, All the nations will drink continually. They will drink and swallow, And become as if they had never existed."

In Obadiah, as well as other sections of the Old Testament, countries are often taken as blocks. There seems to be a sense of collective judgment on countries, in addition to individual judgment after death. From Scripture, several passages imply that God judges countries at specific points, and then presents different (usually negative) situations to try to impel behavior to change. But, there is no collective salvation of a country, just differing circumstances. Moreover, Asaph in Psalm 79 presents a premonition—many countries that once existed will be invaded, and subjected to other rulers. There is no guarantee that a country will survive. This point is evident for many historical countries that once existed and now do not.[26]

---

26. Fazal, *State Death*, 1; Jeremiah, *Agents of Babylon*, 38.

In Numbers 22–24, King Balak of Moab hired a diviner, Balaam, to send a curse on God's people based on a perceived threat. Balaam made three attempts to curse God's people, but God intervened and blessed them instead.[27] Numbers 24:1–2 reads: "When Balaam saw that it pleased the Lord to bless Israel, he did not go as at other times to seek omens but he set his face toward the wilderness. And Balaam lifted up his eyes and saw Israel camping tribe by tribe, and the Spirit of God came upon him."

There is an obvious connection here on the issue of nationalism. Not only does Balaam become inflicted with the Spirit of God, but his nationalistic desires to hurt Israel are overcome by this heart change. The Israelites did not, in nationalistic fervor, attempt to kill Balaam, but rather waited for God to change his heart. Where possible, leaders of a given country should show patience to those in other countries—to seek peace where possible (Matthew 5:9).[28]

On the other side of the coin, the Book of Lamentations outlines the distress of the people when a country is conquered. The prophet Jeremiah, the author of Lamentations, paints a vivid picture of destruction and victimization, which plagues the people of Judah. Lamentations 4:17b reads, "In our watching we have watched, for a nation that could not save."

Furthermore, in Lamentations 5:21–22,

> "There is great mourning when sin is abundant, and the protections of God are taken away from the people—the prophet Jeremiah beseeches God at the end of the book, "Restore us to You, O Lord, that we may be restored; renew our days as of old, unless you have utterly rejected us and are exceedingly angry with us."

The context of the Book of Lamentations is that it was written in the aftermath of the fall of Jerusalem to the Babylonian Empire in 587 B.C.[29] In this context, the Kingdom of Judah was formally annexed as part of Babylonian Empire such that Israel and Judah ceased to exist as independent countries,[30] but were now incorporated as part of a foreign empire. It was a time for intense mourning, and the prophet cries out for restoration—an event that would not happen for centuries.

The annexation of Judah to the Babylonian Empire in Lamentations does not happen in a vacuum. Ultimately, the Israelite peoples slowly descend in their governance, and move—step by step—away from God. In the

---

27. Pray for ISIS, prayforisis.com

28. Sider and Knippers, *Toward an Evangelical Public Policy*, 288

29. Hill and Walton, *A Survey of the Old Testament*, 434.

30. Hill and Walton, *A Survey of the Old Testament*, 434.

Book of Hosea, as an example, there is a foreshadowing of this time. Hosea 4:1 reads, "Listen to the word of the Lord, O sons of Israel, For the Lord has a case against the inhabitants of the land, Because there is no faithfulness or kindness or knowledge of God in the land." In the New International Version, "no acknowledgment of God in the land." God is patient with the peoples of Israel and Judah (see chapter 5 on secession for an in-depth discussion of the division of the Kingdom). Yet, through the prophets in particular, there are numerous warnings for the people to change their ways, and to worship God. In the end, God's chosen people opt not to select God en masse—for this major reason, they are divided and incapable of adequately defending themselves when world politics shifts towards larger empire in the east—the Assyrians, Babylonians, and Medo-Persians. God also allows the events to bring together a broader story of redemption that will occur physically, but most importantly, spiritually, through his son Jesus Christ.

Countries surrounding Israel

The intonation in all of these passages of Scripture in the above section is that nations (countries) exist, and that God has plans and purposes for each country. Israel is the focus in all of these passages, but the borderlines with other countries are more clearly extrapolated in other parts of the Old Testament. This distinction is the focus of this section of the chapter.

In Amos 1, for example, there is a clear distinction between Israel, Judah, and many surrounding countries.[31] In this particular section of Scripture, the prophet Amos starts his book by rebuking neighboring countries before turning his attention to Judah, then Israel.[32] What is most apt here is the distinction of various different countries. Consider again the 30,000-foot definition of nationalism offered at the start of the chapter—that the world is simply divided into countries, rather than other sorts of arrangements. Amos 1 highlights, approximately 2,800 years ago, that the known world at that time was distinctly divided along national lines. Also, in Amos 1 is a greater sense of distinction between positions of patriotism and nationalism. Both are biblically acceptable pending the circumstances. The Lord has consternation against Damascus (verses 3–5), Gaza (verse 6), Edom (verse 6), Ashdod and Ashkelon (verse 8), Ekron (verse 8), Tyre (verses 9 and 10), Edom (again in verses 11 and 12), and Ammon (verses 13 to 15). This is a clear vision of nationalism given the need to protect Israel from its surrounding enemies. There is no specification that any of these surrounding

31. Hill and Walton, *A Survey of the Old Testament*, 481.
32. Sider and Knippers, *Toward an Evangelical Public Policy*, 145.

countries would be subject to colonial or hypernationalist policies, so nationalism is, in this specific case, biblically supported. Amos 1 reads:

> "1 The words of Amos, who was among the sheepherders from Tekoa, which he envisioned in visions concerning Israel in the days of Uzziah king of Judah, and in the days of Jeroboam son of Joash, king of Israel, two years before the earthquake. 2 He said,

> "The Lord roars from Zion and from Jerusalem He utters His voice; and the shepherds' pasture grounds mourn, and the summit of Carmel dries up." 3 Thus says the Lord, "For three transgressions of Damascus and for four I will not revoke its punishment, because they threshed Gilead with implements of sharp iron. 4 "So I will send fire upon the house of Hazael and it will consume the citadels of Ben-hadad. 5 "I will also break the gate bar of Damascus, and cut off the inhabitant from the valley of Aven, and him who holds the scepter, from Beth-eden; So the people of Aram will go exiled to Kir," Says the Lord. 6 Thus says the Lord, "For three transgressions of Gaza and for four I will not revoke its punishment, because they deported an entire population to deliver it up to Edom. 7 "So I will send fire upon the wall of Gaza and it will consume her citadels. 8 "I will also cut off the inhabitant from Ashdod, and him who holds the scepter, from Ashkelon; I will even unleash My power upon Ekron, and the remnant of the Philistines will perish," Says the Lord God. 9 Thus says the Lord, "For three transgressions of Tyre and for four I will not revoke its punishment, because they delivered up an entire population to Edom and did not remember the covenant of brotherhood. 10 "So I will send fire upon the wall of Tyre and it will consume her citadels." 11 Thus says the Lord, "For three transgressions of Edom and for four I will not revoke its punishment, because he pursued his brother with the sword, While he stifled his compassion; His anger also tore continually, and he maintained his fury forever. 12 "So I will send fire upon Teman and it will consume the citadels of Bozrah." 13 Thus says the Lord, "For three transgressions of the sons of Ammon and for four I will not revoke its punishment, because they ripped open the pregnant women of Gilead in order to enlarge their borders. 14 "So I will kindle a fire on the wall of Rabbah and it will consume her citadels amid war cries on the day of battle, and a storm on the day of tempest. 15 "Their king will go into exile, He and his princes together," says the Lord."

In places, the language in Amos 1 is very nationalistic. In some sense, the language is difficult to hear in the twenty-first century given modern, western notions of peace and tranquility. However, war is a more regular part of the human experience when examined through the lens of time and history. As Solomon notes in Ecclesiastes 3:8b, "(there is) a time for war and a time for peace." Conflict abounds, and is an unfortunate part of the human experience, but one that must be subjection to personal rumination in order to find God-honoring political positions.

Amos 2 continues in the same vein as Amos 1 with further deterrent language against other neighboring countries such as Moab (verses 1–3) and Judah (verses 4 and 5).[33] Following verse 5, the Lord turns His anger towards Israel itself.

> "1 Thus says the Lord, "For three transgressions of Moab and for four I will not revoke its punishment, because he burned the bones of the king of Edom to lime. 2 "So I will send fire upon Moab and it will consume the citadels of Kerioth; and Moab will die amid tumult, with war cries and the sound of a trumpet. 3 "I will also cut off the judge from her midst and slay all her princes with him," says the Lord. 4 Thus says the Lord, "For three transgressions of Judah and for four I will not revoke its punishment, because they rejected the law of the Lord and have not kept His statutes; Their lies also have led them astray, those after which their fathers walked. 5 "So I will send fire upon Judah and it will consume the citadels of Jerusalem."

Amos 1 and part of Amos 2 present a situation where the Lord is unhappy with the actions of Israel, Judah, and many surrounding countries. In relation to the issue of nationalism and patriotism is war. The purpose of this book is not to investigate whether it is biblically acceptable for Christians to engage in war, but the subject matter is tangential to a discussion on nationalism.[34] In Amos 1 and 2, among other examples, Israel fights, competes, gets involved in diplomatic disputes with its neighbors. These neighboring countries existed, and were significant points of concern in the governance of the Kingdom of Israel (and later Judah).

National Identity

In tandem with the above discussion on God's view of countries surrounding Israel, especially in times of belligerence, it is useful to engage in a discussion on national identity. This discussion will buttress the definition laid

---

33. Sider and Knippers, *Toward an Evangelical Public Policy*, 146.
34. Clouse, *War: Four Christian Views*.

out in chapter 1 and the start of chapter 2. The following two sections dissect some differences in national identity between the Old Testament and New Testament. It is important to note that God is the same across the two testaments and that His characteristics do not change over time (Hebrews 13:8). With the framework in mind, the next two sections explore the different contexts of national discussion in the two testaments.

Old Testament National Identity

In the midst of a discussion on governing options of nationalism and patriotism, the issue of national identity is an important one, in this case through the lens of the Old Testament. In Deuteronomy 20 and Judges 3, there are major points of discussion over when and how to maintain this identity. The caveat here, again, is that the Israelites were special to God, but He also allowed them to be conquered by neighboring kingdoms in later centuries. Nonetheless, national identity is an important facet of maintaining a functioning and vibrant country. The case of Deuteronomy 20 is more extreme because it presents part of the history of the Israelite people. Deuteronomy 20:1, for example, reminds the Israelites of their time in Egypt, and how they maintained their national unity despite being enslaved. Then, the Israelites escaped, and found the Promised Land. Deuteronomy 20 reads:

> "1 When you go out to battle against your enemies and see horses and chariots and people more numerous than you, do not be afraid of them; for the Lord your God, who brought you up from the land of Egypt, is with you. 2 When you are approaching the battle, the priest shall come near and speak to the people. 3 He shall say to them, 'Hear, O Israel, you are approaching the battle against your enemies today. Do not be fainthearted. Do not be afraid, or panic, or tremble before them, 4 for the Lord your God is the one who goes with you, to fight for you against your enemies, to save you.'"

In the first four verses of Deuteronomy 20—essentially a passage of Scripture that provides instructions for warfare—there is a spiritual component in protecting national identity, at least in a limited sense. Recalling the definition of nationalism, under specific circumstances, it is biblical for Christians to defend their country. The emphasis here is on a defensive war as a means to protect one's family members. Although Deuteronomy 20 is offensive in nature in the context of the Israelites, it is under a very specific circumstance—the Lord brought them out of captivity in Israel, and is now showing them the Promised Land. There are no modern equivalents where this is a viable position biblically. Thus, to take Deuteronomy 20, in the context of New Testaments teachings to love one's neighbor, there is an ability to engage in defensive wars that serve to protect one's family and neighbors. Take, for example, the Armenian Genocide, wherein between 100,000[35] and 300,000[36] Armenian Christians were slaughtered by the Ottomans between 1894 and 1896, and perhaps upwards of 1.5 million between 1914 and 1923.[37] Avoiding a repeat of the Armenian Genocide is obviously important for all of humanity.

In Deuteronomy 20:1–4, the admonition is for soldiers to be brave in the midst of war, but not to forget that God is sovereign. Verse 4 cannot be taken as a guarantee of victory—again, this section is specific to Israel. The broader lesson is that war, fought by different countries, is at times necessary for defensive purposes. Deuteronomy 20:5 continues:

> "5 The officers also shall speak to the people, saying, 'Who is the man that has built a new house and has not dedicated it? Let him depart and return to his house, otherwise he might die in the battle and another man would dedicate it. 6 Who is the man that has planted a vineyard and has not begun to use its fruit? Let him depart and return to his house, otherwise he might die in the battle and another man would begin to use its fruit. 7 And who is the man that is engaged to a woman and has not married her? Let him depart and return to his house, otherwise he might die in the battle and another man would marry her.' 8 Then the officers shall speak further to the people and say, 'Who is the man that is afraid and fainthearted? Let him depart and return to his house, so that he might not make his brothers' hearts melt like his heart.' 9 When the officers have finished speaking to the people, they shall appoint commanders of armies at the head of the people."

War is a serious undertaking. Deuteronomy 20:5–9 is a descriptive text, but given examples in throughout history, there is a possible prescriptive application: there is an importance to volunteerism in the military as a means of best protecting the population. Put simply, a successful outcome in war is more likely if it is fought by people that want to serve their country. National identity is therefore a key facet here because without people willing to stand up and defend the country, it will be invaded and conquered. Nationalism is acceptable under limited circumstances as a means of fending off enemy invasion. National identity is a critical component

---

35. McMeekin, *Ottoman Endgame*, 25.
36. Evans, *Pursuit of Power*, 689.
37. McMeekin, *Ottoman Endgame*, 223–245.

here, because to defend one's neighbors implies a broader connection to them to the point of being willing to sacrifice one's life in defense of the country. Deuteronomy 20:10 continues:

> "10 When you approach a city to fight against it, you shall offer it terms of peace. 11 If it agrees to make peace with you and opens to you, then all the people who are found in it shall become your forced labor and shall serve you. 12 However, if it does not make peace with you, but makes war against you, then you shall besiege it."

The first pledge in Deuteronomy 20:10 is to offer peace. This obviously depends on circumstances and motives. Nevertheless, the overarching desire is to restore peaceful relations between countries. In verse 11, peace is subject to taking the territory, but this, again, is specific to Israel in a historic time and place. The wider application for Christian leaders within any country (whether there is a large Christian population or not) is to seek a peaceful resolution to conflict (Matthew 5:9). War may ensue if peace is spurned as a viable option for resolution. At some point, Christian leaders need wisdom to diagnose whether a given situation is particularly volatile. The situation of British Prime Minister, Neville Chamberlain, is instructive in confronting Adolf Hitler, the Führer of Nazi Germany. Infamously, Chamberlain obtained "peace in our time" in an agreement with Hitler in September 1938, in his view, to stave off further Nazi expansionism. In exchange for "peace," Hitler was allowed to annex sections of Czechoslovakia known as the Sudetenland (where high percentages of ethnic Germans resided).[38] It was a decision that Chamberlain would come to regret, and unfortunately be known as a central part of his legacy. Christians, therefore, must be careful with peace offers. The advice of the former American President, Ronald Reagan, is particularly apt: "trust, but verify." Christians must be "shrewd as serpents and innocent as doves" (Matthew 10:16b). Deuteronomy 20:13 continues:

> "13 When the Lord your God gives it into your hand, you shall strike all the men in it with the edge of the sword. 14 Only the women and the children and the animals and all that is in the city, all its spoil, you shall take as booty for yourself; and you shall use the spoil of your enemies which the Lord your God has given you. 15 Thus you shall do to all the cities that are very far from you, which are not of the cities of these nations nearby."

---

38. Metaxas, *Bonhoeffer*, 314.

In Deuteronomy 20, the Lord is in the midst of giving instructions for taking the Promised Land through the sword.[39] He is clear to delineate this space from other countries. There is no instruction to attack other countries that are not subject to this specific section of territory.

> "16 Only in the cities of these peoples that the Lord your God is giving you as an inheritance, you shall not leave alive anything that breathes. 17 But you shall utterly destroy them, the Hittite and the Amorite, the Canaanite and the Perizzite, the Hivite and the Jebusite, as the Lord your God has commanded you, 18 so that they may not teach you to do according to all their detestable things which they have done for their gods, so that you would sin against the Lord your God. 19 "When you besiege a city a long time, to make war against it in order to capture it, you shall not destroy its trees by swinging an axe against them; for you may eat from them, and you shall not cut them down. For is the tree of the field a man, that it should be besieged by you? 20 Only the trees which you know are not fruit trees you shall destroy and cut down, that you may construct siege works against the city that is making war with you until it falls."

Sections of Deuteronomy 20 are amongst the most challenging in Scripture as it denotes an instruction to completely conquer the land.[40] The central idea that can be taken for Christians in the twenty-first century is to be cognizant of national identity and to maintain a level of unity as a means of military preparedness. There is no instruction to conquer or kill all the inhabitants of a land, but these elements may be an unfortunate outcome in warfare. Tangentially, this is a reason why diplomacy is so important because preventing conflict from starting is a preferred outcome. Otherwise, in cases of "Total War," as most recently evidenced by some of the most bloody theatres of World War II, it present the need for a military to be sufficiently ready to combat a population that is intent on waging total conflict.[41] Again, in order to protect one's family and neighbors, careful conduct in warfare is necessary.

Switching to another example in Judges 3, the idea of national identity is a prominent one. Under specific circumstances—namely the threat of war, particularly the invasion of your country by an outside force—defensive

---

39. Grudem, *Politics according to the Bible*, 189.

40. Some critics will argue that God is a moral "monster" citing passages like Deuteronomy 20, or God's people capturing the Holy Land. For those interested, Paul Copan's 2011 book, "Is God a moral monster?" provides the cultural and historical background to show why these events occurred.

41. Duerr, "*War*," 549.

warfare is acceptable. In Judges 3, the storyline provides examples of both nationalism and patriotism. The Israelite people are, on several occasions, mobilized for war against enemy surrounding countries. The book of Judges is notorious for the cyclical nature of the Jewish people's faith, oscillating from an in-depth yearning for God to worshipping idols and false gods. In tandem with this oscillation is the peace-war dichotomy that afflicts the Israelites. The vicissitudes of their freedom, even in the short chapter of Judges 3, is enough to induce a vomit-plagued rollercoaster ride. On several occasions, the Israelites are defeated and enslaved.[42] After they cry out to God for mercy, He delivers them from their enemies and restores their freedom—the process then repeats. Judges 3 starts:

> "1 Now these are the nations which the Lord left, to test Israel by them (that is, all who had not experienced any of the wars of Canaan; 2 only in order that the generations of the sons of Israel might be taught war, those who had not experienced it formerly). 3 These nations are: the five lords of the Philistines and all the Canaanites and the Sidonians and the Hivites who lived in Mount Lebanon, from Mount Baal-hermon as far as Lebo-hamath. 4 They were for testing Israel, to find out if they would obey the commandments of the Lord, which He had commanded their fathers through Moses."

In the opening verses of Judges 3, the wider narrative is that the surrounding countries to Israel provide an ongoing test to governance in the country. National identity remains a prominent feature to unite the people as different from others. Again, this specific circumstance is based on worship of the Lord. In the modern era, people from every country can become Christians. Thus, neighboring countries can naturally maintain a disposition of peace if Christ followers act in peaceful ways. Take, for example, the relationship between Canada and the United States. Even though the War of 1812 (that lasted through 1814) pitted the two countries against each other (what is now the Canada was a British colony until 1867 with the British North America Act).[43] Both sides attempted to some degree to conquer the other.[44] Yet, today, friendly relationships continue between the two countries. Christians in both countries contribute to a peaceful environment such that conflict between Canada and the United States is currently considered a very strange idea. This type of peaceful relationship can

---

42. Hill and Walton, *A Survey of the Old Testament*, 195.

43. Hickey, *The War of 1812*.

44. Mearsheimer, *The Tragedy of Great Power Politics*, 244.

be procured by Christians across national lines. Yet, there are important reminders in what to avoid. Judges 3:5 continues:

> "5 The sons of Israel lived among the Canaanites, the Hittites, the Amorites, the Perizzites, the Hivites, and the Jebusites; 6 and they took their daughters for themselves as wives, and gave their own daughters to their sons, and served their gods. 7 The sons of Israel did what was evil in the sight of the Lord, and forgot the Lord their God and served the Baals and the Asheroth. 8 Then the anger of the Lord was kindled against Israel, so that He sold them into the hands of Cushan-rishathaim king of Mesopotamia; and the sons of Israel served Cushan-rishathaim eight years. 9 When the sons of Israel cried to the Lord, the Lord raised up a deliverer for the sons of Israel to deliver them, Othniel the son of Kenaz, Caleb's younger brother. 10 The Spirit of the Lord came upon him, and he judged Israel. When he went out to war, the Lord gave Cushan-rishathaim king of Mesopotamia into his hand, so that he prevailed over Cushan-rishathaim. 11 Then the land had rest forty years. And Othniel the son of Kenaz died."

In Judges 3: 5–11, many specific events happen. The Israelites, in verse 5, allowed their national identity to be watered down to the point of losing all compulsion to defend themselves. The King of Aram, in verse 8 attacks and conquers Israel. It is only after Othniel is installed as Israel's judge that the people return to God, and then they are in a position to regain their sovereignty. The Lord allows these events to transpire. Yet, the cyclical nature of worshipping God and then denying him in the Book of Judges, begins to spin its nefarious wheel again. Starting in Judges 3:12, Scripture shows how the Israelites changed once again:

> "12 Now the sons of Israel again did evil in the sight of the Lord. So the Lord strengthened Eglon the king of Moab against Israel, because they had done evil in the sight of the Lord. 13 And he gathered to himself the sons of Ammon and Amalek; and he went and defeated Israel, and they possessed the city of the palm trees. 14 The sons of Israel served Eglon the king of Moab eighteen years. 15 But when the sons of Israel cried to the Lord, the Lord raised up a deliverer for them, Ehud the son of Gera, the Benjamite, a left-handed man. And the sons of Israel sent tribute by him to Eglon the king of Moab. 16 Ehud made himself a sword which had two edges, a cubit in length, and he bound it on his right thigh under his cloak. 17 He presented the tribute to Eglon king of Moab. Now Eglon was a very fat man. 18 It came about when he had finished presenting the tribute,

that he sent away the people who had carried the tribute. 19 But he himself turned back from the idols which were at Gilgal, and said, "I have a secret message for you, O king." And he said, "Keep silence." And all who attended him left him. 20 Ehud came to him while he was sitting alone in his cool roof chamber. And Ehud said, "I have a message from God for you." And he arose from his seat. 21 Ehud stretched out his left hand, took the sword from his right thigh and thrust it into his belly. 22 The handle also went in after the blade, and the fat closed over the blade, for he did not draw the sword out of his belly; and the refuse came out. 23 Then Ehud went out into the vestibule and shut the doors of the roof chamber behind him, and locked them. 24 When he had gone out, his servants came and looked, and behold, the doors of the roof chamber were locked; and they said, "He is only relieving himself in the cool room." 25 They waited until they became anxious; but behold, he did not open the doors of the roof chamber. Therefore they took the key and opened them, and behold, their master had fallen to the floor dead.26 Now Ehud escaped while they were delaying, and he passed by the idols and escaped to Seirah. 27 It came about when he had arrived, that he blew the trumpet in the hill country of Ephraim; and the sons of Israel went down with him from the hill country, and he was in front of them. 28 He said to them, "Pursue them, for the Lord has given your enemies the Moabites into your hands." So they went down after him and seized the fords of the Jordan opposite Moab, and did not allow anyone to cross. 29 They struck down at that time about ten thousand Moabites, all robust and valiant men; and no one escaped. 30 So Moab was subdued that day under the hand of Israel. And the land was undisturbed for eighty years."

The rest of Judges 3 presents a longer narrative on Israelite national identity. In verse 12, the neighboring Moabites conquer Israel. The Ammonites and Amalekites join the Moabites in fighting against the Israelites. Ehud is raised up as a new leader in Israel, and he has to use a range of guile and moxie to circumvent Eglon, the king of the Moabites. There is a long narrative of how the Moabites are ultimately defeated with a fascinating story of how the King is slain by a left-handed man in the restroom. The major lesson, though, is maintaining allegiance to God, and a national identity that can defend the population. This is not to imply animosity towards neighboring countries. In many parts of the world today, peaceful relations are the norm.

The Old Testament is full of scenarios, typically involving the Israelite people in conflict with others. Patriotism is the default mode where the

Israelites attempt to live peaceably with their neighbors. As discussed in more detail in chapter 5, in 1 Kings 3, for example, King Solomon creates a pact with Egypt; in 1 Kings 5, he created a pact with Tyre. Both instances present a desire to live peaceably with one's neighbors. There are many other situations in the Old Testament, though, where Israel is at war with one or more of its neighbors. In these cases, nationalism replaces patriotism, and is biblically acceptable provided that war is for the purposes of defense. Ethnic nationalism is not supported. In many scenarios, non-native born people help Israel, and are welcome within their ranks (see chapter 3).

New Testament National Identity

In the New Testament, the national unit of focus is no longer Israel (or Judah). All 27 books of the New Testament are written under the rule of the Roman Empire. Yet, there are guiding principles regarding national identity that can be instructional. One is the Great Commission in Matthew 28:16–20—Christians are to make disciples of all nations, an admonition that is still relevant today[45]—if the government of a country so chooses with the consent of their population, immigration and asylum policies can be relatively open (at least within economic reason in a democratic fashion) in order to evangelize people from different parts of the world. In some regards, it is easier to make disciples if people from around the world come to you. Thus, as a corrective to the Old Testament vision of national identity should be balanced by some allowances for immigration and asylum that are debated by the people of a country. As noted earlier this chapter, there is no requirement to allow immigrants or asylum-seekers, because the needs of the poor and disenfranchised within the country must be considered alongside the issue of debt. But, as is the case with the Good Samaritan, charity is an important virtue that can be extended to immigrants, asylum seekers, and/or refugees. The requisite balance between the aforementioned factors should be debated. A country's leaders can close its borders whenever it deems necessary, but a more open, civic version of nationalism follows as what the Bible most closely teaches on the issue—again with numerical limits, and with consent from the population.

In John 6:15, people expected that Jesus would be a strong military ruler, and wanted to sweep Him into power by force.[46] It is noted that many Jews in the Roman Empire anticipated a hero along the lines of Judas Maccabaeus—a revolutionary leader who was nationalistic in the sense that he

45. Piper, *Let the Nations be glad!*, 160.
46. Ladd, *A Theology of the New Testament*, 138.

wanted to overthrow the empire by leading a rebellion in 167–160 B.C. His focus on purifying the Second Temple was viewed as a way to make it Jewish again by removing all Greek influences. As a result of this expectation to be like Judas Maccabaeus, Jesus had to withdraw to the mountainside (again in John 6:15) in order to obviate the notion that He had come to provoke a nationalist-type revolt, instead of a salvific ministry. In all likelihood, the expectation on the part of many people was to accomplish this goal of overthrowing the Roman Empire by force, which would have led to widespread violence across many segments of society.

Instead, Jesus sets up a new vision for state-society relations. The most frequently cited section of Scripture in the New Testament when it comes to a Christian's interaction with government is Romans 13:1–7. It reads:

> "1 Every person is to be in subjection to the governing authorities. For there is no authority except from God, and those which exist are established by God. 2 Therefore whoever resists authority has opposed the ordinance of God; and they who have opposed will receive condemnation upon themselves. 3 For rulers are not a cause of fear for good behavior, but for evil. Do you want to have no fear of authority? Do what is good and you will have praise from the same; 4 for it is a minister of God to you for good. But if you do what is evil, be afraid; for it does not bear the sword for nothing; for it is a minister of God, an avenger who brings wrath on the one who practices evil. 5 Therefore it is necessary to be in subjection, not only because of wrath, but also for conscience' sake. 6 For because of this you also pay taxes, for rulers are servants of God, devoting themselves to this very thing. 7 Render to all what is due them: tax to whom tax is due; custom to whom custom; fear to whom fear; honor to whom honor."

The first seven verses of the book of Romans provide a rich overview of how a Christian should interact with government.[47] In sum, every single person is "exhorted to be subject to the governing authorities."[48] What is interesting in context of a discussion of nationality, though, is verse one where, Paul notes, (the authorities) "which exist established by God." This means that the government has been established by God, and tangentially, the country has been allowed to exist by God. Verse 2 spells out this idea more clearly noting that Christians should not rebel against what God has instituted, or risk being judged for their actions—"they who have opposed will receive condemnation upon themselves." This discussion is especially interesting

---

47. Grudem, *Politics according to the Bible*, 188–9.
48. Ladd, *A Theology of the New Testament*, 502.

in light of chapter 5 on secession and any right of rebellion, but, for now, the central idea is that a national identity is something presented by God in the form of a government over a particular territorial jurisdiction. Concomitantly, the expectation is also that the government does not terrorize the population—this is an integral component of governing justly. Verse 4 counterbalances this idea of subservience to the government by highlighting that governance should be for the "good" of the population. A definition of good, however, is not given here. Nevertheless, throughout Scripture, there is ample evidence as to what good entails. This is why this work often cites the concept of gaining consent from the population. Democracy is not inherent within Scripture, but governing for the good of people at least infers some level of consent, and a move away from tyranny.[49]

Adding to this discussion from Romans 13, a prominent historical example is the role of Christians in Nazi Germany. The German theologian, Dietrich Bonhoeffer took personal responsibility for the actions of Germany in World War II.[50] As a Christian, this view ultimately brought him to a point of trying to disrupt, and then expel, the leadership of his country.[51] Bonhoeffer understood the detrimental effects of hypernationalism, and knew that this position was not supported biblically, thus, he had to act in order to protect the German people, and those afflicted by the German people. After action, Bonhoeffer sought repentance and forgiveness for not doing more to prevent the rise of Hitler.[52] Ethnic nationalism, in this case, led to hypernationalism wherein Nazi Germany attempted to conquer and subjugate the conquered people. Moreover, ethnic Jews and many others were slaughtered largely on racial and ethnic grounds. Bonhoeffer knew that his personal actions went against the German (Nazi) government, but he did so in order to try to protect people, and serve a greater good.

Examining nationalism more broadly, national identity is an important issue to comprehend, especially in light of the fact that human life is limited with life expectancy across the world somewhere in the realm of 50–80 years depending on the country, in comparison to eternity. The writer, Richard John Neuhaus, for example, argues that:

> "Once upon a time it was the 1976 bicentennial of the American founding, to be precise I wrote a book on the American experiment and the idea of covenant. *Time* magazine picked up on it and reported, "On the day of judgment, Neuhaus wants to meet

49. Johnson-Sirleaf, *This Child will be great.*

50. Metaxas, *7 Men*, 92.

51. Metaxas, *Bonhoeffer*, 399.

52. Sider and Knippers, *Toward an Evangelical Public Policy*, 303.

God as an American." Neuhaus continues, "That's not quite right. What I wrote is that I expect to meet God as an American. And that for the simple reason that, among all the things I am or have been or hope to be, I am undeniably an American. It is not the most important thing, but it is an inescapable thing. Nor, even were I so inclined, should I try to escape it. It is a pervasive and indelible part of what is called one's "identity." Among American thinkers, and not least among American theologians, one frequently discerns an attempt to escape one's time and place. It is a very American thing to try to do. We are never more American than when we believe we have transcended being American. America is, after all, as some like to say, the world's first "universal nation."[53]

Neuhaus makes an important point here. If one experiences life through the lens of residing within a specific country, then that is the frame of reference through which one can interact with God. If human beings are held to account for their lives by their creator, then part of that interaction must be distilled through the culture and mores of said country. Across time and space, this interaction will look different, but for many people, they will meet God through a specific national lens.

Nationalism versus Patriotism

As noted in chapter 1, for the layperson, the terms nationalism and patriotism largely overlap and are often conflated. Even for the academic, these terms are likewise often immingled, or hard to disentangle. So, what is nationalism? And, what is patriotism? In chapter 1, rudimentary definitions of nationalism and patriotism were offered to the reader, but more unpacking is necessary in order to uncover more nuances in the subject matter.

Nationalism and patriotism have a lot in common, but nationalism has harder edges, and implies a greater sense of rigidness towards foreigners and engagement in military actions. Depending on the situation, selecting nationalism as the optimal government policy over patriotism may be warranted. At most other times, patriotism is the preferred overarching vehicle for policy. In some senses, nationalism is useful when it comes to the question of national defense. Obviously, this is a contentious subject—whether or not Christians can go to war, and in what capacities? But, if non-Christians rulers are in power, and opt to go to war, then Christians

---

53. Neuhaus, *Our American Babylon.*

have to, at a bare minimum, respect those in office.[54] Moreover, if Christ's admonition to love one's neighbor is in place, does this involve defending one's neighbor, or willfully allowing them to suffer and die? On that question, Christians can participate in war, especially if it is waged in defense of the community as a means of loving that community.[55] The bounds of what a Christian soldier can or cannot do are strictly limited, and extend to showing mercy and love to one's enemies.

Nationalism, then, can be useful to a Christ-follower, but only in a very limited capacity. The appropriate circumstances for nationalism are twofold: 1) when one's country is under attack, Christians may mobilize as an expression of love to one's neighbors, assuming that they are part of the government's military, 2) where a people, somewhere in the world, are experiencing genocide—Christians cannot lovingly sit back and allow for ethnic cleansing to take place unchecked.[56]

In many respects, nationalism depends on how it is mobilized. The models of civic nationalism and ethnic nationalism are the most noteworthy. Scholars have, for some time, debated the existence, viability, and definitions of these terms. It is not a foregone conclusion that either one exists in practice. But, in theory, the civic/ethnic dichotomy is useful because it highlights how governments may act differently towards its people.[57] Civic nationalism, for example, is much more open, and citizenship is based on constitutional principles wherein any person can theoretically join the country.[58] Ethnic nationalism is much more dependent on blood and soil forms of identity wherein someone has to be born into citizenship.[59] Thus, under a definition of nationalism, the sharper edges are much more dangerous under ethnic nationalism because the road to colonialism and hypernationalism are facilitated by making a racialist argument of ethnic superiority. Nationalism still has harder edges under a civic form, but it much less likely to devolve into colonialism or hypernationalism because all people are intrinsically valued by the state as citizens. In practice these academic definitions are imperfect, but a sense of civic equality under the constitution retards any overt move towards jingoism; thus, civic nationalism helps to curtail the tendency towards the harder edges of nationalism.

54. Clouse, *War: Four Christian Views*, 25
55. Holmes, "Just War," 118
56. Brown, "The Crusade or Preventive War," 159
57. Duerr, *Secessionism and the European Union*, 6.
58. Ignatieff, *Blood and Belonging*, xiii.
59. Duerr, *Secessionism and the European Union*, 6–8.

As noted at the beginning of this chapter, the definitions of nationalism and patriotism differ in several ways. One of these differences includes the nature of the state. Patriotism almost certainly has to be defined in civic terms because the idea is to include everyone in creating an allegiance to the state. There are some exceptions, but this is only because a given country might be very homogenous. Iceland or Japan, as examples, are very homogenous because the boundaries of the state are concrete since both countries are islands. It is hard to define a country in civic terms when there is virtually no ethnic diversity. A civic form of identity can encompass both nationalism and patriotism, but it depends on the circumstances within the country. Patriotism most strongly aligns with civic identity, but civic nationalism is pervasive when the country is under attack, or the threat of attack, and requires a robust national defense.

Nationalism can therefore be either civic or ethnic. Civic nationalism brings together people of different ethnic, linguistic, and/or identity backgrounds, and provides them with a reason to be within the circle of belonging. Civic nationalism differs from patriotism in that a territorial and defensive element might exist.[60] For example, the United States military is composed of people from many different ethnic groups—Caucasian, Hispanic, and African-American being the three largest. All of these groups, collectively fighting for the United States in a defensive conflict, would form a civic nationalist community.

As noted earlier, the situation is more worrisome when ethnic nationalism is present. When a particular ethnic, linguistic, and/or identity group is mobilized as representative of the state, to the exclusion of other minorities within that country, the pathway to colonialism or hypernationalism is more likely. Ethnic nationalism, once mobilized, can be the cause of vicious and bloody military campaigns,[61] some of which historically were carried about by some Christians. Two earlier examples include Christians in the Nazi military, or Hutu militiamen perpetrating the Rwandan genocide. Ethnic nationalism can escalate quickly to a violent hypernationalism if left unchecked. Historically, colonialism was an output of ethnic nationalism. And, while overt colonialism is no longer physically present in the world today, colonial practices could always return or reemerge.

---

60. Duerr, *Secessionism and the European Union*, 6–8.

61. Ignatieff, *Blood and Belonging*, xiii.

Contemporary Examples—Nationalism or Patriotism?

On Wednesday, November 9, 2016—the day after the US presidential election—in the sleepy town of Clifton, Ohio, a middle aged woman holds aloft a sign for Republican candidate, turned President-elect Donald J. Trump. The small town of approximately 150 residents bisects Greene and Clark counties, which, especially for the latter, serves as a "swing" county within a "swing" state—in essence, Ohio's 18 Electoral College votes are a major prize for both Republican and Democratic candidates alike. Swing counties like Clark County serve as the true bellwethers as to which candidate will likely win the state of Ohio, and with it greatly increase the prospects for said candidate winning the presidency.

Passing along Route 72 through Clifton, streams of motorists honked in support of the middle-aged woman standing aloft outside of one of the businesses—in this case, a small, homely restaurant—through the town. For residents of Clifton, which include some evangelical Christians, the presidency of Donald Trump and his "America First" platform resonated with people, some of whom had witnessed sharp job losses as particularly evidenced with the closure of major employment centers in nearby Dayton and Springfield, Ohio. The region lost one manufacturing plant after another, in part, due to globalization. The question, then, is where does President Trump fit? Whether or not President Trump became a Christian in 2016 is a subject of debate, but, if he is a follower of Christ, he is very new to the faith.

First, it is important to situate President Trump within the Constitution of the United States. Everything he says and does is in context of a Constitution that is civic in nature. On the one hand, President Trump has outlined policy platforms that fit with a definition of patriotism because he espouses a desire to help the economic needs of Caucasians, African-Americans, Hispanic-Americans, and all other groups, alike without regard to skin color. On the other hand, Trump made some very inflammatory comments towards a range of different groups, especially as a candidate. Some readers will find it very difficult to disentangle these negative comments from their view of the president. Additionally, Trump's policy of "American First" exhibits an expression of jingoistic overtones, which more closely align with a definition of nationalism or perhaps worse. Both policies—patriotism and nationalism—are acceptable positions for Christians to hold; although, patriotism, in my view, aligns most closely with Scripture. Overt nationalism has its dangers.

President Trump has also pitched policy positions opposed to globalism. In my view of Scripture, globalism is fraught with potential dangers as outlined in Genesis 11. However, there are benefits of working with other countries, and developing interdependent linkages. Christian supporters of President Trump should carefully walk this line between maintaining an openness to cooperation (as outlined in chapter 4) and pushing back against globalism (as discussed in chapter 7).

The U.S. President, Donald Trump, therefore, borders the line between patriotism and nationalism. His "America First" brand is laced with nationalistic elements, but, given that African-Americans, Hispanics, and Caucasians can all fit under the banner of his America First policy, he retains some elements of patriotism. Trump is walking a fine line, however. And, where he engages in overt military action, he would fall into the nationalism category. He could argue for civic nationalism if he provides for people regardless of ethnicity in his policy outcomes.

To cite another recent populist example, the 2017 French presidential candidate from Front National, Marine Le Pen, describes herself as patriotic. Her nationalism, however, is linked to French identity based on ethnicity, and, to a lesser degree, of secularism, or not being Muslim.[62] This is an oversimplification of her position, but the general tone of her campaign lurches more closely towards nationalism than patriotism. Le Pen is not in power, so she does not have the ability to make executive level decisions like going to war, but the general tenor of her campaign bends more closely towards nationalism. This is an acceptable position for a Christian to hold, but the requisite dangers of sliding towards colonialism or hypernationalism remain present, and must be held in check to avoid governing in a way that is unbiblical and unbecoming of Romans 13:1–7.

To present another recent example, in Nigeria, Presidents Olusegun Obasanjo and Goodluck Jonathan came to power as avowedly "Christian" leaders. In fact, the Nigerian presidency is based on consociational governance—that is, Christian and Muslim leaders are expected to rotate every eight years, and also counterbalance religious differences within the executive branch. Put simply, if a Christian president is in power, the vice-president must be a Muslim. And, if said Christian president governs for two, four-year terms, then he is expected to vacate the office, and a Muslim president then takes power. The situation is a delicate balance in order to maintain peace in Nigeria between the two largest religious groups. Therefore, Obasanjo and Jonathan were expected to govern as Christians with the overarching need in their country to avoid sectarian conflict between Christians and Muslims. Policies were thus enacted to provide societal goods to all people within Nigeria, whether Christian or not.

62. Duerr, "*Identity, Tradition, Sovereignty*" 117.

To cite an older example, former U.S. President George W. Bush, when he came to office in 2001 showcased patriotism. As an avowed Christian, he utilized a position that respected people of different ethnic backgrounds.[63] After the 9/11 attacks on September 11, 2011, Bush transitioned from a definition of patriotism to nationalism; utilized to keep the country safe as explicated in the American Constitution.[64] Bush prayed through Psalm 23 on 9/11, a day in which most Americans felt heavily under attack.[65] In arming U.S. and North Atlantic Treaty Organization (NATO) forces to declare war on the Taliban government in Afghanistan, the government that protected al-Qaeda—the terrorist organization responsible for the 9/11 attacks. Given the multilateral approach to the war in Afghanistan,[66] and fulfilling the core tenets of just war theory,[67] Bush transitioned from patriotism to nationalism in a biblical, and limited manner.

Obviously, the Iraq War in 2003 was much more contested, especially in the aftermath of the "Axis of Evil" statement at the 2002 State of the Union address.[68] President Bush's use of the term evil in the speech connected three brutal regimes—Iraq, Iran, and North Korea—noting the potential to threaten world peace.[69] The fear, at the time, was one of these rogue regimes assisting a terrorist organization in the procurement of a nuclear weapon. Preventing a nuclear version of 9/11 was at the forefront of President Bush's mind, with the desire to uphold the Constitution's primary goal—protect American citizens.

For the Iraq War, Bush did not obtain NATO support or a United Nations Security Council Resolution (although a previous UNSCR dealt with the issue of Saddam Hussein's misgivings in Iraq).[70] Here, Bush should have taken more time to make a more robust case for a temporary nationalism. Certainly, Bush and British Prime Minister, Tony Blair, spent copious amounts of time discussing and praying through the implications of war against Saddam Hussein's rogue regime.[71] Yet, longstanding allies like France, Germany, and Canada among others refused to join the coalition of the willing.[72] Whether the

63. Bush, *Decision Points*, 65–105.

64. Grudem, *Politics according to the Bible*, 393.

65. Bush, *Decision Points*, 138.

66. Duerr, "*A Proposal for the Future of US counterinsurgency*"; Duerr, "*War*" 559.

67. Holmes, "*Just War.*"

68. Duerr, "*Evil Empire and Axis of Evil.*"

69. Aikman, *A Man of Faith*, 168.

70. Fasulo, *An Insider's Guide to the UN*, 56.

71. Aikman, *A Man of Faith*, 169.

72. Kagan, *Of Paradise and Power*, 75.

Iraq War was biblically justified is a still a matter of great debate. Hussein was a recalcitrant leader who murdered thousands of his own people including Kurds.[73] He also maintained a nascent nuclear weapons program, and frequently dodged international inspections from the UN's nuclear watchdog, the International Atomic Energy Agency. Yet, despite these despicable acts and policies, was the U.S.-led coalition's war on Iraq justified biblically? The answer is contested since it is biblical to stand against genocide, but there was no clear attack from Iraq on the United States.

The US-led coalition stayed in Iraq for a decade. Bush—and the US in general—did not set-up a colony in Iraq. The expectation is that the American government will not maintain a presence in Baghdad indefinitely, but there are dangers in staying for decades. Furthermore, with the rise of ISIS in 2014,[74] the United States sent troops back to Iraq to quash the heinous aggression of ISIS against minorities in Iraq and Syria.[75]

Of course, Christian leaders can make decisions that reflect unbiblical principles. General Efrain Rios Montt, the former president of Guatemala, engaged in a scorched earth campaign against Mayan people in the northern parts of the country during the decades-long civil war in the Central American country.[76] Montt was trying to protect Guatemala against the scourge of Communism in the Cold War era, but overstepped his duties as a Christian leader by inflicting such damage on people with a death toll of an estimated 140,000 to 200,000 through the deployment of "death squads."[77] Decisions look easy in retrospect. The fog of the Cold War made decisions difficult, especially when the greater good was defeating communism. But, an effusive nationalism is enough for any Christian leader to protect his people—colonialism or hypernationalism spread only war and pestilence that do not promote the good of the people under Romans 13. Again, this point is easy to discuss, yet difficult to implement. Take the historic example of Athanasius, the fourth century church leader who defended the doctrine of the Trinity. As a political leader in Alexandria he diverted grain supplies in order to defend his position from opposition, and also engaged in tactics to stop his ecclesiastical rivals.[78] At what point are the actions of Athanasius defensible?

73. Shlaim, *War and Peace in the Middle East*.

74. Belz, *They say we are infidels*, 255–267.

75. Other governments also sent troops to fight ISIS. Russia, for example, has been extensively engaged in the Middle East under the premise of defeating ISIS (Trenin, *What is Russia up to in the Middle East?*).

76. Garrard-Burnett, *Terror in the Land of the Holy Spirit*.

77. Jelen and Wilcox, *Religion and Politics in Comparative Perspective*, 232.

78. Letham, *The Holy Trinity*, 127.

Across the world, most democratic countries fall under a definition of patriotism. Christian leaders who happen to hold the highest elected office in these countries also typically maintain positions of patriotism. Tangential to this point is that relatively few world leaders are willing to say that they are nationalists, or nationalistic. Many, instead, will argue that they are patriotic. In authoritarian countries in the world, some Christian leaders lurch more closely towards nationalism rather than patriotism. In some cases, where civil wars are enacted, the Christian leader engages in nationalist behavior, which may border on a form of colonialism, especially if he attempts to repress groups within his society. Thus, democracy is useful in maintaining a more sensible form of nationalism that is juxtaposed on self-defense where necessary.

Jesus' own experience with nationalism and patriotism

Jesus was rooted, in his upbringing, in the Jewish cultural context. He regularly went to the synagogue as a boy, and as a man. He was comprehensively Jewish—Israeli in a modern sense; although, there is technically a difference between the terms: Jewish, Hebrew, and Israeli. In a sense, Jesus' position on nationality was one of allegiance to the Jewish people, especially in his early years. Of course, there is no record of any form of national attachment, only a sense of his cultural upbringing, and the desire of many around him to protect Jewish identity under the yoke of the Roman Empire. Jesus, as God, already knew Scripture, but "learned" alongside other young men of his era. In this way, He lived in a way that a young Jewish boy might be expected. His connection was one of patriotism at this time.

Jesus also had to flee with his parents to Egypt when he was very young. Although this was not Jesus' decision, the idea of cross-national connections is one that impacted his life. Without a level of protection in Egypt, Herod's men may well have found Jesus. This point presents a counterfactual to the gospel, and we can assume that God would have delivered the family from Herod's sword, but, by seeking refuge in Egypt, Jesus lived in different "national" contexts under the Roman Empire.

Furthermore, as the ministry of Jesus continues into the future, there is no sense of national boundaries. Jesus accepts disciples from a range of different ethnic and national backgrounds, provided that they know the Old Testament scriptures. In conclusion, Jesus knew of, and experienced, national boundaries, but his ministry was so much more complex than the dichotomy of nationalism and patriotism. For this major reason, and for application to the twenty-first century, it is worth exploring other elements of national identification in chapter 3.

Nationalism and Patriotism in Democratic and Authoritarian States

As already established, the Bible calls Christians to honor those in power, regardless of the circumstances. However, the Bible is also explicit about sin, and, in tandem with this point, following sinful governments. One of the great challenges of the human experience is that everyone is sinful, and every government is sinful. There is a significant difference, though, in whether or not Christians have the ability to influence government.

In democratic countries where the government is not Christian, or perhaps anti-Christian to some degree, provided that Christians can still run for office, vote their consciences, and lobby for Christian issues, there is an ability to have a Christian influence within the society. This is highly preferably to an authoritarian society wherein Christian voices are quashed, and followers of Jesus are persecuted. Surveying the World Watch List of persecuted Christians, disseminated by *Open Doors*, the top four countries on the 2020 list are all authoritarian: North Korea, Afghanistan, Somalia, and Libya.[79] The fifth and tenth countries on the list Pakistan and India respectively, are both democracies on paper, with India being more entrenched than Pakistan. Other top ten countries on the World Watch List include: Eritrea, Sudan, Yemen, and Iran, all of which are authoritarian.[80]

In general, democracies tend to better protect Christians and all other minorities, but this is clearly not always the case with Pakistan and India both listed in the top ten. The admonition of honoring those in power remains, but the inability to openly lobby government is a shortcoming, and a way in which authoritarian states continue to engage in sinful policies without being checked.

As an example, the Islamic Republic of Iran's government specifically seeks to follow Twelver Shia Islam with explicit instructions prohibiting religious conversion from Islam to any other faith, as well as proselytizing on behalf of that other faith.[81] Even though people in Iran believe many different things about religion, society, economics, and politics, this authoritarian government maintains a tight level of control on who can serve in government. This is not to argue that there is a complete absence of public debate,

79. Open Doors. World Watch List, 2020.

80. Open Doors. World Watch List, 2020.

81. Rostampour and Amirizadeh, *Captive in Iran*, 6.

rather that it is closely monitored.[82] However, sharing the Christian faith is a charge for which people can be sent to prison because it constitutes, "participating in political activities against the government."[83]

Democratic states are also prone to any number of misgivings. There are no perfect countries or people. Christians still need to check sinful displays of power within democratic countries, but there is more room to be patriotic since a Biblical worldview can be argued for within the greater society, even if it is rejected by those in power.

Concluding Points

As established in chapter 1, nationalism and patriotism are two forms of identity. This chapter has provided examples of how the two terms differ, examples from the Old and New testaments, as well as engaged in different examples. In general, the preferred option is patriotism over nationalism, but this assumes a comfortable world in which to reside. Realist scholars, for example, argue that the world is anarchic, that is, there is no central governing authority to arbitrate disputes, thus powerful countries and rulers can take advantage of the weak.[84] Nationalism, as defined with the component of engaging in conflict for either defensive or protective purposes, is useful in that less people are likely to die, and there is a greater sense of freedom and justice in the world. Of course, there are limitations as to what any given Christian can do in the world. The example of Jesus living under the Roman Empire is an example of this point wherein he conducted his entire ministry under outside occupation. Christians, therefore, need not worry about every circumstance in the world, but should seek to help fellow believers, and to pray for them where persecuted.

The concepts of nationalism and patriotism, though, are more complex than the dichotomy laid out in this chapter. Chapter 3 builds upon this discussion, and tangentially describes situations pertaining to people with multiple national identities, allegiances, or ancestries. The modern world, as well as the ancient world, is/was full of complexities regarding how people lived, worked, and governed.

---

82. As an example, I have been interviewed on several Iranian media outlets. I have always been free to share my view without censure, at least to my knowledge.

83. Rostampour and Amirizadeh, *Captive in Iran*, 73.

84. Mearsheimer, *The Tragedy of Great Power Politics*.

Chapter 3

Multiple National Identities

Then David sent to Joab, saying, "Send me Uriah the Hittite."
So Joab sent Uriah to David. When Uriah came to him, David asked concerning the welfare of Joab and the people and
the state of the war. Then David said to Uriah, "Go down to
your house, and wash your feet." And Uriah went out of the
king's house, and a present from the king was sent out after
him. But Uriah slept at the door of the king's house with all
the servants of his lord, and did not go down to his house.

—2 SAMUEL 11:6–9

IN 2 SAMUEL 11, the reader is introduced to the overt sin of King David in
his sinful relations with Bathsheba, outside of marriage—the core message of
the text. But, underlining this discussion is Bathsheba's husband, Uriah.[1] On
several occasions, Uriah is referred to as a Hittite. This is interesting because
Uriah is clearly of a minority ethnic group, but also fights for the military
of the Kingdom of Israel. After all, King David, later in 2 Samuel 11 calls
Uriah back from the front to Jerusalem as a means of trying to cover his sin.[2]
Hittites are historically from the modern-day region of Anatolia in southern
Turkey, but their historic kingdom was wider. Clearly, Uriah was accepted as
part of Israel's society, even to the point of being allowed to serve faithfully in
the military. But, as noted above, he is often referred to in the text as Uriah

1. Grudem, *Politics according to the Bible*, 125.
2. Hill and Walton, *A Survey of the Old Testament*, 224.

the Hittite, someone from modern-day Turkey, Syria, or Lebanon, as was the extent of the Hittite Empire during its heyday. Deuteronomy 7:1 mentions the Hittites alongside six other nations that are described as "greater and stronger than you (Israel)." Historically, the Hittites were an enemy of Israel, and were known as a powerful kingdom.

This chapter primarily discusses the issue of multiple national identities. As introduced in chapter 1, I hold citizenship in three countries. Many followers of Christ in the modern era have some form of history in a second, or third, country, even if they were born and raised in a single country. Whether a parent or a grandparent is from another country, or a person has a strong ancestral connection to a country, or they have traveled for work, or been on missions trips, there are many cross-national connections in the modern world. The purpose of this chapter is to examine how Christians can utilize their unique situations for the gospel.

As noted at the beginning of chapter 1, the world of the 2000s looks remarkably different from the world of the 1900s, especially for the Christ-follower. Although globalization was at a new high in 1910, the onset of the Great War in 1914 quickly reversed the interactions of people across different national boundaries.[3] Nationality was often described along racial and/or linguistic lines. The hierarchy of racial groups was (and is) an unbiblical practice that most people followed in this era. Unfortunately, many Christians also followed this hierarchy. National units, therefore, were more often ascribed to particular racialist features. Moreover, most of the recognized countries of 1900 including the countries of Europe and Japan, held colonies in various parts of the world.

The 2000s by comparison, however, have largely been devoid of war and ongoing conflict, bar a few select areas of the world, such as Syria, which have been befallen by fissiparous ethnic and ideological conflict. Even with such a tragic conflict, the world is much more peaceful at the present, than at virtually any other time in human history.[4] The number of war deaths has declined dramatically from World War II in the 1940s, to the Vietnam era in the 1970s. War deaths still happen, and each loss of life is tragic, but holistically the number has declined dramatically. At one point in the early 2010s, there were no interstate wars—conflicts between two or more countries—anywhere in the world (at least by some metrics).[5]

Globalization hit a high point the 2000s and 2010s decades, but may be beginning to slow. The sheer volume of cross-national movement,

3. Duerr, "War."

4. See Goldstein, *Winning the War on War.*

5. Goldstein, *Winning the War on War,* 4–11.

trade, and communications far exceeds any other point in human history. The world population, in 2020 at 7.8 billion people,[6] in many parts of the globe, has at least some ability to connect through social media to learn about people in other countries, even if they do not have the physical ability to travel elsewhere.

Given all of these connections, and this situation, Christians should be prepared to think about how multiple national identities, or at least multiple national connections can be mobilized for the gospel. This is not an easy endeavor. Take the Chinese graduate student studying in the West. He attends church and studies the Bible, but has limitations in various capacities. When he visits his parents in China, there are a range of governmental level prohibitions on what he can do. Proselytism of the Christian gospel is still illegal in China,[7] even if there is some loosening in select provinces. In his Ph.D. program in the United States, this same Chinese student has every freedom to share his faith, but the atmosphere is much more limited in acceptance of Christians mores compared to what it was even a few decades. Bringing one's faith into the classroom is, in most cases, strictly a difficult endeavor.

What can followers of Christ do? Throughout Scripture, there are excellent examples of how Christians shared the gospel, and mobilized their positions for the sake of the gospel. In fact, the Bible is very well situated to provide guidance in the globalized world of the twenty-first century; many people throughout the world care deeply about the Word of God as it has spread dramatically across the Global South.[8]

The Life of Paul

Biblically, the life of Paul is of special interest in this chapter. Paul, after all, became all things to all people so that he might save some (1 Corinthians 9).[9] Paul was, at the same time, a Greek, a Jew, and a Roman citizen. Moreover, the theologian George Ladd notes that Paul inhabited three worlds: "Jewish, Hellenistic, and Christian."[10] In this way, Paul was able to hold multiple allegiances simultaneously so that he might be able to, through the Holy Spirit, use his words and deeds to convince people of the life, death, and resurrection

6. Population Reference Bureau, "International Data."

7. There are formalized churches in China like the Three-Self Church, but there are strict limitations of what can be preached (Yun and Hattaway, *Heavenly Man*, 54; Aikman, *Jesus in Beijing*.)

8. Jenkins, *The New Faces of Christianity.*

9. Carson and Moo, *An Introduction to the New Testament*, 354–85.

10. Ladd, *A Theology of the New Testament*, 398.

of Jesus Christ. There is no contradiction in holding all of these different identities provided that it is underneath the identity of knowing and following Christ. In practical terms, emulating Paul's situation is a very difficult balance such that a Christian's national identity does not get in the way of the gospel. There were times when Paul's Jewish background is clearly evidenced as in Acts 21:18–26, and he wrote several letters that were included the Bible in Greek. Paul also held all of these identities legally under the prescribed laws of the polity—the Roman Empire, in his case. In fact, Paul's life was used mightily to glorify Christ in his different circles of influence.

This is not necessarily to encourage people to collect citizenships in order to become like Paul, but rather to use one's circumstances in life, to glorify Christ.[11] If a follower of Christ happens to have a parent of one country, and another from elsewhere in the world, there is a natural situation where a person can connect with other people in two different countries. As noted in chapter 1, this might even involve several countries. A Christian who was born and raised in a country, and can trace her ancestry back several generations, may have a burgeoning interest in another country through a collegiate level study abroad program. Even if someone has resided within the same small county for their entire life, migration—whether through legal, illegal, asylum, refugee—has led to opportunities to interact with people from different national and cultural backgrounds. As an example, in the small to mid-size city of Leamington, Ontario, Canada, on the north banks of Lake Erie, thousands of Mexican and Jamaican citizens reside seasonally in the area to work primarily picking tomatoes for the large tomato and ketchup industries in North America. Christians in this community have reached out helping create Spanish language churches, and ministries to help people residing within the city. Moreover, Christians within these Mexican and Jamaican diasporas have added much to the ministry and gospel-proclamation throughout the wider Leamington region.

Returning to Paul to see how he acted in various circumstances, in Acts 22:25, Paul faced an immense problem—he was about to be scourged by a Roman centurion. The situation changes, however, as the centurion is unable to punish him because he learns that Paul is a Roman citizen. In fact, in Acts 22:28, the reader learns that Paul was a Roman citizen by birth; by contrast, the Roman commander actually had to buy his Roman citizenship for a "large sum of money."[12] Paul had multiple allegiances, and was able to utilize them all for the sake of the gospel. The whole passage is worth further investigation. Acts 22: 22–24 reads:

11. Carson and Moo, *An Introduction to the New Testament*, 355.

12. Gundry, *A Survey of the New Testament*, 336.

"22 They listened to him up to this statement, and then they raised their voices and said, "Away with such a fellow from the earth, for he should not be allowed to live!" 23 And as they were crying out and throwing off their cloaks and tossing dust into the air, 24 the commander ordered him to be brought into the barracks, stating that he should be examined by scourging so that he might find out the reason why they were shouting against him that way.

NIV: 22 The crowd listened to Paul until he said this. Then they raised their voices and shouted, "Rid the earth of him! He's not fit to live!" 23 As they were shouting and throwing off their cloaks and flinging dust into the air, 24 the commander ordered that Paul be taken into the barracks. He directed that he be flogged and interrogated in order to find out why the people were shouting at him like this."

Preceding this passage, the account notes Paul's miraculous conversion on the road to Damascus—it recounts an earlier time wherein Saul (now Paul) persecuted Christians with alacrity. He was known as one of the most infamous persecutors of Christians before Jesus himself intervenes asking why he persecuted the church. Then, when Paul preached the gospel, the people turned against him. In verse 22, people start calling for him to be killed because of his preaching. In verse 24, the commander even takes Paul away to be interrogated and flogged. But then a new piece of information changes the situation.

Acts 22:25–29 continues:

"25 But when they stretched him out with thongs, Paul said to the centurion who was standing by, "Is it lawful for you to scourge a man who is a Roman and uncondemned?" 26 When the centurion heard this, he went to the commander and told him, saying, "What are you about to do? For this man is a Roman." 27 The commander came and said to him, "Tell me, are you a Roman?" And he said, "Yes." 28 The commander answered, "I acquired this citizenship with a large sum of money." And Paul said, "But I was actually born a citizen." 29 Therefore those who were about to examine him immediately let go of him; and the commander also was afraid when he found out that he was a Roman, and because he had put him in chains."

The hinge of the passage is verse 25 when Paul reveals himself, in question form, to be a Roman citizen. Immediately, this new piece of information causes the commander to pause given the legal concerns of the treatment of citizens of Rome; after all, "the penalty for a false claim to citizenship" is death.[13] To reiterate, Paul was at the same time a Jew, a Greek, and a Roman citizen. Thus, when the commander came upon Paul, he probably took him to be a Jewish preacher who was causing trouble in the synagogues. He was not yet aware of Paul's Roman citizenship. Even though the commander, in verse 28, had to pay a lot of money for his citizenship, Paul gained his by virtue of his birth. Paul then utilizes his situation for the gospel through legal means under Roman law. He is at the same time subservient to the laws of the empire and respectful of its leadership, whilst simultaneously preaching the resurrection of Jesus Christ.

Millions of people hold multiple passports in the twenty-first century, and many millions more have lived in at least two different countries, in situations with at least some similarities to Paul. When one resides in a country, and then moves to another (and perhaps another), several things may happen. First, a person may remain indwelt in the identity of his former home. Second, a person may quickly adopt the identity of her new home. However, a third option is much more likely even for people who strongly identify with elements of options one and two. In all likelihood, the person has both a "push and pull" sense of identity between the two homelands. There is a longing, and a sense of nostalgia for the place that has been left, but also a simultaneous embracing of what is new. Sometimes the new country is questioned and critiqued, but, ultimately, over time, there is often a recognition of what is good and enjoyable about the new country; otherwise, the person would eventually seek to leave.

Of course, this discussion is further complicated by a few factors. Perhaps the person is now living in a third or fourth different country. Depending on the allegiance to that country, in terms of citizenship, a person may have a stronger sense of connection. Business transactions may also overlay the situation in that a Christian may have a bank account or a business entity within a third or fourth country. The sense of identity becomes further splintered, but still no less important to wrestle through.

Perhaps the sense of multiple national identities comes through marriage to someone from another country, or to whom some of the above apply. The covenant of marriage might connect people across borders. For example, if one's spouse's parents are in need of help, the Christian has a Biblical sense of duty to honor those parents (Exodus 20:12), which might involve individualized care, and/or financial assistance. Navigating different governments, especially related to health care and social security related questions produces many specific concerns.

---

13. Gundry, *A Survey of the New Testament*, 336.

The discussion could also revolve around ancestry. Perhaps a person was born in a particular country, but of an ethnic minority background. There are many strongly-held ethnic backgrounds that may assert themselves within a given family. As an example, Italian-American identity in the United States, or Italian-Canadian identity in Canada, especially as connected to festivals and events in the cities of Boston, New York, and Toronto. The allegiance this person feels might be to the homeland of her parents or grandparents or great-grandparents. In general, there is no biblical mandate to maintain a national allegiance based on one's bloodline, but a sense of identity might be particularly strong among some ethnic groups. As another example, Chinese identity in Singapore, which have strongly connected business linkages through the ethnic Han Chinese diaspora.[14]

In sum, there are a range of different possibilities as to how a given person will live, act, and feel when it comes to nationality. This situation could become immeasurably more complex depending on residence, familial relations, and ancestry. In these cases, often a tension exists in balancing allegiances between countries and ethnic heritage(s). This is the blessing and the curse of multiple national identities. Scripture compels Christians to obey the governing authorities under which one finds themselves. Yet, residence matters since allegiance is partly implied given the payment of taxes to a given leader. Jesus himself instructs his followers to pay their taxes (Matthew 22:21; Mark 12:17); in general, more tax is paid to one governing authority. Dual nationals may have to pay income or other taxes in multiple countries, but there is generally a primary residence in one country. Thus, people with multiple national identities usually reside primarily in one location. There are exceptions, especially people who work in multinational corporations or missionaries, but even with frequent travel, only the very wealthy have two or more residences across two or more countries.

Adoption: A Practical Application

The topic of adoption is a complex one on many levels, especially when considering adoption from abroad. Yet, followers of Christ are instructed to care for orphans and widows in several sections of Scripture (see James 1:27). Christians are also called to help the poor. Layered on top of this issue is that the Bible speaks clearly about issues related to life, pro-life positions, but often with significant nuances that are generally underexplored by the public; preventing infant mortality is an important issue for followers of Christ.

14. Chua, *World on Fire*, 23–48.

Ultimately, adoption by Christian parents is an outer working of the Holy Spirit in their lives. No single source can dictate what these parents should do, whether they are able to conceive their own biological children or not. There are, however, a few points to consider, especially as it relates to nationality. On the one hand, there are generally thousands of poor children in the foster care system even in the most affluent countries of the world. Issues of the heart become important here because some people opt to adopt babies rather than older children. There are different sets of issues that come with adopting babies versus older children in terms of life events, mental state, and a host of other potential issues from physical to sexual abuse that may have transpired. On the other hand, there are myriads of children in need of adoption especially in less wealthy countries throughout the world. American parents, for example, historically adopted many babies and children from China and Russia. All of these children are presented with great life opportunities in the United States.

For Christian parents of adopted children, the issue of multiple national identities remains a potent force in the lives of most young people. The children realize that they are citizens of one country, but were born (and potentially raised for a few years) in another country. That sense of national identity is one that many adopted children want to explore. From a biblical standpoint, there are mechanisms through which the gospel can disseminate as a result of that child who straddles two countries via adoption. This should be the ultimate goal of the adopted child, if he accepts Christ for himself, and for his adoptive parents, to explore: how can the gospel be mobilized among other members of the adopted child's country of birth?

Old Testament Examples

At this stage of the chapter, several other examples are useful in a discussion of multiple nationalities in order to get a sense from Scripture as to what earthly allegiances should look like. There are three major biblical characters—Joseph, Ruth, and Daniel—who, for different reasons, had to leave their homeland to live in another country. In all three cases, these people live very well in their new circumstances. Additionally, there are other examples like Joshua, Uriah, and Solomon who have to decide how they will serve God in a cross-national context. They are all a testament to faithfulness in God, and loyalty to God's people.

Joseph

The story of Joseph in Genesis 37–50 is a tragic one in which a man is sold into slavery by his jealous brothers. In context, Joseph is the eleventh of twelve brothers from his father, Jacob. The tragedy of Joseph's story is that he was the favorite son of his father, Jacob; Genesis 37:3 notes that Joseph was favorite "because he was the son of his old age." Joseph is the oldest son from Jacob's favorite wife, Rachel. Yet, because of this perception as favorite, Joseph was despised by his brothers. In part, this dislike was due to Joseph's dreams in which he saw his bothers bowing down to him on two occasions (Genesis 37:5–9).

There are several daunting points of the story, especially where Joseph could easily have fallen into despair. When Joseph was sold into slavery, he entered the house of Potiphar, an officer of Pharaoh in Egypt. In spite of working diligently for Potiphar, Joseph is falsely accused of attempting an extramarital affair by Potiphar's wife even though he actually rejected her sexual advances. Joseph is then summarily thrown in prison and has to start his life over again (Genesis 39:20). Most people would fully despair at this point, but Joseph continued to work hard, and he gained favor in the eyes of the prison guards, and ultimately, the chief jailer. At one point Joseph is effectively forgotten even when there was an opportunity for his redemption. Finally, when Pharaoh is troubled sufficiently by a number of dreams that a call is made for someone to interpret said dreams. It is at this point when the chief jailer recalls Joseph's special, God-given ability to interpret dreams. Pharaoh then retells Joseph two different dreams in which he is wracked by fear over the future. Joseph then responds that both dreams represent the same future concern: seven years of plenty followed by seven years of famine (see Genesis 40). As a result of his interpretation, Joseph is not only released from prison, but he is elevated to the second-most powerful position in the empire following Pharaoh. In some senses, Joseph becomes vice president or prime minister or head of several areas of government policy (see Genesis 41). Moreover, Joseph enacts a policy to store food and grain from the seven years of plenty so that when the seven years of famine arrive, Egypt is well placed to not only survive,[15] but to be of assistance to neighboring countries.

During the seven years of famine, the people of Israel (another name for Jacob and his family), leave their homeland to seek food elsewhere. To condense the story, Joseph helps his brothers in spite of their selling him into slavery. It is the summation of a powerful story of redemption and the

---

15. Hill and Walton, *A Survey of the Old Testament*, 74.

power of forgiveness, speaking to Joseph's high moral character and ongoing diligence in the midst of very difficult circumstances. Joseph celebrates with his brothers, reconciling with them, and making sure that the rest of the Israelites do not die as a result of the ongoing famine.

The story of Joseph in the Book of Genesis is best summed up by quoting Genesis 50:20 wherein Joseph is responding to the concerns of his brother who sold him into slavery, "As for you, you meant evil against me, but God meant it for good in order to bring about this present result, to preserve many people alive." Thus, Joseph, by no choice of his own, was connected to Israel and Egypt simultaneously. Once elevated by Pharaoh of Egypt to oversee agriculture and significant aspects of the economy, Joseph was charged with helping first and foremost the citizens of Egypt.[16] Yet, given his favor in the eyes of Egypt's Pharaoh, Joseph was able to help foreigners, in particular, his family members from Israel that sought food aid. Joseph thus serves both Egypt and Israel to the best of his ability, and helps both peoples in their time of need.

Naomi and Ruth

Another story is of Naomi and Ruth in the book of Ruth. To summarize, Ruth stays with Naomi and adopts Yahweh as her God.[17] Ruth stays with her mother-in-law, Naomi, even when the latter decides to move back to Israel. This point is so powerful that Ruth is recorded in the book of Matthew as an ancestor of Jesus (Matthew 1:5).[18] Through Boaz, the kinsman redeemer, Ruth manages to provide for Naomi even in her old age.[19] She is both loyal and generous. Moreover, she juggles the sense of dual allegiances whilst under God. I noted, dual allegiances, because, in most parts of the world, ethnic differences are quite obvious in homogenous societies. Although the average person in a multicultural society would probably not think too much about the ethnic background of a person, the issue is one that remains pertinent through the modern era. Ethnicity, in many countries then and now, provides a point of distinction between national groups.

The story of Ruth is perhaps one of the most intriguing in all of Scripture. The book of Ruth centers on a tragic story wherein a mother, Naomi, loses her two sons in a foreign land. Ruth starts with the story of said widow, Naomi, who left Judah to live in the land of Moab, with her

16. Hill and Walton, *A Survey of the Old Testament*, 74.

17. Hill and Walton, *A Survey of the Old Testament*, 204.

18. MacArthur and Mayhew, *Biblical Doctrine*, 441.

19. Hill and Walton, *A Survey of the Old Testament*, 206.

husband, Elimelech, and her sons, Mahlon and Chilion. Moab is noteworthy because this was a country that oppressed Israel prior to being driven
out by King Ehud in Judges 3.[20]

Verses 1–5 of Ruth 1 present a very tragic overview of Naomi's life in
Moab. There are numerous lessons contained within the Book of Ruth that
have been interpreted in light of "famine, refugee status, tribal or ethnic
loyalties, levirate marriages, and polygamy are not ancient biblical practices,
but the normal realities of today."[21] National status and citizenship have long
been malleable depending upon famine, war, and a range of other factors
that cause people to leave their homes.

Today, the country of Moab does not exist, but the kingdom is located
in modern-day Jordan, the area to the east of the Dead Sea. The Kingdom
of Ammon also overlaps with modern-day Jordan, but Ammon is north of
Moab. Ruth 1:1–5 reads:

> "1 Now it came about in the days when the judges governed,
> that there was a famine in the land. And a certain man of Beth-
> lehem in Judah went to sojourn in the land of Moab with his
> wife and his two sons. 2 The name of the man was Elimelech,
> and the name of his wife, Naomi; and the names of his two
> sons were Mahlon and Chilion, Ephrathites of Bethlehem in
> Judah. Now they entered the land of Moab and remained there.
> 3 Then Elimelech, Naomi's husband, died; and she was left with
> her two sons. 4 They took for themselves Moabite women as
> wives; the name of the one was Orpah and the name of the
> other Ruth. And they lived there about ten years. 5 Then both
> Mahlon and Chilion also died, and the woman was bereft of
> her two children and her husband."

Unlike Orpah, Ruth opts to take a different approach to her mother-in-
law, Naomi. The story of Ruth is one of devotion and loyalty, but also one
that shows a foreshadowing of when the gospel would be dispensed to all
peoples of the world. For example, Naomi provides the option to Orpah and
Ruth to return to the homes of their own mothers. Orpah takes the offer, but
Ruth opts to stay with Naomi. Ruth 1:6–22 continues:

> "6 Then she arose with her daughters-in-law that she might
> return from the land of Moab, for she had heard in the land of
> Moab that the Lord had visited His people in giving them food.
> 7 So she departed from the place where she was, and her two
> daughters-in-law with her; and they went on the way to return

20. Hill and Walton, *A Survey of the Old Testament*, 205.

21. Jenkins, *The New Faces of Christianity*, 80.

to the land of Judah. 8 And Naomi said to her two daughters-in-law, "Go, return each of you to her mother's house. May the Lord deal kindly with you as you have dealt with the dead and with me. 9 May the Lord grant that you may find rest, each in the house of her husband." Then she kissed them, and they lifted up their voices and wept. 10 And they said to her, "No, but we will surely return with you to your people." 11 But Naomi said, "Return, my daughters. Why should you go with me? Have I yet sons in my womb, that they may be your husbands? 12 Return, my daughters! Go, for I am too old to have a husband. If I said I have hope, if I should even have a husband tonight and also bear sons, 13 would you therefore wait until they were grown? Would you therefore refrain from marrying? No, my daughters; for it is harder for me than for you, for the hand of the Lord has gone forth against me." 14 And they lifted up their voices and wept again; and Orpah kissed her mother-in-law, but Ruth clung to her. 15 Then she said, "Behold, your sister-in-law has gone back to her people and her gods; return after your sister-in-law." 16 But Ruth said, "Do not urge me to leave you or turn back from following you; for where you go, I will go, and where you lodge, I will lodge. Your people shall be my people, and your God, my God. 17 Where you die, I will die, and there I will be buried. Thus may the Lord do to me, and worse, if anything but death parts you and me." 18 When she saw that she was determined to go with her, she said no more to her. 19 So they both went until they came to Bethlehem. And when they had come to Bethlehem, all the city was stirred because of them, and the women said, "Is this Naomi?" 20 She said to them, "Do not call me Naomi; call me Mara, for the Almighty has dealt very bitterly with me. 21 I went out full, but the Lord has brought me back empty. Why do you call me Naomi, since the Lord has witnessed against me and the Almighty has afflicted me?" 22 So Naomi returned, and with her Ruth the Moabitess, her daughter-in-law, who returned from the land of Moab. And they came to Bethlehem at the beginning of barley harvest."

At the conclusion of the first chapter of Ruth, Naomi's daughter-in-law supports her despite her Ruth's husband/Naomi's son dying. Ruth, a Moabite woman by birth, heritage, and culture, decides to stay with Naomi who has now tragically lost everything.

For Israel, Moab was oftentimes a contentious neighboring country with whom they went to war on several occasions in Scripture.[22] The

---

22. Hill and Walton, *A Survey of the Old Testament*, 205.

animosity between the two countries was heightened at certain points in history, but obviously did not stand between the marriage of an Israelite to a Moabite. In this case, both of Naomi's Israelite sons married Moabite women. The passage also clearly states that the Moabites had different gods from the God of Israel, so there are spiritual implications as well as political, cultural, and national ones. Yet, given Ruth's faithfulness, she is elevated in Scripture, and also becomes part of the lineage, through King David,[23] into which Jesus is born. Therefore, the lineage of Jesus is not exclusive Israelite, it also include gentiles.

Daniel

Daniel was taken to Babylon as a young man, probably at around the age of 14, where he was called into the diplomatic service of King Nebuchadnezzar[24] in what was the center of learning and knowledge in the world.[25] Much like the account of Joseph wherein God allowed for the power to interpret dreams and granted wisdom,[26] Daniel was likewise exalted in Babylon.[27] At first, he was a "high official" in King Nebuchadnezzar's court.[28] Later, in Daniel 2:48, he was called to serve as the prime minister of the entire Babylonian empire.[29] Even when King Nebuchadnezzar was out-of-service for seven years, Daniel effectively ran the entire empire despite not being a Babylonian. He knew that he was acting in the service of God to teach the most powerful person on the planet—King Nebuchadnezzar—a lesson on submitting to the Lord.

In Daniel 5, approximately sixty years after the account of Daniel 1, when Babylon was replaced by the Medo-Persian Empire,[30] once again, Daniel was elevated to serve as one of the three main governors over the 120 provinces of the empire (Daniel was in charge of 40). When insurrections grew under the other two main governors, Daniel was placed in charge over all of the Medo-Persian Empire (under the King), just the same role as he held over the Babylonian Empire.[31] Throughout his time

23. Hill and Walton, *A Survey of the Old Testament*, 204.

24. Hill and Walton, *A Survey of the Old Testament*, 452.

25. Jeremiah, *Agents of Babylon*, 17.

26. Feinberg, *No One Like Him*, 322.

27. Jeremiah, *What in the World in Going On?* 54–5.

28. Grudem, *Politics according to the Bible*, 58.

29. Jeremiah, *Agents of Babylon*, 24.

30. Jeremiah, *Agents of Babylon*, 148.

31. Hill and Walton, *A Survey of the Old Testament*, 452.

in exile, probably around sixty years, Daniel worked diligently unto God under four gentile rulers, and was rewarded for his faithfulness.[32] This is not to imply that work definitively leads to positive outcomes, just to note that Daniel had God's favor.

The major narrative surrounding Daniel, though, starts at the beginning of the book. Even as a young man, Daniel makes a decision to serve God. He has been taken away from his home in Israel to now serve in the court of the King of the Empire, the most powerful person on the planet, Nebuchadnezzar. Ultimately, Daniel opts to serve the foreign kingdom, but to preserve his witness and desire to serve the Lord God of Israel. In this sense, Daniel takes on the role of multiple allegiances while maintaining his integrity before God, even if opposed by the most powerful earthly kingdom. Daniel 1:1–6 reads:

> "1 In the third year of the reign of Jehoiakim king of Judah, Nebuchadnezzar king of Babylon came to Jerusalem and besieged it. 2 The Lord gave Jehoiakim king of Judah into his hand, along with some of the vessels of the house of God; and he brought them to the land of Shinar, to the house of his god, and he brought the vessels into the treasury of his god. 3 Then the king ordered Ashpenaz, the chief of his officials, to bring in some of the sons of Israel, including some of the royal family and of the nobles, 4 youths in whom was no defect, who were good-looking, showing intelligence in every branch of wisdom, endowed with understanding and discerning knowledge, and who had ability for serving in the king's court; and he ordered him to teach them the literature and language of the Chaldeans. 5 The king appointed for them a daily ration from the king's choice food and from the wine which he drank, and appointed that they should be educated three years, at the end of which they were to enter the king's personal service. 6 Now among them from the sons of Judah were Daniel, Hananiah, Mishael and Azariah."

Daniel 1:1–6 sets the scene of Babylonian captivity, and explicitly lists four Israelite young men that have been tasked with serving the king.[33] It is a key point because Israel is a subservient province within a much wider empire—at that time, the most powerful empire in the world. In verse 4, there is a clear order for the Israelites to learn the literature and language of the Chaldeans. In effect, these young Israelite men have to learn and truly understand the culture of the ruling empire. Daniel 1:7 continues:

32. Jeremiah, *Agents of Babylon*, 334.
33. Hill and Walton, *A Survey of the Old Testament*, 455.

> "7 Then the commander of the officials assigned new names to them; and to Daniel he assigned the name Belteshazzar, to Hananiah Shadrach, to Mishael Meshach and to Azariah Abednego. 8 But Daniel made up his mind that he would not defile himself with the king's choice food or with the wine which he drank; so he sought permission from the commander of the officials that he might not defile himself."

In verses 7 and 8, it is clear that the Babylonian culture is more prominent than that of a small province on the edge of the empire, Israel. The four young men, for example, are assigned new names to fit their new place within Babylonian society. However, the account describes the forthrightness of Daniel in his decision not to defile himself. Daniel 1:9 continues:

> "9 Now God granted Daniel favor and compassion in the sight of the commander of the officials, 10 and the commander of the officials said to Daniel, "I am afraid of my lord the king, who has appointed your food and your drink; for why should he see your faces looking more haggard than the youths who are your own age? Then you would make me forfeit my head to the king."
> 11 But Daniel said to the overseer whom the commander of the officials had appointed over Daniel, Hananiah, Mishael and Azariah, 12 "Please test your servants for ten days, and let us be given some vegetables to eat and water to drink. 13 Then let our appearance be observed in your presence and the appearance of the youths who are eating the king's choice food; and deal with your servants according to what you see." 14 So he listened to them in this matter and tested them for ten days."

Daniel takes an important stand in Daniel 1:9–14. Ultimately, Daniel and his friends could partake in the finest food and drink of the empire. But, because this act would contravene Jewish law, they opt to avoid indulging. The commander of the officials obviously has some level of compassion on the four Israelites as he gives them 10 days to try to make amends for not indulging in the food and drink of the king. Daniel 1:15 reads:

> "15 At the end of ten days their appearance seemed better and they were fatter than all the youths who had been eating the king's choice food. 16 So the overseer continued to withhold their choice food and the wine they were to drink, and kept giving them vegetables. 17 As for these four youths, God gave them knowledge and intelligence in every branch of literature and wisdom; Daniel even understood all kinds of visions and dreams. 18 Then at the end of the days which the king had specified for

presenting them, the commander of the officials presented them before Nebuchadnezzar. 19 The king talked with them, and out of them all not one was found like Daniel, Hananiah, Mishael and Azariah; so they entered the king's personal service. 20 As for every matter of wisdom and understanding about which the king consulted them, he found them ten times better than all the magicians and conjurers who were in all his realm. 21 And Daniel continued until the first year of Cyrus the king."

God blessed Daniel and his friends for their decision to stand firm in their faith.[34] Their rigorous studies also helped them gain a greater understanding of their new host culture. The circumstances of being raised in a foreign culture against the will of the people of Israel was obviously a national disappointment. Yet, in this scenario, the four young men make the best of the difficult circumstance—they serve as an example of serving God and, in this case, the country in which they had been called "without compromising his loyalty" to the Lord.[35] Daniel's example serves as a powerful lesson to many persecuted believers in the world today. Much obviously depends upon individual circumstances, but God's glory was illuminated through Daniel. Daniel utilizes his understanding of different national context for the glory of God throughout his life, as listed in the book bearing his name.

Joshua and Rahab

Additionally, there are several other cases wherein a person becomes an Israelite, and serves Yahweh. For example, in Joshua 2, Rahab spies on behalf of the Israelite people and provides sanctuary to the two spies from Shittim (Joshua 2:1).[36] In the end, Rahab's intelligence reports and allowances for the spies provides the Israelites an opportunity to conquer a section of the Promised Land; a directive having been given to Joshua to drive out the Canaanite people occupying the land.[37] In the book of Joshua, the key theme is taking possession of the Promised Land and trusting God. As noted in chapter 2, there is a specific case of Israelite nationalism, which, under God, allowed for the aggressive taking of this territory. This concept is not extending to anyone else in the modern world. Ultimately, the greater narrative of Joshua was to purge the land of non-believers, and to purify the

---

34. Hill and Walton, *A Survey of the Old Testament*, 456.

35. Jenkins, *The New Faces of Christianity*, 145.

36. MacArthur and Mayhew, *Biblical Doctrine*, 441

37. Grudem, *Politics according to the Bible*, 457.

population so that Yahweh could be worshipped. In real life, a directive is always murkier than a direct order—even when it comes from God.

In Joshua 2, the reader is introduced to Rahab—a prostitute (verse 1) who views the Israelites with kindness, and develops an allegiance for the one true God. She proves to be instrumental in taking Jericho (in Joshua 6), which becomes a lynchpin for taking other areas of the Promised Land. Joshua 2:1 starts:

> "1 Then Joshua the son of Nun sent two men as spies secretly from Shittim, saying, "Go, view the land, especially Jericho." So they went and came into the house of a harlot whose name was Rahab, and lodged there. 2 It was told the king of Jericho, saying, "Behold, men from the sons of Israel have come here tonight to search out the land." 3 And the king of Jericho sent word to Rahab, saying, "Bring out the men who have come to you, who have entered your house, for they have come to search out all the land."

Joshua 2:1–3 sets the scene of the Israelite nation entering the Promised Land from the east after years in the wilderness. Jericho, a city to the east of Jerusalem, that still exists today, is the location of the account. Joshua 2:4 continues:

> "4 But the woman had taken the two men and hidden them, and she said, "Yes, the men came to me, but I did not know where they were from. 5 It came about when it was time to shut the gate at dark, that the men went out; I do not know where the men went. Pursue them quickly, for you will overtake them." 6 But she had brought them up to the roof and hidden them in the stalks of flax which she had laid in order on the roof. 7 So the men pursued them on the road to the Jordan to the fords; and as soon as those who were pursuing them had gone out, they shut the gate. 8 Now before they lay down, she came up to them on the roof, 9 and said to the men, "I know that the Lord has given you the land, and that the terror of you has fallen on us, and that all the inhabitants of the land have melted away before you."

From Joshua 2:4–9, Rahab provides favor for the two Israelite spies. Although the spies were in physical danger being in an enemy city, Rahab expresses her faith in God, and agrees that the Promised Land should belong to them. Rahab hides the spies and tries to make sure that they are able to fulfill their mission without being found.

"10 For we have heard how the Lord dried up the water of the Red Sea before you when you came out of Egypt, and what you did to the two kings of the Amorites who were beyond the Jordan, to Sihon and Og, whom you utterly destroyed. 11 When we heard it, our hearts melted and no courage remained in any man any longer because of you; for the Lord your God, He is God in heaven above and on earth beneath. 12 Now therefore, please swear to me by the Lord, since I have dealt kindly with you, that you also will deal kindly with my father's household, and give me a pledge of truth, 13 and spare my father and my mother and my brothers and my sisters, with all who belong to them, and deliver our lives from death."

As most would expect in a circumstance like this one, Rahab asks for special favor since she has helped the spies to infiltrate Jericho. She also expressed faith in God, and notes how the Israelites are gaining traction in their quest to gain the territory of the Promised Land.

"14 So the men said to her, "Our life for yours if you do not tell this business of ours; and it shall come about when the Lord gives us the land that we will deal kindly and faithfully with you." 15 Then she let them down by a rope through the window, for her house was on the city wall, so that she was living on the wall. 16 She said to them, "Go to the hill country, so that the pursuers will not happen upon you, and hide yourselves there for three days until the pursuers return. Then afterward you may go on your way." 17 The men said to her, "We shall be free from this oath to you which you have made us swear, 18 unless, when we come into the land, you tie this cord of scarlet thread in the window through which you let us down, and gather to yourself into the house your father and your mother and your brothers and all your father's household. 19 It shall come about that anyone who goes out of the doors of your house into the street, his blood shall be on his own head, and we shall be free; but anyone who is with you in the house, his blood shall be on our head if a hand is laid on him. 20 But if you tell this business of ours, then we shall be free from the oath which you have made us swear." 21 She said, "According to your words, so be it." So she sent them away, and they departed; and she tied the scarlet cord in the window."

In verses 14–21, Rahab's plan with the Israelite spies comes to fruition. They all make an oath to serve God in this situation. Rahab clearly connects with the Israelite nation, and thus utilizes her position within multiple national contexts to serve God. Many outside observers might consider her actions to be treasonous, but her example is one of service to God over her national context, which, by implication, is sinful and falls short of the greater purpose of loving God.

> "22 They departed and came to the hill country, and remained there for three days until the pursuers returned. Now the pursuers had sought them all along the road, but had not found them. 23 Then the two men returned and came down from the hill country and crossed over and came to Joshua the son of Nun, and they related to him all that had happened to them. 24 They said to Joshua, "Surely the Lord has given all the land into our hands; moreover, all the inhabitants of the land have melted away before us."

In Joshua 2, Rahab becomes instrumental in helping the Israelites take the city of Jericho. She, in effect, provides a major assist to the people. This biblical account is important for many reasons, but, in light of the discussion of this book, showcases Rahab's dual national claims. Ultimately, she chooses the side of Israel; she makes a concrete decision to support one side over the other.

Although much of the planning is discussed above in Joshua 2, Joshua's actual conquest of the Promised Land starts in Joshua 6 with the taking of Jericho, a city just across the Jordan River. Next, the Israelites attempt to take the city of Ai, but because of the sin of one man—Achan—their vast military superiority is rebuffed.[38] In Joshua 8, the Israelites are then successful in taking Ai.

Uriah

The start of this chapter introduced Uriah. At this point, it is instructive to return and finish the story in the context of other Old Testament figures who utilized their dual nationality for God's kingdom. Although his story is tragic, Uriah the Hittite (the husband of Bathsheba) is first introduced when away from his home fighting for King David's empire. This section of Scripture is primarily about King David's sin, and his extramarital relations with Bathsheba, but the story of Uriah the Hittite shows that one can hold multiple national allegiances and serve God diligently at the same time. The unfortunate part for Uriah is that David, in an attempt to cover up his multitude of sins, sends Uriah to his death on the frontlines in war. Nonetheless, what can be gleaned

---

38. Hill and Walton, *A Survey of the Old Testament*, 190.

from the story is that Uriah is a faithful man who served the Israelite kingdom well despite the indiscretions of the king. 2 Samuel 11 reads:

> "1 Then it happened in the spring, at the time when kings go out to battle, that David sent Joab and his servants with him and all Israel, and they destroyed the sons of Ammon and besieged Rabbah. But David stayed at Jerusalem."

The start of 2 Samuel 11 sets the scene of Israel at war with the Ammonites, a frequent enemy in the Old Testament. Ultimately, the siege is successful, as noted in 2 Samuel 12:26–27 wherein the Ammonites become subject to Israel. 2 Samuel 11:2 continues:

> "2 Now when evening came David arose from his bed and walked around on the roof of the king's house, and from the roof he saw a woman bathing; and the woman was very beautiful in appearance. 3 So David sent and inquired about the woman. And one said, "Is this not Bathsheba, the daughter of Eliam, the wife of Uriah the Hittite?""

As noted above, the central point of this account is a discussion of David's various sins. The noteworthy focus of this chapter is Uriah's national identity. Uriah is mentioned in verse 3 as a Hittite, and referenced regularly by his ethnic identity. Yet, he is also serving faithfully as a member of Israel's army. Uriah is sacrificing his life for King David and Israel. He is also cruelly betrayed by his king as noted in verse 4:

> "4 David sent messengers and took her, and when she came to him, he lay with her; and when she had purified herself from her uncleanness, she returned to her house. 5 The woman conceived; and she sent and told David, and said, "I am pregnant."6 Then David sent to Joab, saying, "Send me Uriah the Hittite." So Joab sent Uriah to David. 7 When Uriah came to him, David asked concerning the welfare of Joab and the people and the state of the war. 8 Then David said to Uriah, "Go down to your house, and wash your feet." And Uriah went out of the king's house, and a present from the king was sent out after him. 9 But Uriah slept at the door of the king's house with all the servants of his lord, and did not go down to his house."

Note the intensity of Uriah's loyalty to Israel in verse 9. He has been given special leave from the battlefield, but rather than spend time at home, he slept at the King's house with the servants so that he could continue serving his country. Uriah's ethnic, Hittite identity, is mentioned again, but his actions

show someone that has opted to serve his king and kingdom; in effect, his
service is to the place where God has placed him. 2 Samuel 11:10 proceeds:

> "10 Now when they told David, saying, "Uriah did not go down
> to his house," David said to Uriah, "Have you not come from a
> journey? Why did you not go down to your house?" 11 Uriah
> said to David, "The ark and Israel and Judah are staying in tem-
> porary shelters, and my lord Joab and the servants of my lord
> are camping in the open field. Shall I then go to my house to eat
> and to drink and to lie with my wife? By your life and the life of
> your soul, I will not do this thing." 12 Then David said to Uriah,
> "Stay here today also, and tomorrow I will let you go." So Uriah
> remained in Jerusalem that day and the next. 13 Now David
> called him, and he ate and drank before him, and he made him
> drunk; and in the evening he went out to lie on his bed with his
> lord's servants, but he did not go down to his house."

In verses 10–14, David gets ever desperate to cover his sins. Yet, even when
coerced by the king, Uriah maintains his utmost loyalty to the kingdom and
to the Israelite people. This is when King David opts to make an even worse
betrayal by sending his to the frontlines of battle:

> "14 Now in the morning David wrote a letter to Joab and sent
> it by the hand of Uriah. 15 He had written in the letter, saying,
> "Place Uriah in the front line of the fiercest battle and withdraw
> from him, so that he may be struck down and die." 16 So it was
> as Joab kept watch on the city, that he put Uriah at the place
> where he knew there were valiant men. 17 The men of the city
> went out and fought against Joab, and some of the people among
> David's servants fell; and Uriah the Hittite also died."

Uriah makes the ultimate sacrifice that any soldier can make for his country: laying down his life. War is a complex subject under Scripture, but also
a common theme, especially in the Old Testament. The Bible does not give
precise details on what happened, but clearly this was an intense conflict.
There is a great likelihood that others also died in that battle against the
Ammonite kingdom. Yet, were these deaths orchestrated by David to cover
his sin? War results in casualties, but it seems likely that David specifically
ordered this battle so that Uriah would die. 2 Samuel 11:18 continues:

> "18 Then Joab sent and reported to David all the events of the
> war. 19 He charged the messenger, saying, "When you have
> finished telling all the events of the war to the king, 20 and if
> it happens that the king's wrath rises and he says to you, 'Why
> did you go so near to the city to fight? Did you not know that

they would shoot from the wall? 21 Who struck down Abimelech the son of Jerubbesheth? Did not a woman throw an upper millstone on him from the wall so that he died at Thebez? Why did you go so near the wall?'—then you shall say, 'Your servant Uriah the Hittite is dead also.'"22 So the messenger departed and came and reported to David all that Joab had sent him to tell. 23 The messenger said to David, "The men prevailed against us and came out against us in the field, but we pressed them as far as the entrance of the gate. 24 Moreover, the archers shot at your servants from the wall; so some of the king's servants are dead, and your servant Uriah the Hittite is also dead." 25 Then David said to the messenger, "Thus you shall say to Joab, 'Do not let this thing displease you, for the sword devours one as well as another; make your battle against the city stronger and overthrow it'; and so encourage him." 26 Now when the wife of Uriah heard that Uriah her husband was dead, she mourned for her husband. 27 When the time of mourning was over, David sent and brought her to his house and she became his wife; then she bore him a son. But the thing that David had done was evil in the sight of the Lord."

Uriah was loyal to the Kingdom of Israel, and upright in his life. In almost every mention in 2 Samuel, the national marker, Hittite is used with his name. The Hittite people are mentioned in Exodus 33:2 as people who lived in the Holy Land prior to it becoming the land for the Jews. The Hittite Empire was powerful leading up to the start of the Iron Age in 1200 B.C.[39] Although, as mentioned in the introduction of this chapter, the Hittite Kingdom historically spread across various countries in the modern Middle East from Turkey to Syria and Lebanon, there was a portion in the Holy Land, as the Hittites conquered numerous port cities along the Mediterranean Sea.[40] Uriah's birthplace is not noted in Scripture, but he was clearly someone from a different national background that served honorably the Kingdom of Israel under David. Ultimately, Uriah even laid down his life for his kingdom, and for King David. Even though the account of David and Bathsheba has a much more specific meaning about sin, the life of Uriah should not be overlooked. Here is someone referred to as a Hittite throughout the account that becomes a loyal subject of Israel and sacrifices his life for the country.

39. Hill and Walton, *A Survey of the Old Testament*, 155.
40. Hill and Walton, *A Survey of the Old Testament*, 156.

Solomon

Solomon was the King of Israel, and as such provided with an opportunity to expand the border of Israel, and to create new diplomatic ties with other nations. In chapter 4 on Supranationalism, the account of 1 Kings 5–9 is discussed at length specifically regarding Solomon's "trade deal" with King Hiram of Tyre (a port city on the Mediterranean Sea). In the latter part of 1 Kings 2 and in the start of 1 Kings 3, the reader is introduced to a deal made by Solomon with the Pharaoh King of Egypt.[41] The alliance has some problematic features, but Solomon takes an Egyptian wife as a mechanism of solidifying a good relationship with Egypt. 1 Kings 2:46b-3:3 reads:

> "46 So the king commanded Benaiah the son of Jehoiada, and he went out and fell upon him so that he died. Thus the kingdom was established in the hands of Solomon. 3:1 Then Solomon formed a marriage alliance with Pharaoh king of Egypt, and took Pharaoh's daughter and brought her to the city of David until he had finished building his own house and the house of the Lord and the wall around Jerusalem. 2 The people were still sacrificing on the high places, because there was no house built for the name of the Lord until those days. 3 Now Solomon loved the Lord, walking in the statutes of his father David, except he sacrificed and burned incense on the high places."

When King Solomon takes over reign of the Kingdom of Israel following the death of King David, Scripture records that his first act was to make an alliance with the Pharaoh King of Egypt. Although Solomon had multiple wives, this particular wife from Egypt served as a lynchpin between the two kingdoms for the purposes of maintaining peace between the two powerful neighbors. As with much of Scripture, there are other important points in this passage, and a detailed overview of polygamy in the Old Testament is outside of the scope of this discussion. Nevertheless, Solomon, the King of Israel after David starts his reign by obtaining a peace agreement with Egypt—a very powerful kingdom. Throughout David's time as king, his discussions whether in 2 Samuel or throughout the Psalms often note David in the midst of battle or facing death via an enemy. When Solomon becomes king after David, this changes. Scripture notes that the "land is at rest" a euphemism to argue that peaceful relations between Israel and its neighboring kingdoms became the norm.

---

41. Hill and Walton, *A Survey of the Old Testament*, 240.

A Warning in Judges 2:6–23

The discussion in this section of chapter 2 has thus far revolved around positive cases wherein some well-known and some lesser-known characters from the Bible negotiate issues of multiple national allegiances. In these cases, the overarching message is to serve God regardless of the national circumstances, even when under a foreign empire such as the case of Daniel. Rahab, of course, is a different situation in that she serves the purposes of God by supporting the Israelites.

But, it is important to note that there are also dangers in multiple national allegiances—this is another theme found throughout Scripture. In Judges 2:12, for example, the people of Israel adopt gods from surrounding countries; invariably these neighboring countries then conquer Israel within a short period of time.[42] In the case of the Israelites, they adopted the god of Ba'al (a noted theologian describes Ba'al as "one of a pantheon of deities worshipped by the Canaanites").[43] Starting in Judges 2:6, Scripture reads:

> "6 When Joshua had dismissed the people, the sons of Israel went each to his inheritance to possess the land. 7 The people served the Lord all the days of Joshua, and all the days of the elders who survived Joshua, who had seen all the great work of the Lord which He had done for Israel. 8 Then Joshua the son of Nun, the servant of the Lord, died at the age of one hundred and ten. 9 And they buried him in the territory of his inheritance in Timnath-heres, in the hill country of Ephraim, north of Mount Gaash."

When a great leader dies, it is right for a country to mourn said leader. Romans 13:7, for example, admonished Christians to "honor to whom honor (is due)." Joshua had fulfilled his purpose by conquering the Holy Land, for the most part, and for providing the Israelite people with a state to envelope the nation. This is a key advantage because there is recognition on behalf of other surrounding states. Moreover, with continued access to permanent territory, it facilitates the process of defending the territory because there is an advantage to knowing the nuances of the terrain when staving off an enemy attack. Judges 2:10 continues:

> "10 All that generation also were gathered to their fathers; and there arose another generation after them who did not know the Lord, nor yet the work which He had done for Israel."

---

42. Grudem, *Politics according to the Bible*, 92
43. Hill and Walton, *A Survey of the Old Testament*, 469.

Like other sections of Scripture, for example, Exodus 1:8 notes that a new Pharaoh in Egypt arose who did not know Joseph. Even though Joseph effectively saved Egypt and other surrounding countries from famine given his expedient planning, the Israelites become slaves in Egypt because the new pharaoh forgot what Joseph had done. As in verse 10, the Israelites forgot Joshua, and turned away from God when a new generation comes to power. Verse 11 follows:

> "11 Then the sons of Israel did evil in the sight of the Lord and served the Baals, 12 and they forsook the Lord, the God of their fathers, who had brought them out of the land of Egypt, and followed other gods from among the gods of the peoples who were around them, and bowed themselves down to them; thus they provoked the Lord to anger. 13 So they forsook the Lord and served Baal and the Ashtaroth."

Within a generation, Israel moves from faithfully following God to capture the Promised Land to switching allegiance by serving Ba'al. Verse 12 repeats the fact that God brought them out of Egypt to the Promised Land; yet, the new generation overlooks these miraculous events and begins to change.

> "14 The anger of the Lord burned against Israel, and He gave them into the hands of plunderers who plundered them; and He sold them into the hands of their enemies around them, so that they could no longer stand before their enemies. 15 Wherever they went, the hand of the Lord was against them for evil, as the Lord had spoken and as the Lord had sworn to them, so that they were severely distressed. 16 Then the Lord raised up judges who delivered them from the hands of those who plundered them. 17 Yet they did not listen to their judges, for they played the harlot after other gods and bowed themselves down to them. They turned aside quickly from the way in which their fathers had walked in obeying the commandments of the Lord; they did not do as their fathers."

Even in the midst of the Israelite people turning away from God, He raised up judges to protect them from greater plunder. In effect, the kingdom was divided and prone to attack from the outside.[44] Yet, despite these dire warnings, the people did not listen to the judges, or change their sinful ways.

> "18 When the Lord raised up judges for them, the Lord was with the judge and delivered them from the hand of their enemies all the days of the judge; for the Lord was moved to pity by their

---

44. Grudem, *Politics according to the Bible*, 92.

groaning because of those who oppressed and afflicted them. 19 But it came about when the judge died, that they would turn back and act more corruptly than their fathers, in following other gods to serve them and bow down to them; they did not abandon their practices or their stubborn ways."

The corruption of Israel gets worse in verses 18 and 19. Ultimately, national allegiance in Israel as a kingdom that serves Yahweh was watered down by multiple allegiances to Ba'al and other gods. Even though Israel starts out as a relatively homogenous state, there are outside influences from surrounding nations that have an impact on the day-to-day governance of the kingdom. This changes reaches a point where the kingdom is no longer unified in its purpose, and begins to lose its identity. Verse 20 continues:

> "20 So the anger of the Lord burned against Israel, and He said, "Because this nation has transgressed My covenant which I commanded their fathers and has not listened to My voice, 21 I also will no longer drive out before them any of the nations which Joshua left when he died, 22 in order to test Israel by them, whether they will keep the way of the Lord to walk in it as their fathers did, or not." 23 So the Lord allowed those nations to remain, not driving them out quickly; and He did not give them into the hand of Joshua."

The most significant challenge for any Christian in the twenty-first century is comparing oneself to any of the three aforementioned cases. In some ways, the warning of Judges 2 seems apropos. There are dangers to change. Yet, change is a constant in life, so carefully monitoring is important. In the twenty-first century, national identity will change; ideas will shift from one generation to the next. Yet, for Christians, rootedness in Scripture is of the highest importance because it provides instruction on how to live in whatever circumstances God places a person.

As examples in this chapter, Joseph, Ruth, and Daniel all were linked to Israel, and were then forcibly moved to another country, their allegiance to God was paramount. In Joseph's case, he was sold into slavery, then imprisoned, but ultimately maintained his focus on God. For Uriah and Ruth, both were unconnected to Israel initially, but opted to profess allegiance to Yahweh. In both cases, they took their vow seriously, for Uriah resulting in his sacrificial death, for Ruth sacrificing for her mother-in-law, Naomi.

Yet, at the same time, all served with distinction in their respective national governments or societies. Both Joseph and Daniel were so respectful of their respective kings that they were noted for their success and diligence in their roles. Esther managed to change policy in the empire so as to protect her people from destruction against the evil deeds of Haman.

Federalism[45]

Thus far, this chapter has treated states as fairly monolithic—that a centralized national identity exists and that citizens happily accept governance from the capital. The discussion has engaged people who have allegiances to two or more countries, and noted examples found in Scripture. The reality is more complicated. Even someone that is able to trace her lineage back numerous generations in the same country, may have an affinity for a specific region of the country, rather than any connection with bureaucrats in the capital city.

Almost every country in the twenty-first century is not homogenous or monolithic, there are different regional distinctions even if there is a shared ethnic, religious, and/or linguistic heritage. The political scientist, James Ker-Lindsay, for example, argues that only 15 of the 193 member states of the UN are homogenous nation-states wherein the nation essentially aligns with the state.[46] Therefore, it is important, in the midst of this discussion, to engage in the tangent of differences within countries, and, sometimes, between countries. There are regions, in some parts of the world, with very similar cultural threads that run across national borders. Very strong cultural connections exist between people in the north of Mexico and the southwest of the United States,[47] or between ethnic kin within Central Asia, or Central Africa. This point is discussed in greater detail in chapter 5.

Despite cultural elements that overlap different national boundaries, governance is based on recognized, independent countries. In a formalized sense, a wider discussion of federal governance is useful as a means of thinking about how to govern territories that have a mix of different peoples and/or ideas.

Recalling the definitions in chapter 1, the difference between patriotism and nationalism may also be due, in part, to how power is devolved within a country. In situations with a strong, centralized government known as a unitary state, the possibility is more open for nationalism. In

---

45. A global definition of federalism merely infers devolution of power to more localized levels, whether they be states, regions, provinces, cantons etc. To the American reader, federalism typically infers the addition of three co-equal branches of government. (Smith et al., *Rendering to God and Caesar*, 98–101).

46. Ker-Lindsay, *The Foreign Policy of Counter Secession*, 5.

47. Woodard, *American Nations*, 10.

federal states where power is devolved to different groups and/or regions of a state, patriotism might be more widespread since people share a collective banner under the knowledge that their more local allegiance is granted some autonomy within the central state. Thus, even if a person identifies more closely with a region than the country, she may still feel comfortable within that country given significant autonomy from the central government to express her local language and/or culture. Patriotism can flourish more easily when people from various territories group together under a single banner. It can help to prevent zealotry on the part of one, homogenous group.

The issue of multiple allegiances may also be better managed in federal situations. For example, Israel was divided into 12 tribes, each with geographic dispersion across the territory. Deuteronomy 27: 12–13, for example, list the 12 tribes: Reuben, Simeon, Levi, Judah, Issachar, Zebulun, Dan, Naphtali, Gad, Asher, Benjamin, and Joseph. Later, Joseph is split into the tribes of Ephraim and Manasseh, making 13. Some scholars argue that Ephraim and Manasseh comprise "half tribes." When Reuben transgresses, Jacob removes him from the lineage and boosts Ephraim and Manasseh.

In a sense, a federal model allows for all of the people to be part of a wider union such as Israel, but to also hold to a smaller subsection of the territory. Some of the largest countries in the world today such as Russia, Canada, the United States, and Brazil utilize this type of federal model. At the continent level, most of the largest countries are federations. Some examples include (this is not an exhaustive list): North America (Mexico), South America (Argentina), Africa (Ethiopia and Sudan), Oceania (Australia), and Europe (Germany). Other large countries in terms of economics or population such as Nigeria and India also utilize federal models of governance.

Federalism is also employed in some smaller countries with multiple identities such as Belgium, Ethiopia, and Iraq. These are some of the most deeply divided societies in the world, and federalism provides a mechanism to maintain peace. Of course, when communism fell symbolically with the Berlin Wall in November 1989 and literally with the collapse of the Soviet Union in December 1991, multinational federal countries in Eastern Europe had their challenges.[48] All three multinational federal states, Czechoslovakia, Yugoslavia, and the Soviet Union dissolved. In the wake of what had been three countries, 22 emerged by the end of 1995, while several other entities remain mired in a contested status, known as a "frozen conflict."[49] Additionally, Montenegro split from Serbia in 2006, and Kosovo declared

48. Bunce, *Subversive Institutions.*
49. Coyle, *Russia's Border Wars and Frozen Conflicts.*

its independence in 2008[50] (the status of Kosovo under international law is controversial since approximately 2 in every 3 countries recognize Pristina's independence, but it does not have membership in the UN).

Scholars also debate the merits of federalism to solve problems. Is federalism like glue or solvent?[51] That is, is federalism more likely to keep countries together, or facilitate the process of splitting them apart? The academic literature is split on this question, simply because each case study is very different. Moreover, given that different types of federalism exist, the key to learning more is teasing out the differences. For example, some scholars argue that the structure of the multinational federal states in Eastern Europe all collapsed together in the wake of the end of communism.[52] Yet, other federal states like Canada have survived with full territorial integrity despite major secessionist challenges.[53] What accounts for these different outcomes?

There may be methods through which countries can utilize federalism to better serve the multiple identities within an existing country. But, change should be made slowly, and should reflect territorial rather than ethnic boundaries. The Old Testament provides some guidance here, especially under David and Solomon wherein the 12 tribes of Israel all work towards one goal of building a successful kingdom. In many respects, the 40-year reign of Solomon is the "golden era" of the Kingdom of Israel because "the land is at peace" and Israel is a very strong and powerful empire ruled by a very wise ruler. This is not to argue that federalism is a panacea to politics, after all, when Rehoboam takes over from Solomon, the kingdom splits in two. Yet, a discussion of 12 tribes raises the important point that no national identity is monolithic. There are specifics to every circumstance that are worthy of further examination.

Multiple National Identities: Discussion

Jesus' own experience with multiple national identities

As previously stated, Jesus was born into a Jewish family. Bethlehem's location is very close to Jerusalem, and it is clear that there is a very Jewish/Israelite context to Jesus's upbringing. For example, Jesus is referenced as being in a synagogue and sitting with prominent teachers even as a young boy. But, at

---

50. King, *Extreme Politics*, 105.

51. Bird et al., "*Is Decentralization" Glue" or" Solvent" for National Unity?*"

52. Bunce, *Subversive Institutions*; Duerr, "*Peaceful and Mutual Parliamentary Dissolution*"

53. Young, *The Secession of Quebec and the Future of Canada.*

an early age, his parents had to flee to Egypt in order to keep Jesus alive since King Herod decreed that all newborn sons must be killed. Later, when life was safer after the death of Herod, His family returned to Israel to raise Jesus and his siblings. Scripture does not indicate whether or not Jesus maintained any linkages with Egypt after the return. However, the city of Nazareth features prominently in his upbringing. Like Bethlehem, Nazareth is firmly found in a Jewish/Israelite context, albeit under the Roman Empire.

Although Scripture does not provide any indication that Jesus became Egyptian, or anything but a Jew, there is a period in His life when He lived abroad for what is probably a considerable amount of time. Scripture briefly records Jesus as a 12-year old boy, notably on a trip to Jerusalem. Therefore, it is not known how long Jesus lived in Egypt, but living in a neighboring province of the Roman Empire keeps Jesus safe in the short term.

Conclusions

There are two main challenging aspects of dual or multiple national allegiances. First, the question of whether and when a person should shift from the support of one to another. The process can be gradual, and both (or multiple) allegiances can be held at the same time, but what is biblical? In some respects, it depends on the circumstances. For example, in the country of Estonia, it is illegal to hold dual citizenship. Sometimes this is done for historical reasons, and sometimes these types of policies have been enacted in opposition to a group, or due to historical enmity. In the case of Estonia, there is a large ethnic Russian population, especially in the eastern Ida-Veru county. By allowing for dual citizens, a danger arises in terms of significant segments of the population aligning with Russia whilst living within Estonia. For many Estonians, they recall a horrific past of being occupied by the Soviet Union. Therefore, there are circumstances wherein recent historical events further complicate issues of nationality. Specific answers to every situation are not possible, but there are Christian admonitions to love one's neighbors while simultaneously honoring those in power whether they are fellow Christians or not.[54]

Depending on the situation, a given follower of Christ may possess citizenships in two or more countries. This situation brings both blessings and responsibilities. There is a richness to life based on diversity of background—it is a blessing, but not everyone may understand the torn nature of these identities. Some may insist that one identity should be prominent. This is a fair point when one country provides education, social services,

54. Schaeffer, *The Mark of the Christian*, 18.

employment, and opportunities—there should be a sense of gratefulness in the heart of followers of Christ for what has been granted by that single country. There are also points in history that demand national allegiance especially if the country is threatened, for example, in war. If there is an openness to the constitution, however, there should be no prohibition on a person enjoying elements of culture (food, entertainment etc.) from their other citizenship, or country of their birth. In many cases, the host country is enriched by the diversity in language, culture, and lifestyle.

There is also a major responsibility to disseminate and forward the gospel based on the distinction of holding multiple citizenships. When a person is bicultural, or has the ability to almost seamlessly move between cultures, this ability should be used for God's kingdom—a person is a natural point of connection for language skills, connections between peoples, and peace between countries. Recalling the words of Paul that he became "all things to all men, so that I may by all means save some" (1 Corinthians 9:22).

In many countries throughout the world, for example, there are English, Korean, and Chinese language churches (among many other languages), which serve to connect ex-patriot populations. These churches also serve to culturally enrich the local society, and help to connect local believers and seekers who may have an interest in a particular speaker, or culture. In some senses, the prevalence of these linguistic churches throughout the world serves as a beachhead for the country, with all the baggage it brings, but also for cross-national gospel expression akin to Revelation 7, just in an earthly setting.

Ultimately, the lives of Christ followers with multiple national identities should emulate the life of Paul, who used his positions to further the gospel. Not every person will serve as a missionary, and cross borders with regularity, but the position should elevate the gospel, and allow it to be heard in different countries around the world.

Chapter 4

Supranationalism

The Lord gave wisdom to Solomon, just as He promised him;
and there was peace between Hiram and Solomon, and the
two of them made a covenant.

—1 Kings 5:12

Supranationalism, as defined in chapter one, refers to an entity "existing above rather than between states."[1] The term, supranational, is most commonly used as an adjective to describe intergovernmental unions or organizations that transcend but also recognize and order themselves through national borders. In essence, supranational organizations involve two or more different countries in a union wherein they all poll select common goods and/or share the norm of free trade. The term Supranationalism differs in definition from transnationalism where national borders occupy a much lesser role (discussed in more detail in chapter 6).

For some Christians, depending on where they reside in the world, Supranationalism is not really a daily issue in their lives; for others, Supranationalism is a very real part of life that, whether recognized or not, impacts the lives of Christians residing within these areas of the world. Some supranational organizations heavily impact trade within a continent, and control areas of policy like the food that is consumed or the air that is breathed.

The most prominent example of Supranationalism is the European Union (EU), which connects 27 countries in Europe (the Brexit vote of June

1. Archer, *International Organizations.*

2016 and its subsequent ratification in January 2020 means that the United Kingdom exited the organization reducing membership from 28 to 27). The EU government has control over a range of different policy areas;[2] although, it is worth noting that most constitutional powers still reside with national governments. For example, the Spanish government is Madrid is still responsible for all taxation in Spain, and for providing the vast majority of services to its citizens. But, member states agree to accept Europe-wide policies and regulations in a wide range of areas in exchange for access to a large continental market of almost half a billion people. Technically EU law supersedes national law, since national and European law must be harmonized, and any given member state is subject to legal action through the European Court of Justice (ECJ).[3] The political scientist, Anne-Marie Slaughter argues that these relationships between national courts and the ECJ, "enable the supranational institution to be maximally effective."[4] EU member states increasingly intertwine political, economic, judicial, and social policy areas. As an example, 19 of the 27 member states also share monetary policy with the Euro currency, which was adopted in 2002.[5] These numbers have expanded quite dramatically in the twenty-first century, and will likely increase again in the coming years; there are negotiations with several different countries on potential accession in the future.

The EU started as the European Coal and Steel Community (ECSC)—a union forged in the belief that pooling coal and steel resources would reduce the likelihood of another world war.[6] After all, in the span of three decades—from 1914, the start of World War I to 1945, the end of World War II—Europe was the center of two major conflagrations. The Treaty of Paris, the founding document of the ECSC, in 1951 initiated the organization with six member states: West Germany, France, Italy, Belgium, Luxembourg, and the Netherlands[7] with a focus on Franco-(West) German cooperation.[8] In essence, the overarching goal was to change historic enemies into partners.[9] Over time, usually with a new treaty, the organization grew in size and cooperation.

---

2. Gilbert, *European Integration*, 1.

3. McCormick, *Understanding the European Union*, 109.

4. Slaughter, *A New World Order*, 14.

5. Gilbert, *European Integration*, 174.

6. McCormick, *Understanding the European Union*, 56.

7. McCormick, *Understanding the European Union*, 66.

8. Mazower, *Dark Continent*, 182.

9. Gilbert, *European Integration*, 9–11.

After being blocked for membership in the 1960s, the United Kingdom, along with Ireland and Denmark joined in 1973.[10] Greece was added in 1981, as well as Spain and Portugal in 1986. Then, when Austria, Sweden, and Finland joined in 1995, the EU-15 was set.[11] The organization looked much like a rich, western European club; although, some countries like Greece, Ireland, Spain, and Portugal gained significant wealth in that time from the 1970s to the mid-1990s, moving from "medium" income to wealthy. The Irish economy, in particular, grew quickly denoting the title "Celtic tiger" in reference to its strong economic growth and sharp increase in standard of living.[12] Numerous organs were also added to the EU. A European Parliament was first elected in 1979, a European Commission was formed, as well as the European Council and the Council of Europe.[13] A judicial branch—the European Court of Justice—was added, gaining traction in 1963 with a binding decision on the Treaty of Rome as a "constitutional instrument," which "imposed direct and common obligations on member states."[14] Most notably, the Maastricht Treaty of 1992, created the binding idea of the EU with harmonized organs and areas of policy. In 2004, the EU expanded dramatically to become the EU-25 with the accession of ten new members, 8 of which were from behind the Cold War-Iron Curtain including Czech Republic, Slovakia, Poland, Hungary, Slovenia, Estonia, Latvia, and Lithuania, with the small Mediterranean islands Malta and Cyprus also joining.[15] Finally, the EU-25 grew to the EU-27 in 2007 with the entrance of Romania and Bulgaria; the EU-28 was created with the accession of Croatia in 2013. Several other countries have sought to accede to the EU, but are either "in-waiting" or have been blocked. The accession of Turkey, for example, has long been a major point of debate given the large, predominantly-Muslim population, but also that the country sits on the geographic periphery of Europe.[16]

The EU remains a culturally Christian entity in that the vast majority of countries come from some form of Christian heritage—whether Roman Catholic, Protestant, Orthodox, or any other grouping. Yet, the proposed European Constitution, for example, did not have any mention of Europe's

10. McCormick, *Understanding the European Union*, 57.

11. Gilbert, *European Integration*, 182.

12. Gilbert, *European Integration*, 145.

13. McCormick, *Understanding the European Union*, 84–114.

14. McCormick, *Understanding the European Union*, 110.

15. Bale, *European Politics*.

16. Jenkins, *God's Continent*, 115.

Christian heritage within a 70,000-word document[17] suggesting that the continent has become "Post-Christian."[18] Moreover, a Catholic-Italian politician, Rocco Buttiglione, was rejected for a position in the European Commission (Justice, Freedom, and Security), for espousing his conscience regarding Christian views on marriage.[19] Many argue, therefore, that the Europe is culturally Christian, but the EU has tried to position itself as a secular organization.

None of this is new to Christians per se, in that the Bible has no provisions that Christians must possess political power in tandem with their gospel witness. The aforementioned theologian Wayne Grudem argues that government should not compel religion (in this case, Christianity).[20] Therefore, Christians in all EU countries live with an additional, European layer of government that impacts their lives, whether it is noticed or not.

Alongside, the accession of new member states, the EU also harmonized areas of policy, and grew into new areas. The treaties of Amsterdam (1997), Nice (2001), and Lisbon (2009) accomplished these goals,[21] but also, in part, led to the rise of the Brexit movement in the UK, as well as other "Euroskeptic" movements elsewhere in Europe. In 2005, EU member states voted on a new "constitution," which would have radically centralized the organization into a nascent "United States of Europe,"[22] a term borrowed from the British Prime Minister, Winston Churchill, who suggested the idea in the 1940s.[23] Given perceived overreach from Brussels, the twin "non" and "nee" no votes by the French and Dutch voters respectively, cauterized any advance of an EU Constitution in 2005.[24]

Perhaps the most obvious outward sign of Supranationalism in Europe is the Euro currency. Historically, the French Franc, the German Mark, the Dutch Guilder, the Spanish Pesata, among others, were all separate currencies. The new currency was officially launched in 2002 when 12 of the then-15 members gave up their currencies in favor of the Euro.[25] This area of policy—known as monetary policy—is a very important component piece

---

17. Jenkins, *God's Continent*, 38–9.

18. The Peruvian pastor, Samuel Escobar discusses the meaning of the term, Post-Christian, as societies which have "displaced Christianity from role of honor and influence" (Escobar, *The New Global Mission*, 70).

19. Jenkins, *God's Continent*, 40.

20. Grudem, *Politics according to the Bible*, 23.

21. Bale, *European Politics*.

22. Reid, *The United States of Europe*; Rifkin, *The European Dream*.

23. McCormick, *Understanding the European Union*, 63.

24. Bale, *European Politics*.

25. Bale, *European Politics*, 68.

of sovereignty for any national government because it covers currency, printing money, as well as the ability to set interest rates. This is a clear piece of evidence of Supranationalism in Europe.

Of course, there is another side to the argument. The EU, some argue, is not fully supranational because there are still numerous areas of government that belong at the national level.[26] This, according to the argument, impedes cooperation at the continental level because national borders restrict the ability to compete in certain industries, especially the high tech sector.[27]

Another example elsewhere in the world is the Southern Common Market, better known by their Spanish and Portuguese acronyms, Mercosur or Mercosul. Mercosur, as it is best known, encompasses four countries—Brazil, Argentina, Uruguay, and Paraguay—in its organization (Venezuela's membership is on hiatus). The first four countries joined Mercosur in 1991. Venezuela gained full accession to the union in 2012 (having been an associate member since 2006), but was suspended in December 2016.[28] In comparison to the EU, Mercosur is much less supranational because the member states maintain more autonomy across a range of different policy areas. Each member state of Mercosur retains their own currency; as noted previously, 19 of the 27 members of the EU use the Euro.

Beyond the EU and Mercosur, there are numerous other, continental organizations around the world. Most of them have not consolidated powers amongst member states. In general, these organizations seek to cooperate based on trade in order to facilitate the free movement of goods and services—in essence, the major reasoning is to improve business efficiency. For Christians in Canada, Mexico, and the United States, there is aforementioned United States Mexico Canada Agreement (USMCA), formerly the North American Free Trade Agreement (NAFTA); in South-east Asia, the Association of Southeast Asian Nations (ASEAN); in Russia, Armenia, Belarus, Kazakhstan, and Kyrgyzstan, the Eurasian Economic Union (EAEU); in the Caribbean, the Caribbean Community (CARICOM); in West Africa, the Economic Community of West African States (ECOWAS); in East Africa, the Intergovernmental Authority on Development (IGAD); in Central Africa, the Economic and Monetary Community of Central Africa (CEMAC under its French acronym); in Southern Africa, the Southern African Development Community (SADC). Beyond this list, there are also several other organizations that have numerous member states, and varying levels of Supranationalism.

26. Moravcsik, *"Europe, the Second Superpower"* 91.

27. Verhofstadt, *Europe's Last Chance*, 152–54.

28. BBC, *"Mercosur suspends Venezuela over trade and human rights"*

The point here is not to provide an exhaustive list of all supranational organizations in the world, but rather, make a strong case that Christians all over the world reside under various layers of government, including continental blocs. Some of these blocs, like the EU, are quite powerful. How, then, should the Christian live?

Scripture and Supranationalism

As one might imagine, there are very few sections of Scripture that directly relate to the idea of Supranationalism. The Bible discusses the some concepts surrounding the notion of empire in significant detail, but mainly as a descriptor. For example, the New Testament is written, in its entirety, in the reality of the Roman Empire as the authority. Christ himself asks believers to "Then render to Caesar the things that are Caesar's, and to God the things that are God's" (Luke 20:25; Mark 12:17; Matthew 22:21). In the Old Testament, there are numerous empires. Israel becomes an empire under the rule of successive powerful kings, Saul, David, and Solomon. The Egyptian Empire covers much of the latter part of Genesis and the beginning of Exodus. The Assyrian and Babylonian empires are key facets of the exilic period where the people of Israel and Judah are taken into captivity.

Supranationalism, however, differs from empire in that countries voluntarily decide to join a trade bloc like the EU, Mercosur, ECOWAS, or NAFTA. Under an empire, membership is forced, often through very harsh and bloody means. Roman rule in the New Testament is noted as harsh, Jesus himself was killed upon a Roman cross.

One section of Scripture—1 Kings 5—in particular, provides some indication of how Christians should live, and connect to the ideas of governance and trade.[29] This discussion in Scripture can then be connected to Supranationalism. 1 Kings 5: 1–5 reads:

> "1 Now Hiram king of Tyre sent his servants to Solomon, when he heard that they had anointed him king in place of his father, for Hiram had always been a friend of David. 2 Then Solomon sent word to Hiram, saying, 3 "You know that David my father was unable to build a house for the name of the Lord his God because of the wars which surrounded him, until the Lord put them under the soles of his feet. 4 But now the Lord my God has given me rest on every side; there is neither adversary nor misfortune. 5 Behold, I intend to build a house for the name of the Lord my God, as the Lord spoke to David my father, saying,

---

29. Hill and Walton, *A Survey of the Old Testament*, 238.

'Your son, whom I will set on your throne in your place, he will build the house for My name.'"

The opening section of 1 Kings describes the change in leadership in Israel from David to Solomon. David was a sinful leader as noted in Scripture (discussed in some detail in chapter 3), but also "a man after God's own heart" who did much to gain power for Israel through improved governance. David never saw peace in the land, though; this is something that changed with Solomon, as Scripture described, the "land is at rest," peace became more prevalent.

As with any shift in governance, new leaders should carefully and optimistically approach their new counterparts. Hiram, the King of Tyre (roughly equivalent to modern day Lebanon) approaches Solomon. Tyre does not feature prominently in Scripture, even though it was a major city along international trade routes following the coastline of the Mediterranean Sea.[30] For example, unlike Edom, Aram, and Ammon, Israel did not fight numerous wars against the Kingdom of Tyre. Yet, as a near neighbor to Israel, peaceful relations are important, for the simple fact that economic prosperity is much easier in times of peace, rather than war. The new King of Israel, Solomon, seeks to build a more peaceful security environment for Israel—he also inherits a regional security situation that is generally more peaceable than the start or the middle of David's reign (20–40 years earlier). 1 Kings 5: 6–9 continues:

> "6 Now therefore, command that they cut for me cedars from Lebanon, and my servants will be with your servants; and I will give you wages for your servants according to all that you say, for you know that there is no one among us who knows how to cut timber like the Sidonians."7 When Hiram heard the words of Solomon, he rejoiced greatly and said, "Blessed be the Lord today, who has given to David a wise son over this great people." 8 So Hiram sent word to Solomon, saying, "I have heard the message which you have sent me; I will do what you desire concerning the cedar and cypress timber. 9 My servants will bring them down from Lebanon to the sea; and I will make them into rafts to go by sea to the place where you direct me, and I will have them broken up there, and you shall carry them away. Then you shall accomplish my desire by giving food to my household."

In verses six to nine, Solomon and Hiram begin to outline a trade deal. This deal is limited in terms of a precise exchange of wood for food, but, taken more broadly, incorporates several different areas of modern policy.

---

30. Hill and Walton, *A Survey of the Old Testament*, 39.

This deal between Solomon and Hiram, at minimum, involves both the timber and agriculture industries, as well as the service sector, and construction. Although parallels cannot be drawn with modern-day trade deals that envelop every sector of the economy, this tentative deal between Solomon and Hiram provides an outline of how a relationship can blossom, and how it can have a relatively widespread impact on the economy. Trade deals can be narrow, but such agreements can also incorporate a number of government departments and agencies, as is the case in the bilateral deal created by Hiram and Solomon.

The Kingdom of Tyre was renowned for its cedar wood, and, even to the present, the Lebanese flag has a cedar tree emblazoned in the middle. At the time, wood was an integral building material, especially given Solomon's plans to rebuild the temple. For Solomon, building the temple was seen as act of worship to God, and a means of enriching the spiritual well-being of his people, in addition to the economic and diplomatic well-being of his people. Continuing with 1 Kings 5:10–12:

> "10 So Hiram gave Solomon as much as he desired of the cedar and cypress timber. 11 Solomon then gave Hiram 20,000 kors of wheat as food for his household, and twenty kors of beaten oil; thus Solomon would give Hiram year by year. 12 The Lord gave wisdom to Solomon, just as He promised him; and there was peace between Hiram and Solomon, and the two of them made a covenant."

In the next three verses, 10–12, Solomon and Hiram initiate a formal deal between the two kingdoms. The two leaders provide precise measures of what they are each to provide. Every treaty in the modern era should be very specific such that the various different sides know to what degree they are engaging. Changes to the treaty that are discussed later in 1 Kings should also be transparent. 1 Kings 5:13–18 continues to add details to the agreement:

> "13 Now King Solomon levied forced laborers from all Israel; and the forced laborers numbered 30,000 men. 14 He sent them to Lebanon, 10,000 a month in relays; they were in Lebanon a month and two months at home. And Adoniram was over the forced laborers. 15 Now Solomon had 70,000 transporters, and 80,000 hewers of stone in the mountains, 16 besides Solomon's 3,300 chief deputies who were over the project and who ruled over the people who were doing the work. 17 Then the king commanded, and they quarried great stones, costly stones, to lay the foundation of the house with cut stones. 18 So Solomon's

builders and Hiram's builders and the Gebalites cut them, and
prepared the timbers and the stones to build the house."

The end of 1 Kings 5 shows how the treaty between Solomon and Hiram
was carried out in practice. Solomon starts by conscripting laborers to help
with the tasks of taking down the cedar wood, and then transporting it to
Israel. Reading into the text, these laborers needed to be organized, fed,
and transported. Carrying out all of these tasks for 30,000 men would have
been a monumental task requiring widespread coordination. Moreover,
Adoniram was in charge of forced labor, which required an additional
150,000 men split between transporting the cedars, and cutting stone in
the hills. The fact that 3,300 supervisors were required shows the sheer
magnitude of the work.

Not much is said about Hiram's portion of the bilateral agreement. Yet,
in verse 18, Scripture specifically notes that the Gebalites were responsible for
cutting the wood and stone. Gebal, also known as Byblos, was a city just to the
north of modern day Beirut.[31] Given its location as a port city on the Mediterranean, it is safe to assume that many of these men were very skilled in ship
building, and using wood for numerous types of construction.

Notably, in the modern era, when considering verse 13, forced labor is
not an acceptable practice as enshrined under constitutions in many countries
throughout the world. But Scripture is merely stating what happened here.
The larger narrative remains that leaders can sign and implement treaties with
neighboring countries provided that there is a benefit to people.

Despite some shortcomings, there is an initial zest for the bilateral deal
between Israel and Tyre. Solomon constructs the temple, and Israel continues to prosper as an economically developed and peaceful country. In many
respects, this is the "golden era" of the Kingdom of Israel wherein Saul and
David built an empire upon which Solomon consolidates power so that it
becomes a beacon of good governance for surrounding countries.

It is important to follow a story to its conclusion, however. While the
situation was very good for a considerable time, and Solomon succeeded in
his objectives, the situation changes. The optimism of 1 Kings 5 eventually
cedes to pessimism and regret in 1 Kings 9, written approximately 20 years
later. 1 Kings 9:10–14 reads:

> "10 It came about at the end of twenty years in which Solomon
> had built the two houses, the house of the Lord and the king's
> house 11 (Hiram king of Tyre had supplied Solomon with cedar
> and cypress timber and gold according to all his desire), then
> King Solomon gave Hiram twenty cities in the land of Galilee.

31. Hill and Walton, *A Survey of the Old Testament*, 182.

> 12 So Hiram came out from Tyre to see the cities which Solo-
> mon had given him, and they did not please him. 13 He said,
> "What are these cities which you have given me, my brother?"
> So they were called the land of Cabul to this day. 14 And Hiram
> sent to the king 120 talents of gold."

Although the initial deal struck between Solomon and Hiram in 1 Kings 5 worked for a time, including building the house of the Lord and the king's house (verse 10), there are serious problems 20 years later as noted in 1 Kings 9. In verse 12, Hiram is clearly not pleased with the outcome of the deal between the two kings. Even though Solomon gave Hiram 20 towns, the latter questioned the worth and utility of these places. Scripture simply records that Hiram left unhappy. Verse 13 states that Hiram called the towns, the "Land of Cabul," which roughly translates as "good for nothing." To make matters worse, verse 14 records that Hiram paid 120 talents of gold, roughly equivalent to four tons of gold—a massive sum of wealth.

This account in 1 Kings shows that a trade deal can work, but that it must be constantly evaluated to see if it is working for both (or multiple) sides. Supranational organizations can be brought down, or revoked, should they not suit the needs of the rulers (1 Kings 5), or work for the good of people governed by those rulers (Romans 13). Both of these biblical principles should provide a check on the power of supranational blocs.

Is it biblical to form an encompassing social, political, and economic alliance organization with other countries?

As noted in the example of 1 Kings 5 above, there is a biblical framework through which countries can engage in lasting trade union with one another. This is not to argue that Supranationalism is explicitly biblical, but there are examples of when countries work together. Moreover, Christians may simply react to what is happening around them in the political environment. For many Christians today in Europe, they were born under the EU's system, so getting rid of the organization is not under their purview. Of course, British voters in June 2016 voted to leave, so it is possible to exit the EU, albeit after a protracted negotiation between parties (Brexit was completed in January 2020).

The concept of Supranationalism is both new and old at the same time. On a surface level, Supranationalism is largely synonymous with the idea of a confederation, or an alliance between different groups or countries. This idea is also ancient. Joshua 9–12, for example, describes confederations of northern and southern kings in their effort to stave off the invasion of the

Israelites in the land of Canaan. People have always worked together and collaborated for wider ranging goals. The question is to what degree does this collaboration include?

In order to answer this question, it is useful to stop and consider a different, academic question, one that presents a nuance in the discussion. The debate is Intergovernmentalism versus Supranationalism. In some senses, a debate over Intergovernmentalism and Supranationalism is a debate surrounding two similar terms. When examining any given free trade union, there are differences in how much control is granted to the union. Viewed another way, how much power is devolved from a national government to a supranational organization.

Essentially, both terms exist on a continuum when a free trade area exists. In intergovernmental structures, the members of the free trade area still maintain wide latitude; the accumulated power of the organization is limited. Intergovernmentalism is best defined under an organization like the USMCA, formerly known as NAFTA;[32] although the term can be broadly defined to mean "cooperation among member states on matters of common interest."[33] Three member states, the United States, Canada, and Mexico have agreed to trade good and services without restrictions or tariffs; however, there is no pooling of resources, and three countries have not created a shared parliament or commission to oversee governance. Put simply, there is no government overseeing all three countries. Real life is always a little messier than theory, but much of the previous sentences hold in a practical sense.

Supranationalism, as discussed throughout this chapter, is best defined by the EU. A full academic definition of Supranationalism connotes the inability to "maintain complete control over developments" within the organization.[34] However, the member states of the EU still maintain some degree of autonomy; Europe is not a country, it is not a "United States of Europe." Put simply, the EU is not a state with a centralized government. There is a high degree of economic, political, and social integration in Europe, but each member state is still separate. For example, Europe does not have a unified military, nor does Europe supersede the budgets for each country; taxation remains a national power. Compared to the USMCA, though, the EU is much more centralized and harmonized across numerous areas of public policy.

---

32. Pastor, *Toward a North American Community*, 16.

33. Nugent, *The Government and Politics of the European Union*, 558.

34. Nugent, *The Government and Politics of the European Union*, 558.

As an example, the political scientist, Andrew Moravcsik argues that Europe functions in a much more harmonized way such that it can be considered a second superpower (alongside the United States) in the world.[35] Other American Europhiles like Jeremy Rifkin, author of *The European Dream* (2004),[36] and T.R. Reid, author of *The United States of Europe* (2004)[37] concur that Europe has much to offer the world in terms of standard of living and governmental goals. Harmonized policies in Europe, both authors argue, have created a "European Dream"[38] or "European Social Model"[39] that rivals the American Dream. Interestingly, Europe has not invested heavily into the military, and instead chosen to focus on economic and emotional well-being, rather than becoming a geopolitical power.[40]

In some senses, it is natural for countries, especially smaller states to look for alliances in order to secure their borders and people. Policy outcomes can fail dramatically if a government performs poorly. For example, in Lamentations 5:6, the prophet Jeremiah is crying out to God pleading for mercy. The prophet notes that requests have been made to Egypt and Assyria in order that the people of Judah would receive enough bread to live, and to stave off the hunger after the Babylonian Empire took Jerusalem. In this case, it might have behooved the people of Judah to have at least developed rudimentary ties with neighboring countries and empires as a means of gaining help in a time of need. Yet, when Rehoboam refused to listen to the people, Judah was isolated after the division of the kingdom (1 Kings 12)[41] and its leaders did not advocate developing new alliances in the succeeding centuries leaving it prone to attack.

In the life of every country, there are times of plenty, and times of need. Petitioning neighboring countries during a time of famine is a lesson unto itself. Regularly promoting good, working relations with neighboring countries has its uses; especially should hard economic times develop. To return to the account of Pharaoh's dream in Genesis 41 (discussed in chapter 3) is particularly apt when Joseph provides an explanation for the dream. In summary, Joseph discerns that there will be seven years of plenty, followed by seven years of sharp decline and famine. Pharaoh listens to the advice of Joseph, and plans accordingly. Thus, when the land is afflicted during the

35. Moravcsik, "*Europe, the Second Superpower*"

36. Rifkin, *The European Dream*.

37. Reid, *The United States of Europe*.

38. Rifkin, *The European Dream*, 38–40.

39. Reid, *The United States of Europe*, 144–176.

40. Kagan, *Of Paradise and Power*, 53–54.

41. Grudem, *Politics according to the Bible*, 107.

seven lean years, Egypt is very well positioned to survive during this period. Other countries then come to Egypt begging for supplies.

There are Scriptural examples of what happens under different circumstances of governance and diplomacy. God uses various situations to humble peoples and countries, but there are specific examples of when poor governance leads to death and destruction, which, in marked contrast to other situations wherein leaders seek out mutually beneficial working relationships with other leaders. God often raises up "evil" leaders or sends "foreign oppressors" in order to precipitate punishment for countries.[42] For example, Israel's and Judah's destruction via the Assyrian and Babylonian empires respectively was the result of years of sin when the people forgot repentance to the point that they no longer feared God.

Creation and The Tower of Babel

In Genesis 1:28—the "creation mandate" reads as follows: "God blessed them; and God said to them, "Be fruitful and multiply, and fill the earth, and subdue it; and rule over the fish of the sea and over the birds of the sky and over every living thing that moves on the earth." Here, Moses outlines the ability to human beings to be fruitful, to engage in human flourishing.[43] Human beings are given a mandate over the earth, the sea, and the air. Of course, territory (the earth), waterways (the sea), and the air, do not stop and start at contemporary national boundaries—there is no one, universal country or empire. Even the four largest countries of the world (in terms of land mass): Russia, Canada, and the United States, and China, share borders with other countries. For this reason, shared governance and diplomacy with other countries is a useful tool for any wise leader. Despite its size and power, China is still impacted—through the earth, sea, and air—by its neighbors. Beijing might be able to coerce these neighbors through its economic and military power, but its citizens are still impacted from across the various borders, sometimes negatively. For example, if China acts in a bullying way towards its neighbors, the Vietnamese, Taiwanese, or Filipino governments might not be so amendable to trade, and seek to offset Beijing's ambitions with China's great power rival, the United States.[44] For this reason, among several, the United States Navy patrols the South China Sea and conducts freedom of navigation (FONOPS) exercises.[45] This will hurt

42. Hill and Walton, *A Survey of the Old Testament*, 197.

43. Grudem and Asmus, *The Poverty of Nations*, 280–1.

44. Mearsheimer, *The Tragedy of Great Power Politics*, 376.

45. Fabey, *Crashback*, xiv.

certain sectors of China's economy. In this light, some form of negotiation and governance structure is useful in upholding the creation mandate, in every modern national context.

Viewed more broadly, a global organization like the United Nations can have some relevance—even if it has no formal powers—in order to provide a forum to discuss issues that traverse the earth, sea, and air. There are places where governance across national lines is helpful in order to better the lives of human beings under the creation mandate. This is not to say that the UN is explicitly biblical—it is not. But the UN does provide a forum for countries to discuss pressing issues, and to resolve them peacefully.[46] Governance over shared issues does not, however, mean global government. There is no biblical mandate for a structure of global government. Depending on how one reads the Book of Revelation, the Antichrist might consolidate power through some form of global government structure in order to wage the Battle of Armageddon (Revelation 16:14).[47] Thus, Supranationalism can be useful when viewed in the narrowly bounded lens of 1 Kings 5, but should not be applied so broadly as to create a full, global supranational entity.

The Biblical account of the Tower of Babel is a warning against advanced Supranationalism, at least to the point where it attempts to unify all the peoples of the world as a mechanism of becoming god, a means of rivaling, in their minds, the one true God of the universe.[48] Genesis 11: 1–9 reads:

> "1 Now the whole earth used the same language and the same words. 2 It came about as they journeyed east, that they found a plain in the land of Shinar and settled there. 3 They said to one another, "Come, let us make bricks and burn them thoroughly." And they used brick for stone, and they used tar for mortar. 4 They said, "Come, let us build for ourselves a city, and a tower whose top will reach into heaven, and let us make for ourselves a name, otherwise we will be scattered abroad over the face of the whole earth." 5 The Lord came down to see the city and the tower which the sons of men had built. 6 The Lord said, "Behold, they are one people, and they all have the same language. And this is what they began to do, and now nothing which they purpose to do will be impossible for them. 7 Come, let Us go down and there confuse their language, so that they will not understand one another's speech." 8 So the Lord scattered them abroad from there over the face of the whole earth; and they stopped building

---

46. United Nations, *The United Nations Today*, 5.

47. Jeremiah, *The Book of Signs*, 248.

48. MacArthur and Mayhew, *Biblical Doctrine*, 440.

the city. 9 Therefore its name was called Babel, because there the Lord confused the language of the whole earth; and from there the Lord scattered them abroad over the face of the whole earth."

Genesis 11:1–9 should provide a further warning to supranational organizations. In some ways, a supranational organization might have the connotation of trying to be like God, or accomplish the purposes of God through man. Both of these ambitions run counter to the sovereignty of God who alone has power and dominion over humanity.

In verse 4, the people try to build a tower that "reaches to the heavens" as a means of appropriating power that is rightfully God's. It is the height of human arrogance. Supranational blocs face this risk in that when power is consolidated into a vast empire, it is sometimes done as a means of trying to reach par with God. Provided, then, that a supranational bloc has in place appropriate checks and balances to the power that any one person can wield, any Tower of Babel comparison can be avoided.

As established at the beginning of the chapter, the 1 Kings 5 model discusses trade. Trade and economic policy is a major area under the EU, but the organization has grown to encompass many more areas, from currency to full regulations over what can be consumed throughout the continent. The EU can serve its citizens through Romans 13 good governance provided that it avoids consolidating power, and allowing for the rise of consolidated policies that enshrine un-Christian or un-Biblical practices. If free people opt to live their lives counter to Biblical commands, then this is a normal situation since the fall in Genesis 3. However, if the EU mandates peoples' actions, then the governance structure more strongly resembles the fallacies of the Tower of Babel.

In North America, NAFTA/USMCA is the prominent vehicle to promote trade between Canada, Mexico, and the United States. How should Christians in these three countries live? NAFTA's foundation date back to historical discussions between the colonies of British North America (now Canada) and the United States. In fact, the first—albeit rudimentary—agreement was in place in the mid-1850s and lasted through the mid-1860s.[49] Subsequent discussions always faltered usually at a late hour, including the 1911 agreement that saw Canadians vote in their election as a plebiscite on whether or not to sign a trade deal with Washington D.C. It took until 1965 with an Auto Industry agreement for Canada and the United States to create a specific, 1 Kings 5-type deal. Under President Ronald Reagan of the United States, and Prime Minister Brian Mulroney of Canada, the two countries joined in a free trade agreement in 1988. Mexico later petitioned to join the

---

49. Duerr, "*Traversing Borders.*"

union, and signed the initial deal in 1992, which came into force in early
1994, thus creating NAFTA. Americans, Canadians, and Mexicans have long
debated the status of NAFTA and whether or not the organization should become, like the EU, more supranational in nature.[50] Although there are many
voices in the argument, the debate is most acute between two doctorate holding writers. The late-Robert Pastor, a professor and diplomat, supports much
deeper North American integration,[51] whilst writer Jerome Corsi, fiercely
rejects this idea arguing that all three countries will lose substantial freedom
through supranational engagement.[52]

Christians in all three countries of North America should evaluate the
1 Kings 5 model. NAFTA/USMCA, as it currently exists, reasonably reflects
1 Kings 5. In many respects, the renegotiation of NAFTA to become the
USMCA in 2018 and 2019, shows lessons learned from Hiram and Solomon
in 1 Kings 9. NAFTA, founded in 1994, was almost 25 years old when renegotiation started—an appropriate time to check if the tenets of the agreement were still working for all three member states.

Although shared governance across the earth, waterways, and the air
are all important in North America, there is no biblical mandate to support
deeper integration, beyond the need for shared governance under the Genesis
1:28 creation mandate. There is no specific requirement under Scripture for
countries to engage in bilateral, trilateral, or multilateral organizations. But,
where leaders opt to explore good relations through trade with neighboring
countries, the lessons of 1 Kings 5 and 9 can be wisely applied.

To examine one more case, in South America, the Southern Common
Market (Mercosur is the Spanish language acronym) is the largest free trade
bloc. In some respects, it is slightly more integrated than NAFTA—because
there more joint areas of policy and additional supranational commissions—
but not nearly to the extent of the EU. Given that Mercosur is the second most
prominent example of Supranationalism, this includes millions of Christians
in Argentina, Brazil, Paraguay, and Uruguay.

In terms of supranational integration, Mercosur has inter-parliamen-
tary meetings, which rotate amongst host sites, as well as a court and tribu-
nal to arbitrate on concern between member states, and a Common Market
Council, which facilitates compliance under the Asunción Treaty. In many
ways, the role of Mercosur in the lives of the average Argentinian, Brazilian,
Paraguayan, and Uruguayan is limited. But, in other areas, especially connected to commerce, the role of Mercosur is growing.

50. Duerr, "*Traversing Borders*" 187.

51. Pastor, *Toward a North American Community*; Pastor, *The North American Idea*.

52. Corsi, *The Late Great USA*, 8.

Biblical applications of Supranationalism are best noted in the examples of 1 Kings 3 and 1 Kings 5. But, in biblical prophecy, there are some noteworthy points. Biblical prophecy is a complex subject, which does not have widespread uniformity amongst Christians. However, one concrete doctrine is that Christ will return.[53] Jesus foretells of a time when He will return to earth in Mark 13. Returning to the theologian, Wayne Grudem, the gospel will be preached to all nations, the Great Tribulation will occur, false prophets will work signs and wonders, there will be signs in Heaven, the Man of Sin and Rebellion will come, and there will be the salvation of Israel.[54] Whether a Christian agrees with all of these points or not is matter of academic debate to some degree. At the very least, Christ has promised his return. This is a time to which all Christians look forward.

In Zechariah 3:10, the prophet notes that, 'In that day,' declares the Lord of hosts, 'every one of you will invite his neighbor to sit under his vine and under his fig tree.' The interesting reference here is that the vine was a symbol of peace, and the fig tree a symbol of prosperity. This is in reference to verse 8, referencing the branch, which is the messiah. There is a time coming of peace and prosperity under the reign of Christ (Isaiah 9:7; Micah 4:4).[55] In some ways, this idea of peace and economic prosperity, under organizations like the EU and Mercosur provide a glimpse of what life will be like when Christ returns. This is not to argue that Supranationalism is biblical, only to note that a time of unity is coming in Christ. Of all the shortcomings of the EU in particular, the organization has had the notable success of helping to prevent another world war that plagued Europe twice from in a roughly thirty-year period from the outbreak of World War I in 1914 to the conclusion of World War II in 1945. The distance between Sarajevo—the location of the assassination of the Archduke Franz Ferdinand of Austria-Hungary essentially starting World War I—and Berlin—the location of Nazi Germany's surrender after more than half a decade of bloodletting—is less than 900 miles. The EU should take some credit for attaining this time of peace, which has lasted over 70 years.

Of course, the EU should only be granted some credit. Supranationalism cannot be viewed as a mechanism for maintaining peace. Other factors including, but not limited to, a Cold War standoff, a nuclear peace, an American security guarantee, the United Nations system, the Marshall Plan all contributed to the creation of a more peaceful continent.[56] Finally,

53. Grudem, *Systematic Theology*; MacArthur and Mayhew, *Biblical Doctrine*.

54. Grudem, *Systematic Theology*, 1098–1099.

55. MacArthur and Mayhew, *Biblical Doctrine*, 325.

56. Steil, *The Marshall Plan*.

the time of peace may be simply God's kindness on Europe. In Ecclesiastes 3:8, Solomon notes, "(there is) a time to love and a time to hate, a time for war and a time for peace."

Case Study: How Should a Christian live under supranational entities? In particular, how should a German Christian live?

Perhaps the most significant question for Christians in the EU is how to live? The EU has become part of life in most European countries, so it is reality for Christians. The focus of this section is to probe a little deeper on how a German Christian should live in light of the EU? The reasoning is that Germany is the largest member state of the EU, and played a unique role in the Reformation as the home of Martin Luther.[57] Moreover, given the recent history of Germany, especially during the Nazi period, there is still a widespread sense of shame in much of the country, which has caused much reticence when it comes to national identity and any expression of nationalism. Of course, Germany has changed dramatically since 1945, in particular given a new political system designed to reduce the likelihood of extremism and strong leaders like former Chancellor Konrad Adenauer (1949–1963) who worked hard to align West Germany with other democratic countries in the post-World War II era.[58] More so than any country, some Christians in Germany may prefer the option of regionalism (as discussed in chapter 1) over the options of patriotism and nationalism.

Concomitantly, the German economy has also rebounded in major ways, in part due to trade within the EU. Today, Germany is one of the major national driving force behind the EU organization. It is the biggest, in terms of economics and demographics, country in the EU bloc, and arguably the most influential especially in the post-Brexit era. Christians can play a major role in the national life of politics in Germany, so the specific question pertaining to German Christians in the EU seems apropos.

Like any country, Germany has a unique history and backdrop. Formed in the backdrop of three wars against Denmark (1864), Austria (1866), and France (1870–1), the Prussian military unified vast swaths of German-speaking areas in Central Europe into what became Germany. After decades of economic and population growth, Germany became a

---

57. Metaxas, *Martin Luther.*

58. Steil, *The Marshall Plan,* 270.

superpower in the heart of Europe[59] with an ability to gain territory and wealth from weaker, neighboring states. In some senses, this unbalancing of the Concert of Europe (the treaty that held the balance of power[60] peace in Europe following the Napoleonic Wars a century earlier), served as one of the catalysts for the outbreak of World War I.

Germany's loss in World War I after years of trench warfare came with a large cost in terms of reparations (worth approximately $33 billion today), land, and prestige. Germany turned to Adolf Hitler, democratically, after significant election success in the November 1932 election. Yet, Hitler's Nazi Party did not have a majority in the Reichstag (parliament) at the time, but Hitler managed to con the ageing President, Paul Von Hindenberg, into making him chancellor after a prolonged negotiation in January 1933.[61]

The life of Dietrich Bonhoeffer, mentioned earlier, serves as an important Christian counterbalance to the evils of Hitler. Although German Christians did not collectively stop the rise and then subsequent atrocities of Hitler given the descent of the Lutheran Church in collaboration with a Nazified assault on Christianity,[62] many did stand as a means of protesting Hitler even when the Third Reich consolidated power. Bonhoeffer engaged in numerous radio broadcasts wherein he preached against the perils of Hitler in the 1930s.[63] Later, Bonhoeffer made the decision to quietly accept Hitler as a means of trying to subvert the Nazi regime by feigning compromise.

In the aftermath of World War II, German Christians were at the forefront of rebuilding the society into what it is today—a country that has tried to promote peaceful dialogue and interactions between states, whilst pursuing economic growth. Of course, fallen people occupy every country on earth, so Germany has its share of challenges internally.

As the most populous and economically most powerful state in the EU, Germany plays a lead role in the advance of Supranationalism. For decades after World War II, free trade and greater integration were seen as panaceas to violence because "win-win" scenarios were readily available for those specializing in the economy. Thus, Germany became a leader in the EU leveraging its resources to connect with other member states. By pooling its coal and steel resources with the other member states, West

59. Mearsheimer, *The Tragedy of Great Power Politics*, 66.

60. A system wherein multiple great powers divide into two or more groups to "balance" the power of other countries. The goal is to check the growth in power of any one country in order to preserve "relative order, harmony, and peace" (Martin, *Prevailing Worldviews*, 216).

61. Turner, *Thirty Days*.

62. Metaxas, *Bonhoeffer*, 174.

63. Metaxas, *Bonhoeffer*, 287–8.

Germany became much less likely to go to war, and also helped to mobilize the economic recovery of Western Europe.[64] The average German Christian helped with the initiatives to move away from war and towards peace, democracy, and economic growth.

Supranationalism: A Discussion

Jesus' own experience with Supranationalism

Jesus lived under Roman occupation, primarily in Syria-Palestina within the wider Roman Empire. As noted earlier, the Roman Empire was not a voluntary organization, unlike the contemporary groupings of sovereign states like the EU. The Roman Empire gained territory by conquest, and by force, rather than by the complicit pooling of sovereignty over time.

As the name intimates, the Roman Empire centered on the city of Rome. Although a full historical overview of the Roman Empire is not possible here since it is a tangent to the goal of this work, some historical notes are useful. The Kingdom of Rome was founded in 753 BC, and was maintained within a fairly narrow geographic area. After the overthrow of the King, Republican Rome was the successor city-state in the sixth century BC, eventually rising to become an Empire in 27 BC. Throughout every iteration of Rome, the city-state was at war with a very high frequency, expanding its borders throughout much of modern day Italy, into the Mediterranean, also capturing parts of modern day France and Slovenia. Further expansion increased the size of the Roman Republic to include large swaths of North Africa, southern Europe, and the Middle East. At its height, the Roman Empire, under Emperor Trajan in 117 A.D., encompassed modern day England and Wales; southern Europe including the Iberian Peninsula, France, and the Balkans; North Africa, most of the rim of the Black Sea; sections of the Caucasus, and the Middle East.

Thus, when the New Testament is penned, several cities in modern day Turkey and Greece feature prominently in Scripture. For example, Colossae (Colossians), Ephesus (Ephesians), Thessaloniki (I and II Thessalonians), and Corinth (I and II Corinthians), among others, are written by Paul to encourage believers in those cities, and to provide instructions to the broader Christian church. In Revelation 2 and 3, the seven churches mentioned are likewise spread throughout parts of the Roman Empire, specifically Asia Minor (Turkey).

---

64. Bale, *European Politics*.

The Roman Empire took territory by force, and although people, especially soldiers, could gain Roman citizenship, slavery was prominent throughout the territory. In context, this is a reason why the Apostle Paul discusses the role of slaves, because of the methods of violent conquest used by the Romans to gain more territory, as well as to gain the subservience of others. Jesus himself discusses the importance of a godly kingdom as opposed to an earthly kingdom.

Moreover, the apostle Paul, when writing to the church in Colossae, asks the believers to "put on the new self" in chapter 3. Colossians 3:9–11 reads:

> "9 Do not lie to one another, since you laid aside the old self with its evil practices, 10 and have put on the new self who is being renewed to a true knowledge according to the image of the One who created him— 11 a renewal in which there is no distinction between Greek and Jew, circumcised and uncircumcised, barbarian, Scythian, slave and freeman, but Christ is all, and in all."

In the context of this book, verse 11 is particularly interesting. Paul argues that there is no distinction between Christians regardless of ethnic or cultural backgrounds. The terms "barbarian" and "Scythian" are noteworthy. Some commentators argue that a barbarian is anyone who is not a Greek by birth or culture. Others argue that a barbarian is anyone outside of the Roman Empire, especially as a reference to Germanic tribes. The term Scythian refers to a historic ethnic group living around the Black Sea, a reference to modern-day Ukrainians and/or Russians.[65] Some commentators argue that the Scythians could be described as "ultra" barbarians in the context of the Roman Empire. Again, the overarching concept is that they outside the empire, but also specifically located on the north side of the Black Sea. Nevertheless, all Christians are unified in Christ whether within the Roman Empire or not, whether Greek or Jew, circumcised or uncircumcised, barbarian, Scythian, slave or free—there is only unity in Christ.

When Jesus gained popularity in the early days of his ministry around the Sea of Galilee, observers noted the connections to prophecy as well as the miraculous signs and wonders displayed by Christ. Yet, many assumed that Jesus would be a political leader with the ability to overthrow the Roman Empire, and sought to install him in to power.[66] This was not his mission, nor what was prophesized in Scripture. Jesus never attempted to take on the role of a political leader, and frequently told his disciples not to tell anyone about some of his early miracles. Given the potential for significant

65. Plokhy, *The Gates of Europe*, 7–8.
66. Ladd, *A Theology of the New Testament*, 138

misunderstanding, Jesus humbly healed people, and instructed His disciples not to spread his message until they properly understood who He was—the Messiah—as well as His mission to save people from their sins, rather than to rid the world of the Roman Empire.

In Jesus' time, the idea of empire was more predominant than a supranational entity. Nonetheless, some parallels can be drawn. Christ was asked what to do in relation to Caesar—Jesus responded, "Render unto Caesar what is Caesar's, and unto God what is God's" (Mark 12:17). Connected to this point, Wayne Grudem argues, though, that civil government, regardless of the nature of the union, should not be controlled by any religion.[67] Thus, Grudem argues, government should compel religion in the sense that a state religion should be rejected so as to allow citizens to freely worship God and read Scripture without compulsion. Likewise, if a supranational entity has power, it should be maintained by people underneath a framework to which there is an agreement allowing for freedom of worship. In Jesus' era, there were very few forms of democratic rule, with the notable exception of some of the Greek city-states.

Romans 13:1-7 notes the responsibilities of a follower of Christ under government. 1 Peter 2:13-14 also provides significant insight as to how to act as a Christian within a country, and under a government. If that government happens to obviate some areas of its sovereignty to a supranational organization, how should a Christian respond?

Defensive alliances

At times in Christian history, defensive-based alliances have been created in order to provide for joint military protection. An extensive examination of Just War theory is not the purpose of this section, but the works of Augustine and Thomas Aquinas have built a historic Christian response to the issue of warfare and military defense. As connected to a discussion of Supranationalism, two examples of this point come from the time of the Reformation and Counter-Reformation periods in Europe, in the sixteenth and seventeenth centuries in particular. Recalling the continuum on national identification in chapter 1, Supranationalism falls under the broader umbrella of regionalism. Regionalism is a grouping in which different separate countries can come together for a specific purpose—in a tangent related to Supranationalism, it is worth exploring a slightly different usage of regionalism, in this case, common defense. For countries/entities that adhere to a regional grouping, related to an alliance, the only shared areas of policy

67. Grudem, *Politics according to the Bible*, 23

might be defense and foreign policy. Otherwise, the countries still continue to govern themselves independently of one another.

The first example if the Schmalkaldic League. Since Supranationalism connotes the pooling of sovereignty on the part of different countries usually for trade purposes, what about other areas of policy, most strongly connected to the preservation of one's life: security? Can Christian countries/regions/entities join in an alliance for the purpose of security? Once again, the goal in this book is to discuss nationalism, not war, but since the two conversations are linked, some investigation is useful.

Martin Luther, a monk who lived in what is now Germany grew uncomfortable with a number of the practices of the Roman Catholic Church. In his reading of Scripture, he argued for changes, especially to practices like indulgences and the corruption of the church.[68] Thus, he nailed his 95 theses to the church door in Wittenberg in 1517.[69] Luther's goals for doing so are debated, but the American writer, Eric Metaxas, argues that Luther was trying to engage in a conversation over reform, much like others including John Wycliffe and Erasmus.[70] In general, the view up until Luther's excommunication was for reform within a unified HRE, not an insurrection.[71] The Pope, Leo X, played a role in changing this uniformity when he opposed Luther's proposed changes, and ultimately excommunicated him from the church at the Diet of Worms of 1521.[72] Luther's goal was not to hurt the church, but, when found outside of the church, his followers began to include Lutheran aspects to their church services, only some of which were approved by Luther himself. In the end, Luther changed Europe, and also, "more than any other person, created the modern German language."[73] In this sense, Luther had a major spiritual and geopolitical impact.

Throughout the decade of the 1520s, Lutheran beliefs began to proliferate. Some of these changes were intertwined with political and cultural grievances in German-speaking areas against the HRE, leading to the 1524–25 Peasants' Revolt, which Luther opposed, even though many of the protesters took up Luther's positions found in the 95 Theses.[74] When the Peasants' Revolt was violently put down by the emperor, some Lutheran and protest-based principalities began to question under what circumstances,

68. McGregor, *Germany*, 94.

69. Metaxas, *Martin Luther*, 108.

70. Metaxas, *Martin Luther*.

71. Kuyper, *Wisdom & Wonder*, 86.

72. Marsh, *Martin Luther on Reading the Bible as Christian Scripture*, 6.

73. McGregor, *Germany*, 94.

74. Metaxas, *Martin Luther*.

biblically, should they join together in order to provide security for their families—an extension of love thy neighbor.

The Schmalkaldic League was formed on February 27, 1531 as a means of providing common defense for Lutheran entities under the HRE.[75] Centered in the small city of Schmalkalden, which had a population of approximately 4,500 people, the goal was to present a united front for protection against the Emperor, Charles V.[76] Sovereignty was not pooled, but regions provided for a common defense of regions allied to the teachings of Luther during the Reformation. In particular, the Schmalkaldic League was centered on connecting dukes/rulers who possessed political power around the modern-day German regions of Hesse, Saxony, Brunswick-Grubenhagen, Brunswick-Lünenburg, Anhalt, Mansfeld, and, additionally, the towns of Strasbourg, Ulm, Constance, Reutlingen, Memmingen, Lindau, Biberach, Isny, Magdeburg, and Bremen.[77] The city of Lübeck joined the league on 3 May, and Bavaria on 24 October 1531; France joined the alliance in 1532, and Denmark in 1538.[78] The Schmalkaldic League was not exclusively for Lutherans as evidenced by the connection with predominantly-Catholic France, but a means for protecting those protesting the HRE and/or the Roman Catholic Church.

The Augsburg Confession of 1530 was a central tenet for membership in the Schmalkaldic League, which united Lutherans theologically.[79] The 21 articles of the Diet of Augsburg on June 24, 1530 set the parameters of the Schmalkaldic League as a defense against the HRE. The League set-up a fighting force of 10,000 infantrymen as well as 2,000 cavalries split amongst member units.[80] The League was proactive in nature helping leaders convert to Lutheranism, by involving themselves in local matters; the Schmalkaldic League had some noteworthy successes, but also began to decline in the 1540s as Charles V engaged in negotiation and alliances with specific princes as a means of dividing and ultimately stopping the growth of an explicitly Lutheran Empire developing from within the HRE.[81] Charles V also waged war against the Schmalkaldic League in 1546 resulting in the League's dissolution in 1547.[82]

75. Weber, *Schmalkaldic League.*

76. Brady, *"Phases and Strategies of the Schmalkaldic League,"* 162.

77. Weber, *Schmalkaldic League.*

78. Weber, *Schmalkaldic League.*

79. Brady, *"Phases and Strategies of the Schmalkaldic League,"* 162.

80. Wilde, *"The Schmalkaldic League."*

81. Wilde, *"The Schmalkaldic League."*

82. Metaxas, *Martin Luther,* 433.

Although Charles V defeated his primarily Protestant adversaries, the wider scope of protest against Catholicism forced the hand of the HRE to provide a greater level of recognition and freedom of worship to certain regions of the empire. In 1555, the Religious Peace of Augsburg was signed as a mechanism to recognize the Lutheran areas of the HRE alongside Catholicism.[83] This established a key norm in international relations: to decrease conflict around Christian doctrine in Europe. A defensive alliance, like the Schmalkaldic League, did not stop sectarian wars, nor did it protect Protestant areas, but the Religious Peace of Augsburg set in place the idea that Catholic doctrines could be challenged and that Lutherans could live under more peaceable terms, at least for the time being.[84]

Membership in an organization like the Schmalkaldic League is a matter of debate. Should Christians engage in mutual defense pacts? This question is outside of the scope of this project, but let us assume that, yes, under Scripture, Christians can serve in the military (Acts 10) and Christian political leaders can sign agreements of protection. The brief premise here being that a definition of love encompasses taking care of a family and also a set of people under a government (Romans 13:1–7). Many Christians support the Just War concept, or some variant thereof.[85] Here, I argue that a "Just War Plus" model is acceptable in that Christians can engage in defensive wars befitting of Just War parameters,[86] but offensive conflicts are also justified to stop ethnic cleansing and genocide. The Schmalkaldic League was, in some ways, justifiable biblically because it sought to prohibit the slaughter/genocide of Protestant peoples within the HRE.

Unfortunately, the nascent "peace" within the HRE did not last in the long term, and the norms created by the Religious Peace of Augsburg began to fray. The Evangelical/Protestant Union was created in a similar vein to the Schmalkaldic League; the Protestant Union was formed in 1608 in order to defend Protestant entities within the HRE. This did not stop the start of the Thirty Years' War, which started with the Defenestration of three Catholic dignitaries in Prague in 1618. The Thirty Years' War is far too complex to detail extensively here, but the output of the conflict is one that still impacts today's world. It is estimated that over eight million people died as a result of the war.[87] This number may sound low in comparison to World Wars I and II, but consider that the eight million deaths represented approximately 25

---

83. McGregor, *Germany*, 225.

84. Metaxas, *Martin Luther*, 433.

85. Niebuhr, *Christian Realism and Political Problems*.

86. Holmes, "*Just War.*"

87. Wilson, *The Thirty Years War*.

percent of all of the HRE, with German-speakers being particularly impact-ed. The conflict ended with the Peace of Westphalia in 1648, which brought to a conclusion to the conflict.[88] For many historians, the war was a disaster because it did little to end animosity within the HRE, and the Franco-Spanish War continued until 1659, 11 years after the conclusion of Westphalia. For political scientists, however, the silver lining is that the Peace of Westphalia introduced the motion of the modern-state system, especially the develop-ment of primarily Protestant countries in Europe such as England, the Neth-erlands, France, Switzerland, Sweden, and Denmark.[89] Although imperfect, religious toleration within countries (rather than empires) became the norm across Europe, then the rest of the world. Of course, the HRE itself lasted until 1806 when Napoleon ended the empire with the forced abdication of Francis II after defeating him at the Battle of Austerlitz.

Following the end of the Thirty Years' War, and the signing of the Peace of Westphalia, greater religious toleration increased across Europe. Conflict stemming from the Reformation and Counter-Reformation was still evi-dent, but much less drastic. Later European conflagrations such as the Wars of Spanish Succession (1701–1714), Seven Years' War (1856–1863), Napole-onic Wars (~1803–1815), and the Crimean War (1853–1856) among others, had sectarian elements, but were based more heavily on power struggles, dynastic succession, and territorial gains. Even though many laypersons to-day blame the Thirty Years' War on religious strife, historians typically draw more nuanced conclusions. Some, including the British historian Peter Wil-son, argue that the conflict had much more to do with maintaining power within the HRE than explicit religious reasons for bloodshed.[90]

In the modern era, there are no Protestant, or Christian specific enti-ties that play the same role in world affairs as served by the Schmalkaldic League or the Evangelical/Protestant Union of the sixteenth and seven-teenth centuries. The Holy Alliance, formed in 1815 by Russia, Prussia, and Austria in the aftermath of the Napoleonic Wars committed to peace in Eu-rope, and allowed smaller states to join if they agreed to govern according to the "principles of the Christian Gospel."[91] This Holy Alliance later became the Quadruple, then Quintuple Alliance—the Congress of Vienna/Concert of Europe, responsible for keeping peace in Europe in the nineteenth cen-tury. Outside of this loose connection between historically and culturally Christian states in Europe, there are no explicitly Christian defense pacts.

88. Wilson, *The Thirty Years War*.

89. Hazony, *The Virtue of Nationalism*, 23–4.

90. Wilson, *The Thirty Years War*.

91. Evans, *Pursuit of Power*, 22.

Nonetheless, there are more heavily "Christian" areas of the world that tend to work together in military defense alliances.

For example, although the North Atlantic Treaty Organization (NATO) is not an explicitly Christian organization, the member states of the now 30-country bloc have a shared Christian heritage in common. Moreover, the bloc was designed to make the advancement of communism,[92] and by extension, atheistic communism, very difficult, and not without a confrontation. NATO is ultimately backed by American military power[93] as a means of simultaneously keeping the world safe for democracy and commerce.

When the Berlin Wall fell in 1989, it marked a major change in Europe, and served to symbolically end the Cold War era. The western security alliance, NATO, served several purposes during this period of approximately 40 years, most notably the containment of the Soviet Union.[94] However, when the Soviet Union dissolved into fifteen separate countries in December 1991, the main security threat of NATO decreased in size, stature, and as a perceived threat.[95] NATO was left without a clearly defined role.

Yet, NATO has remained resilient, and re-defined its role in the Post-Cold War era.[96] A generation or so later, NATO continues to conduct missions and is building a new headquarters on the outskirts of Brussels. NATO has also grown dramatically, from 16 countries in 1991, to 30 members today (in 2020), including several new members from Eastern Europe.

Despite the illusion of lasting peace in the North Atlantic region, geopolitics is rarely peaceful for long periods of time. Several factors such as economic interdependence, EU Supranationalism, international law, and nuclear deterrence, all decrease the likelihood of conflict, but war remains an unfortunate part of human life.

NATO persists—and will likely continue to persist—because it is a bureaucracy, and because conventional forces are still needed. Once a bureaucracy is in place, its workers/employees are very reluctant to accept any decrease in their role. Without major political will to abolish NATO, the organization will find ways to sustain itself. Conventional forces have been used by NATO on several occasions even after the end of the Cold War. NATO missions were useful in Europe during the Yugoslav wars of the 1990s, specifically in the cases of Bosnia-Herzegovina in 1995 and Kosovo in 1999.[97] Although

92. Duignan, *NATO*.

93. Marshall, *Prisoners of Geography*, 79.

94. Duignan, *NATO*.

95. Duignan, *NATO*, 49–50.

96. Moore, *NATO's New Mission*.

97. Duerr, "*A Proposal for the Future of US counterinsurgency*"

critics note that success in these missions was limited, the end result is impressive. The Balkans is a much more peaceful region today. Violence could still return, but for present at least, it is largely peaceful. NATO also played a role in the war in Afghanistan, given that Article V of the NATO Treaty—an attack on one is considered an attack against all, and necessitates a military response—was invoked for the first and only time after the 9/11 attacks on the United States.[98] NATO conducted a military operation in Libya in 2011, and served an important purpose in the removal of a brutal dictator, Muammar Gaddafi.[99] Although NATO is criticized for conducting costly exercises, and for only achieving limited successes, the organization generally completes baseline objectives for its respective missions. This provides greater security for the citizens of NATO member states.

The continued existence of NATO, therefore, maintains unity within North American and European democratic states, most of which have a historically Christian connection. Predominantly Muslim states like Turkey and Albania have been reliable partners, for the most part, until more recently when Turkish President, Recep Erdoğan significantly took steps towards authoritarian rule.

Conclusion

Put simply, Supranationalism is particularly difficult to assess biblically—there are no specific sections of the Bible that explain what to do with regards to the EU in the twenty-first century. To some extent, that is the point: that Christians should wrestle with Scripture and to ascertain how to apply the Word of God.

There is no mandate for a supranational bloc, but Christians should be reverent to forms of government. The entirety of the New Testament is set under the harsh authoritarian governance of the Roman Empire. Jesus himself admonished His followers to provide due reverence for Caesar. The apostle Paul, in Romans 13, describes the necessary respect owed to one's rulers who have been placed in that position by God, whether liked by the people or not. Supranationalism provides a different model of regional identity, which provides a counter to the Genesis 11 idea of organizing humanity towards global government, globalism. Regionalism is advocated under Supranationalism, not globalism; although the creation of supranational entities moves national identification closer to globalism than nationalism or patriotism on the continuum presented in chapter 1.

98. Moore, *NATO's New Mission*, 97.

99. Duerr, *"A Proposal for the Future of US counterinsurgency"*

The best evidence for Supranationalism in Scripture comes from the book of 1 Kings. 1 Kings 5, whilst beneficial for 20 years, began to unravel by the time the 1 Kings 9 account is written. The initial, bilateral deal did not equally benefit both trading partners. Additionally, the 1 Kings 5 account merely acknowledges trade between the kingdoms of Israel and Tyre; one assumption is that people have to move and live in the other kingdom, but Scripture does not record anyone moving permanently to the other kingdom to live and work, as compared to the EU model of open borders for travel under the Schengen zone. The example in Scripture also connotes that a trade deal must be updated periodically in order to work for the parties. While the EU in particular is regularly updated with new treaties; for example, Maastricht in 1992, Amsterdam in 1997, Nice in 2001, and Lisbon in 2009; there is not a regular opportunity to leave the organization willingly. The Brexit vote of June 2016 may have changed this oversight, but there are potential pitfalls of Brexit. Seemingly, membership should be more fluid, and less bureaucratic. The EU should respond to the governance needs of the citizens, rather than serving as an increasingly bureaucratic layer of governance over the lives of people. But, provided that the organization is voluntary, and in the 1 Kings 5 model, there is a very limited but still noteworthy biblical precedent for trade deals.

Christians must nonetheless be reverential to the governing authorities over their lives. As with Paul, every situation can present itself as an opportunity to minister the gospel. Under the EU's Schengen zone,[100] in essence, a borderless Europe where citizens can live and work in any Schengen country (some EU countries like Ireland maintain an opt-out, whilst some non-EU countries like Switzerland have signed the agreement) provides an opportunity for pastors, missionaries, and all followers of Christ to utilize the free movement of people to preach and disciple. Much like the Roman Empire of the New Testament, a similar opportunity is available to Christians to move freely, disseminate the gospel, meet the tangible needs of people, and disciple people in the faith. For as long as supranational blocs exist, Christians must see the opportunity presented, and work to proclaim a message of faith, hope, and love.

---

100. Gilbert, *European Integration*, 150–151.

Chapter 5

Secessionism, Irredentism, and Rebellion

> Now when Rehoboam had come to Jerusalem, he assembled all the house of Judah and the tribe of Benjamin, 180,000 chosen men who were warriors, to fight against the house of Israel to restore the kingdom to Rehoboam the son of Solomon.
>
> —1 Kings 12:21

IN MANY RESPECTS, REBELLION is an idea often found in the Bible; rebellion is a significant component of a definition of sin, which can be defined as "any failure to conform to the moral law of God in act, attitude, or nature."[1] It is not biblical to rebel, nor is it a sign of a mature follower of Christ to be rebellious, but the desire to rebel is weaved into the DNA of every human being. A presupposition of the Christian faith is that every human being is sinful, and given that reference point, every human being is separated from God because "sin permeates every aspect of our existence."[2] In Genesis 3, for example, we see the fall of humankind wherein sin enters the world. At the individual level, rebellion is part of the fabric of humanity, even if it is usually faulty, or inherently sinful. At the domestic level, governments face rebellious populations. And, at an interstate level, countries will rebel/fight against one another, or the perceived structure of a system, or rule.

Although definitions vary, secession is defined by the Canadian political scientist, John Wood as "referring to a demand for formal withdrawal

1. Grudem, *Systematic Theology*, 490.
2. MacArthur and Mayhew, *Biblical Doctrine*, 451.

from a central political authority by a member unit or units in the basis of a claim to independent sovereign status."[3] In essence, a subnational unit desires to become an independent country in its own right replete with sovereign protections, and a seat at international organizations such as the United Nations.

In light of this subject, this chapter examines 1 Kings 12 as its central section of Scripture. After a discussion of the 1 Kings 12 model,[4] the chapter investigates the tangential issues of irredentism and rebellion, including questions such as whether it is biblical to rebel, or secede; including, for example, whether the US declaration of independence was biblical? This chapter also examines historic Christian movements that have sought secession. Finally, this chapter flips the viewpoint on secession, and approaches the concept from the viewpoint of international organizations. Ultimately, the chapter purports the argument that even though secession is not explicitly biblical, secessionism provides an option for the international community to be peacemakers (Matthew 5:9) through the partition of states in very specific purposes. Secession can be mobilized, under very limited circumstances, for the good of the people being ruled (Romans 13:4).

1 Kings 12

The account of 1 Kings 12 is both a blessing and a curse at the same time. It is ultimately a blessing, at least in the short term, because the people of Israel and Judah decided to separate rather than to engage in a bloody civil war. Despite the arrogance of King Rehoboam, he stops short of ordering his troops to advance upon the rebellious territories thus avoiding a deadly conflict. However, the account of 1 Kings 12 is also a curse in that it divides the kingdom and opens the door for the occupation of Israel, and then Judah, by the Assyrians and the Babylonians respectively. If the kingdom would have remained united, would either region have been conquered? And, would the Israelite people have been exiled in foreign lands? Obviously, the question is one that cannot be answered, and it is clear that God had other plans for His people, but the lessons of 1 Kings 12 are useful in several respects.

1 Kings 11 ends with the death of Solomon in verses 41–43. Then, 1 Kings 12 starts with King Rehoboam as Solomon's replacement. This succession concludes a line of approximately 120 years of strong—but not perfect—rule over the Kingdom of Israel by Saul (32 or 42 years),[5] Ish-bosheth (2

3. Wood, "*Secession,*" 110

4. Grudem and Asmus, *The Poverty of Nations*, 237.

5. Hill and Walton, *A Survey of the Old Testament*, 233.

years), David (40 years), and then Solomon (40 years).[6] Like any new leader, Rehoboam comes to the throne with a range of different options. It must have been difficult to follow such revered kings as Saul, David, and Solomon, so it is clear that Rehoboam wants to assert his own leadership onto the kingdom. In 1 Kings 12:6–7, Rehoboam consults Solomon's former advisors who give him prudent advice on his governance. However, in 1 Kings 12:8–11, Rehoboam also seeks the advice of younger advisors who argue the opposite of verses 6 and 7. Rehoboam opts to accept the advice of the younger advisors and then enforces a much harsher campaign of taxation on the people.[7] In this sense, Rehoboam's rule becomes much more tyrannical.[8] Obviously, it does not take long for dissention to stir. In fact, within the matter of a short period of time, 10 of the 12 tribes are willing to break free to Rehoboam's kingdom and follow Jeroboam instead. 1 Kings 12: 1–5 reads:

> "1 Then Rehoboam went to Shechem, for all Israel had come to Shechem to make him king. 2 Now when Jeroboam the son of Nebat heard of it, he was living in Egypt (for he was yet in Egypt, where he had fled from the presence of King Solomon). 3 Then they sent and called him, and Jeroboam and all the assembly of Israel came and spoke to Rehoboam, saying, 4 "Your father made our yoke hard; now therefore lighten the hard service of your father and his heavy yoke which he put on us, and we will serve you." 5 Then he said to them, "Depart for three days, then return to me." So the people departed."

These opening verses of 1 Kings 12 set the stage for confrontation between Rehoboam and Jeroboam—a former member of Solomon's governance structure who sought to an increase of his own power in 1 Kings 11, but was forced into exile in Egypt for his growing aspirations. Further, as mentioned earlier, Rehoboam is seeking guidance in terms of how to rule the kingdom. 1 Kings 12:6–11 continues:

> "6 King Rehoboam consulted with the elders who had served his father Solomon while he was still alive, saying, "How do you counsel me to answer this people?" 7 Then they spoke to him, saying, "If you will be a servant to this people today, and will serve them and grant them their petition, and speak good words to them, then they will be your servants forever." 8 But he forsook the counsel of the elders which they had given him, and consulted with the young men who grew up with him and

---

6. Hill and Walton, *A Survey of the Old Testament*, 232.

7. Grudem, *Politics according to the Bible*, 107.

8. Grudem and Asmus, *The Poverty of Nations*, 237.

served him. 9 So he said to them, "What counsel do you give that we may answer this people who have spoken to me, saying, 'Lighten the yoke which your father put on us'?" 10 The young men who grew up with him spoke to him, saying, "Thus you shall say to this people who spoke to you, saying, 'Your father made our yoke heavy, now you make it lighter for us!' But you shall speak to them, 'My little finger is thicker than my father's loins! 11 Whereas my father loaded you with a heavy yoke, I will add to your yoke; my father disciplined you with whips, but I will discipline you with scorpions.'"

After consulting with two sets of advisers, Rehoboam opts to take the counsel of the younger members. Instead of dealing well with the people and considering their concerns, Rehoboam instead opts to make life, work, and taxes more burdensome for the people. Moreover, he attempts to brazenly contradict his father's rule by asserting himself as a more powerful ruler. In trying to cultivate a sentiment of respect, Rehoboam instead lays the foundation for rebellion against his rule in 1 Kings 12:12–20:

"12 Then Jeroboam and all the people came to Rehoboam on the third day as the king had directed, saying, "Return to me on the third day." 13 The king answered the people harshly, for he forsook the advice of the elders which they had given him, 14 and he spoke to them according to the advice of the young men, saying, "My father made your yoke heavy, but I will add to your yoke; my father disciplined you with whips, but I will discipline you with scorpions." 15 So the king did not listen to the people; for it was a turn of events from the Lord, that He might establish His word, which the Lord spoke through Ahijah the Shilonite to Jeroboam the son of Nebat.

16 When all Israel saw that the king did not listen to them, the people answered the king, saying,

"What portion do we have in David? We have no inheritance in the son of Jesse; To your tents, O Israel! Now look after your own house, David!"

So Israel departed to their tents. 17 But as for the sons of Israel who lived in the cities of Judah, Rehoboam reigned over them. 18 Then King Rehoboam sent Adoram, who was over the forced labor, and all Israel stoned him to death. And King Rehoboam made haste to mount his chariot to flee to Jerusalem. 19 So Israel has been in rebellion against the house of David to this day. 20 It came about when all Israel heard that Jeroboam had returned, that they sent and called him to the assembly and made him king over all Israel. None but the tribe of Judah followed the house of David."

Very quickly, the scene shifts dramatically. Rehoboam was planning to implement a strong rule over the kingdom, but he is quickly met with strong, and forceful opposition. The people of the northern ten kingdoms rally around Jeroboam as their ruler. Already the kingdom is showing signs of splintering with the ten northern tribes aligned against Judah and Benjamin. 1 Kings 12:21–24 reads:

> "21 Now when Rehoboam had come to Jerusalem, he assembled all the house of Judah and the tribe of Benjamin, 180,000 chosen men who were warriors, to fight against the house of Israel to restore the kingdom to Rehoboam the son of Solomon. 22 But the word of God came to Shemaiah the man of God, saying, 23 "Speak to Rehoboam the son of Solomon, king of Judah, and to all the house of Judah and Benjamin and to the rest of the people, saying, 24 'Thus says the Lord, "You must not go up and fight against your relatives the sons of Israel; return every man to his house, for this thing has come from Me." So they listened to the word of the Lord, and returned and went their way according to the word of the Lord."

In the final verses of 1 Kings 12, a lot of crucial events occur. First, a large army is amassed by King Rehoboam to quell the rebellion—in total, 180,000 young men are ready to go to battle. This position follows with the arrogance of Rehoboam in 1 Kings 12:10 wherein he rebukes Solomon's rule. It takes the intervention of God through Shemaiah to avoid the civil war, and to peacefully conclude the conflict.[9] In essence, the tense standoff ends with the northern ten tribes seceding to form a new country that is separate from the remaining two tribes: Judah and Benjamin, henceforth, the Kingdom of Judah. About five years later, in 1 Kings 14:25–26, the King of Egypt opts to invade Rehoboam's kingdom,[10] an attack that probably would not have happened against a united kingdom. This proves to be a foreshadowing of the conquering of Israel and Judah later in the Old Testament.

---

9. MacArthur and Mayhew, *Biblical Doctrine*, 87

10. Hill and Walton, *A Survey of the Old Testament*, 31.

Is secession biblical?

For many Christians throughout history, the account of 1 Kings 12 is the justification for their rebellion against a government.[11] This raises the question as to whether or not secession is biblical? The simple answer is no, in the vast majority of circumstances, but there are some complications to this answer worth investigating. Although there is a biblical example of secession in 1 Kings 12, secession itself is not explicitly biblical. However, there are areas that are more complex—for example, one subject that is frequently raised between American and British Christians is whether the U.S. Declaration of Independence, and the War of Independence thereafter, was biblical? This question will be answered more thoroughly in the next section. In the debate, though, the 1 Kings 12 model was part of this discussion and many sermons in the lead up the American Revolution.[12] This is not to imply uniformity on the part of Christian churches in the Thirteen Colonies; there were at least ten known denominations in 1776.[13] The shift towards independence was a radical departure, though, from the historic loyalty of Protestants in pre-revolutionary America who fought for the expansion of British territory.[14]

Although the American Revolution is still emotional, the issue is essentially settled because the United States has existed as a sovereign territory since 1776 with recognition by other countries since 1783 under the Treaty of Paris (Morocco was the first country to recognize the United States in 1777, followed by France in 1778; the Netherlands then led wider recognition starting in April 1782). The subject is emotional because it is a marker of American identity, and the July 4th Independence Day holiday reminds people of their citizenship in the United States. The signers of the declaration were, in the eyes of the British Crown, guilty of treason, and could therefore expect a punishment of death.[15]

Interestingly, the previous question on whether or not the American Revolution was biblical is further nuanced by the American Civil War. In a bloody conflict from 1861–1865, the Confederate States of America sought independence from the United States over several areas of policy conflict, notably slavery, but indelibly pegged to economic factors. An estimated 750,000–1 million people died in the conflict, "according to the Department

11. Byrd, *Sacred War, Sacred Scripture*, 170.
12. Byrd, *Sacred War, Sacred Scripture*, 170
13. Jelen and Wilcox, *Religion and Politics in Comparative Perspective*, 290.
14. Byrd, *Sacred Scripture, Sacred War*, 5.
15. Maier, *American Scripture*, 59

of Defense, 364,511 people on the Confederate side died including 140,414 battle deaths. On the Union side, 359,528 people perished in the conflict, 138,154 in battle."[16] This conflict also spawned massive refugee movements, especially across the southern states. Some members of the clergy in the south were attacked by Union supporters for not recanting their secessionist views.[17] Given that it is very difficult to argue for Confederate secessionism without slavery, this case is clearly not biblical. However, it raises an interesting tangential question on who has the right to govern if the consent of the people is not present? President Lincoln arguably made the correct decision biblically to preserve the union, because it meant ending slavery in the United States, yet the death toll from the conflict is still a reason for mourning.

What about a contemporary issue of secessionism? Take the case of Nigeria, the largest population on the continent of Africa, 201 million people in 2020.[18] Although an oversimplification, much of the northern part of Nigeria is Muslim, and much of the southern part of Nigeria is Christian. Both Islam and Christianity have grown dramatically since 1900; in the case of Christianity, the 1 percent in 1900 grew to 44 percent by 1970.[19] Significant violence has occurred between members of these two parts of Nigeria wherein tens of thousands of people are periodically killed or expelled, with much higher death tolls against Christians.[20]

On top of this simplistic Muslim north-Christian south bifurcation is significant complexity—Nigeria is one of the most diverse countries in the world with over 250 recognized ethnic minorities, as well as a significant, historic animist population. And, of course, there are significant Muslim communities in the largely Christian south, and significant Christian communities in the largely Muslim north. How, then, should Nigerian Christians live? And, tangentially, how should a Nigerian Christian act if there is an imposition of sharia law across Nigeria?

The question is a difficult one because there is nothing explicit in the Bible that Christians should live in countries wherein the principle of religious freedom is upheld. It also depends on the degree of sharia law. For example, some countries like Morocco and Jordan have a form of sharia law, but, in general, it is much less burdensome than in other countries like Iran and Saudi Arabia where sharia law is much more stringently imposed. It is much more difficult to read the bible, share one's faith, and to attend

---

16. Duerr, "War," 553.

17. Massey, *Refugee Life in the Confederacy*, 17.

18. Population Reference Bureau, 2020.

19. Jenkins, *The New Faces of Christianity*, 101.

20. Jenkins, *The New Faces of Christianity*, 129

worship services in the latter countries, rather than the former. It is still not easy to be a Christian in Morocco or Jordan, but the government is generally less repressive.[21] So, a more nuanced question could be posed: is it biblical for Nigerian Christians to rebel if a severe form of sharia law is imposed, which leads to the deaths of Christians across the country? In this case, much depends on the situation, but there is an increased case for secession especially when a Christian is to seek justice (Micah 6:8) and look out for the afflicted. Secession for Nigerian Christians is not explicitly a goal, but is an option depending on the severity of the situation. Of course, the downside of seceding is creating a lasting fracture between the two (or more) Nigerias, and also leading to a limited Christian witness in the northern part of the country. In many ways, there is usually an unintended outcome for every action. What might seem sensible for the protection of Nigerian Christians in the south of the country may make witnessing difficult in the predominantly-Muslim north.

One of the reasons for the position asserted here is the outcome of Sudan after the secession of South Sudan in July 2011. Since part of the reasoning for South Sudan's independence referendum in January 2011 was to provide the Christian and animist communities of the south a plebiscite to decide their own future as negotiated in the 2005 peace agreement to bring to an end the civil war in the country (fought from independence in 1956 to 1972, and then again from 1983 to 2005).[22] Thus, when South Sudan gained its independence, the government in Khartoum argued that Sudan was to be strictly Muslim since the Christians and animists had gained their own independent homeland.

As a largely Christian and animist region fighting against a significantly Islamic government in Sudanese capital of Khartoum, the South Sudanese seceded as a means to protect their population.[23] While the secession of South Sudan could be argued as biblical because it sought to institutionalize the protections of Christians and other minorities who, otherwise, had been killed in the millions in a longstanding civil war, there are still shortcomings. In particular, in the aftermath of war, two negative issues have emerged. First, Sudan is now a much more homogenous Muslim country with far fewer Christians available to share the gospel. In some ways, the people who would have shared the gospel are no longer there, or, if they still live in Sudan, are viewed as if they should leave for the "Christian" South Sudan. Second, South Sudan has been in a state of war almost every day

21. Open Doors, *World Watch List*.

22. United Nations. *The United Nations Today*, 100–104.

23. Hertzke, *Freeing God's Children*, 246–50.

since its independence in July 2011. If the biblical rationale to secede is one of protecting people, it has not been fulfilled in the creation of an independent South Sudan because the people are not well governed, nor are they governed for the good of the people.

A tangential issue to the example in South Sudan and East Timor (discussed in the next section) does, however, run through these cases: ethnicity. And, ethnic issues are not biblical issues in that they do not provide a biblical reason to secede. The bible argues the opposite, that all human beings, regardless of ethnicity should come to know God (Revelation 7:9).[24] Where ethnicity and secessionism become entangled, the biblical case for schism becomes even weaker because, as already mentioned in Colossians 3:11, there should be no "distinction between Greeks or Jew, circumcised or uncircumcised, barbarians, Scythians, slave and freeman, but Christ is all, and in all."

Was the American Declaration of Independence biblical?

Recalling the discussion on descriptive versus prescriptive uses of Scripture, there is a descriptive example of rebellion, but no explicit prescription of why 1 Kings 12 applies to the Thirteen Colonies in 1776. In light of this point, the answer to the question is no, there is not an explicitly biblical rationale for the independence of the United States. On a human and societal level, there are many prudent justifications for rebellion in the American case as noted with the oft-cited cry of "taxation without representation." In Scripture, Jesus simply says that Christians should pay their taxes, not be given representation because of taxation.

The question of whether or not the American Declaration of Independence is biblical, outside of any context, is also the wrong question. First, let us start with the no answer. In particular, there is nothing explicitly biblical about the United States exiting the British Empire. Although the British violated certain biblical principles in their governance of the Thirteen Colonies, such as governing for the good of the people, there is no explicit favor that God bestows upon the United States; only Israel is viewed as a country that belongs to God in the Old Testament and is therefore worthy of special consideration. Having said that, British rule was clearly tyrannical.[25] As noted in chapter 2, Romans 13 notes that rulers should rule for the good of the people, this case was clearly in violation. Looking historically, from the Plymouth Rock declaration of 1620 to 1770, most Americans felt that

24. Piper, *Let the Nations be glad!*, 193.
25. Grudem and Asmus, *The Poverty of Nations*, 238.

some form of connection to the British Empire was suitable; most were loyal British subjects. The political position of an outright schism only gained significant widespread traction in the 1770s. It could be argued that had the British offered the United States some form of dominion status (quasi-independence within the confines of the Empire), most Americans would have accepted the offer even as late as 1774 or 1775.[26] As evidence of this point, the American preacher, John Allen, for example, presented a "revolutionary" sermon in 1772 against King George III, which was thought to be a radical departure for the typically American view of the British Empire at the time.[27] The relationship between the British Empire and the Thirteen Colonies was generally in good standing in the early 1770s.

In his book on what was being preached in the pulpit in the lead up to the American Revolution, the American historian James Byrd shows that seven biblical passages were most commonly used. Of particular interest here is 1 Kings 12, which was the sixth-most used passage of Scripture.[28] It is evident that many American preachers and Christians thought that secession was biblical on the grounds of the British Empire acting like a modern day Rehoboam. Under King George III, there is some evidence that this is fair. For most Americans, he is still viewed as a tyrannical ruler bent on subjugating the people of the Thirteen Colonies with burdensome taxes. It is worth noting that King George III actually ruled the British Empire for 60 years, from 1760 to 1820. Even though his legacy in the United States is one of an overbearing tyrant, this is the same monarch that led the British through the Napoleonic Wars, 1803–1815, and helped to structure the Congress of Vienna (also known as the Concert of Europe), which maintained the balance of power in Europe until 1914, the start of World War I. History is always more complex than any one political position at any one given point in time.

Byrd also notes that other biblical passages were more commonly preached during the lead-up to the American Revolution. The commonly preached passages were typically aligned with the idea of submitting to the rulers that God had placed in charge, especially Romans 13;[29] in essence, it was more common for the average American pastor (found within Byrd's dataset) to note the importance of submission to the governing authorities, rather than rebellion.

26. My colleague, Dr. J. Murray Murdoch, Distinguished (Senior) Professor of History at Cedarville University, has often purported this position. He served full-time at the university from 1965–2020, a total of 55 years.

27. Byrd, *Sacred Scripture, Sacred War*, 35.

28. Byrd, *Scared Scripture, Sacred War*, 170.

29. Byrd, *Sacred Scripture, Sacred War*, 170.

Of course, when the American Revolution started, it did cause a significant change to the structure of world events. The French Revolution of 1789 is viewed by some historians as the "twin" to the American Revolution in the advocation of political rights for commoners. These revolutions sought to disentangle the overt relationship between church and state (throne and altar) as a means of projecting popular sovereignty.[30] This is the period in which the notion of citizenship, rather than divine right of kings, became more popular in world affairs.

More territories soon after began gaining their own sovereignty in the next few decades; in fact, significant swaths of the Western Hemisphere gained independence from British, French, and Spanish rule. Tangentially, there is nothing explicitly biblical per se about other cases. Take the example of Haiti winning its independence from France in 1804, the French certainly did not govern the Haitians in a manner that can be described as for "their good"—as is instructed in the bible. Even when Haiti won its independence, the government in the capital, Port-au-Prince still had to pay France in order for Paris not to meddle in their affairs—a cost that made life very difficult in Haiti, and arguably still impacts the small Caribbean country today.[31]

What then is the correct question? The correct question is whether the British had a biblical right to expand their Empire? Genesis 1:26 provides a mandate for human beings to populate the earth, and have dominion over it, but nowhere does it give the British the sole right to do so. Of course, the British are people, and people thus have the mandate to respectfully rule over the world under the Genesis 1 dominion mandate.[32] But, there is no special caveat that the British have the exclusive right to do this. Therefore, the answer to the original question is difficult: no, the United States did not have a biblical right to exit the British Empire, but the British Empire had to explicit right to rule or colonize in the first place.

In sum, this discussion provides a difficult endpoint for the Christian. Secession is difficult to argue as something that is explicitly biblical. But, what should Christians do when rulers do not govern justly? Much of this depends on how one defines biblical goodness or biblical justice in regards to a ruler and the subjects/citizens, depending on the time and context. Rebellion exists in the heart of every person given the fall of humanity in Genesis.

In the twenty-first century, Christians across the world live in a variety of different contexts. Some are violently oppressed because of their

30. Baker, *The End of Secularism*, 59.

31. Bellegarde-Smith, *Haiti*.

32. Moreau, Corwin, and McGee, *Introducing World Missions*, 28.

faith in harshly authoritarian states. In other cases, Christians live in highly democratic and economically developed countries with minimal hardships, but significant concern over what is happening politically. Secession as an option could be more widely used if it is used for the altruistic purpose of better governing people—something that is very difficult to implement in practice.

Justifiable, biblical examples of secession?

In some senses, the conclusions from the last sections of this chapter remain nebulous and unsatisfying. Obviously, secession—and any related form of rebellion—is a complex subject especially when considering whether the action is biblical or not. However, the next question could help to better draw distinct lines as to when secession is biblical and when it is not.

There are several cases that could best fall in the category of biblical support for secession; in particular, one that has happened recently. The country of East Timor (also known as Timor Leste) in south-east Asia is similar to South Sudan, in that they were under governments that persecuted them, in part for their faith. When the Netherlands withdrew from the majority of their colonial possessions in 1948, the Dutch East Indies became an independent country now known as Indonesia. The country of Indonesia consists of a vast archipelago of different islands, and encompasses the world's fourth largest population in 2020 at 268.4 million.[33] When the Portuguese government withdrew from most of their global colonial possessions in 1975, the island of Timor became contested. The eastern half of the island was under Portuguese rule, while the west of Timor was Indonesian. Sensing an opportunity to gain territory, the Indonesian military took the eastern half of Timor killing one-third of the 600,000 population in a genocide. This was the most brutal element of a 24-year period of occupation.[34] The eastern Timorese were different from the people in the west by ethnicity as well as their (generally) shared Roman Catholic faith. In short, a campaign of genocidal violence conducted by the Indonesian government in the mid-to-late 1970s.[35] Effectively, Indonesia (a former Dutch colony) sought to annex East Timor (a former Portuguese colony) over what Jakarta viewed as territorial rights—after all, Indonesia comprised the western portion of the island of Timor, so common sense,

33. Population Reference Bureau. *Indonesia.*
34. D'Souza and Rogers, *On the Side of Angels*, 30.
35. Jolliffe, *East Timor.*

they argued, dictated that East Timor become part of Indonesia.[36] However, over time, pressure mounted to provide East Timor with a different relationship with Jakarta. In 1999, the Indonesian government opted to deflect some of this international condemnation by allowing the East Timorese to vote in a referendum on provisions for special autonomy, whilst remaining within Indonesia.[37] The referendum vote was overwhelmingly rejected by 78.5 percent of voters. Violence erupted again after the referendum as Indonesia sought to maintain its power over the territory. The UN and Australia then moved to stop the violence, and granted East Timor the right to pursue independence. East Timor then became an internationally recognized member state of the UN in 2002.

In pushing back against Indonesian rule, the East Timorese were subject to mass violence. Moreover, the disparate ethnic groups in East Timor, comprising approximately a dozen, were lumped into a group—now known as East Timorese. Not only were the East Timorese ethnically different from the Indonesian rulers, but, as Roman Catholics and other minorities, their faith distinctly deviated from the Islamic rule of Indonesia.[38]

As of the time of writing in 2020, East Timor is the world's third newest country. One of the reasons why I argue here that the secession of East Timor was biblical is for two reasons: 1) The international community, writ large, condemned the actions of Indonesia, and provided the East Timorese with the option of a referendum, which overwhelmingly rejected overtures by the Indonesian government (and tacitly supported independence), and 2) The people of East Timor would have been obliterated without statehood. I would argue that where a Christian (or any other linguistic, ethnic, social, and/or religious community) population faces genocide, there is a biblical justification for secession.

As a result of East Timor's secession, the Indonesian government has clamped down upon other predominantly Christian areas of the country, notably West Papua, to avoid losing more territory. The West Papuan Christians (and others) rebel because they do not want to die en masse, in a genocide akin to the East Timorese in the 1970s. This is the reason why secession is a difficult subject biblically. Christians have every right to protect their families as in a definition of love, but there are always unintended consequences.

Ultimately, the gospel can spread regardless of the international boundary or governing authorities put in place. Christians are also called to

---

36. Dunn, *East Timor*; Robinson, "*If you Leave us Here, We Will Die.*"

37. Fasulo, *An Insider's Guide to the UN*, 132.

38. Dunn, *East Timor*.

sometimes live in less than perfect circumstances, and sometimes those circumstances are extremely difficult. Statehood/independence, on the other hand, provides many benefits such as legal equality with the other countries of the world, as well as institutional recognition for a group. But, statehood should also provide security, which is typically more difficult for smaller countries—the population of East Timor has benefitted immensely from the bestowing of this privilege. Prior to the twentieth century, for example, the premise was to create countries large enough to fend for themselves. It is a big reason why countries with more "artificial" boundaries that encompass two or more (sometimes conflicting) language groups like Czechoslovakia, Yugoslavia, Syria, and Iraq were created in the aftermath of World War I. Because larger countries, so the thinking went, were more likely to survive. This type of thinking is less prominent today as many small countries not only survive, but thrive in the modern economy. However, the more recent thinking may have its presumptions of peace given that it is based on 75 years of significant peace in much of the world since the end of World War II. Small countries have survived (and thrived) since 1945 because the United States and other countries put in place the norm that borders must not change—territory should not be annexed. Obviously, there are exceptions to this point such as Russia's militaristic actions in Georgia in 2008 and Ukraine in 2014, but largely the norm holds—stronger countries should not simply annex the territory of weaker countries.

Like many contemporary political issues, there is a nuance here. What about annexing uninhabited islands? Or, unclaimed islands? The South China Sea has become a bastion of contention in recent decades given China's ambitions to control a great swath of territory. The UN Convention of the Law of the Seas (UNCLOS)[39] technically governs international legal claims over the seas and oceans, but this is subject to contestation. China has "reclaimed" reefs from the sea, and effectively counted them as the sovereign territory of Beijing.[40] These actions are effectively designed to annex territory from some of China's neighbors on the South China Sea, but technically does not involve taking any territory; rather, this method involves creating new territory within the territorial waters of a neighboring country.

Even though the norm of protecting small states from annexation is relatively new, and could reverse if the world order changes, the creation of small, Christian-majority countries might provide better institutional protection for Christians (this logic should extend to any linguistic, ethnic, social, and/or religious community, within reason). The reason for this is that if a

39. Fabey, *Crashback*, 101.
40. Fabey, *Crashback*, 228.

country is a recognized member state of the UN, there is a forum through which a country can appeal if a larger and more powerful neighbor threatens the sovereignty of this predominantly-Christian country. Put simply, being a country helps to stop annexation and genocide. Where an ethnic group, like the Kurds in the Middle East, do not have a state (and recognition in the UN), their people are often subject to violence, which periodically leads to genocide.[41] This ongoing campaign of genocide against the Kurds is clearly unbiblical—tangentially meaning statehood has some biblical justification.

However, there are numerous pitfalls that have to be weighed. By allowing for secession, it is possible that the number of countries in the world may increase dramatically. Moreover, by arguing that secession is biblical, this could encourage every Christian enclave in the world to demand independence. For example, when Jesus rebuked Peter in the Garden of Gethsemane for cutting off the ear of the Roman guard (John 18:10–11), any justification of rebellion is strongly limited to protecting one's population from ethnic cleansing or genocide. Supporting all cases of Christian or other secessionist movements would exacerbate existing conflicts, and plausibly make the world much more violent. The number of member states in the UN could double or triple very quickly.[42] Every disparate group may seek to "fence off" its small part of a territory, leading to an untenable situation wherein there are thousands of city-states in the world, resembling the situation in the HRE (much of modern day Germany) that lasted from Charlemagne in 800[43] until their defeat by Napoleon in 1806. Therefore, the central argument in this chapter is that secession, under very narrow and limited circumstances, is justifiable biblically. The most significant justification is to protect the lives of people from genocide. If independence is the only way to stop genocide, then a biblical expression of secession is justified.

Throughout Scripture, there is little explicitly biblical to support seceding from an existing state, especially under Romans 13:1–7, which implies that the existing government has been placed there by God. It does, however, assume that said government does "good" for the people. At the very least, genocide cannot be considered good.

---

41. Belz, *They say we are Infidels*, 56.

42. The political scientist, Ryan Griffiths, shows how the number of secessionist movements has increased dramatically from 1816 to the present era. At the end of the Cold War in 1991, for example, there were over 8- movements as compared to 10 in 1816 (Griffiths, *Age of Secession*, 51).

43. Fried, *Charlemagne*.

Is rebellion justified against a "Christian" leader or country?

This previous section of the chapter has investigated if any biblical support is available to the idea of secession, but it is important to examine the other side of the argument. How should a Christian leader respond to secessionism or rebellion in his/her country? Take for example, a professing Christian leader in west, central, or southern Africa, or Central America who may be facing an insurrection or secessionist claims? Should he/she try to keep his/her country together at all costs knowing that doing so could cost the lives of citizens, possibly in the thousands. Or, what if the example of East Timor was reversed: if East Timor was predominantly non-Christian, while the Indonesian government was largely Christian?

This type of situation where a professing Christian is the president/leader of the country has arisen in all of these geographic regions even since 1990. In many cases, the professing Christian tries to hold onto power; at times, this has exacerbated the conflict, and led to increased atrocities by government forces, or government-backed militias. Ultimately, the Christian leader should have more reasons than non-Christians to seek the "good" of all the people that are under his/her leadership—after all, the central objective for any Christian leader should be to govern for the "good" of the people in Romans 13. A Christian leader should also be a model for all non-Christians that happen to reside within a territory—his/her leadership in government could be a catalyst for investigation of the truth of God's Word.

As established in chapter 2, Christians can go to war, and Christian leaders can lead their people into war, but only under the very strict parameters outlined earlier, described as the "just war plus" model. Even with the ability to wage war, another, immediate objective should be to work towards peace (Matthew 5:9). This may involve limiting the use of force, providing regular opportunities to find a peaceful resolution, and sharing power amongst opposing factions to bring an end to bloodshed.

This may also involve flexibility in some areas because governance that burdens the people, as evidenced by animosity towards Rehoboam in 1 Kings 12, can lead to serious consequences. Even though a leader, even a Christian leader, is, according to Scripture, placed in that position by God, at what point should said leader step down in the face of rebellion? Or civil war? Christian leaders should seek peaceable agreements under all circumstances, even in the face of secessionist rebellion, or by leaders who specifically seek to purport policies that run counter to biblical teachings. These questions, obviously, are dependent upon circumstances, but some guidelines can be presented. Killing people, en masse, in order to quell a secessionist rebellion runs counter to the central admonition to Jesus to love people. A range of options exist that could pacify a secessionist rebellion long before it increases such as power-sharing, the sharing of resources, or greater autonomy. In general, autonomy agreements "usually de-escalate the fighting, but not always completely or permanently."[44] A wise, Christian ruler should consider the gospel in his/her actions over retaining their own power. It would be more prudent to allow for the secession of a territory, rather than for a Christian leader to engage in a brutal campaign of bloodletting, that might eventually be considered genocide. This point raises more questions, though: what if the new territory is populated primarily by non-Christians who would govern their country in ways explicitly counter to any moral form? What if the new country was governed by atheistic communists? Every human being is made in the image of God, so any form of war/campaign of violence has to be carefully weighed, but there are largescale considerations that have to be assessed. To provide an example, should Christian leaders in South/Central America or Southern Africa have allowed for secession on the part of communist rebel groups in the Cold War era, as in Colombia, Guatemala or Mozambique? There is no justification for widespread bloodshed, nor communist governance—thus discernment on the part of the Christian leader is the most important conclusion.

When is secession acceptable, but not necessarily biblical?

In some cases, Christians living within a given country might be well treated, and face no major persecution. Yet, secessionist movements may abound, as is the case with the United Kingdom, Spain, and Belgium, among other cases, where major pro-independence agitation has been increasing.[45] As with earlier cases, secessionism is not explicitly supported in the Bible, so Christians should exercise caution when considering this idea. Where substantial power-sharing exists such as in a federal state, or unitary state with devolution, Christians should align with the existing governing power where said governing power earnestly desires to govern for the "good" of all the people. In federal states, or unitary states with devolution, the model is similar to the twelve tribes of Israel, which all functioned with some autonomy, but were in union with the other subnational units of the Kingdom of Israel.

Addressing Christianity in the United Kingdom, the former British Prime Minister, David Cameron (2010–2016), made statements on December 16, 2015 during his weekly Prime Ministers Question time. In back-to-back questions on Scotland (referring to Scotland's independence

---

44. Goldstein, *Winning the War on War*, 296.

45. Duerr, *Secessionism and the European Union*.

movement), and then the situation of Christians around the world, PM Cameron made two noteworthy statements:

> "Like the honorable gentleman, I am passionate about our United Kingdom. I believe we can (make) it stronger by accepting that it is a partnership of nations, and a partnership of nations where we should treat each other with respect. [Interruption.] I do not want to listen to Scottish National Party (SNP) Members: they do not want a partnership; they want a separation. Actually, one of the things that is so strong about the United Kingdom—I think other countries, frankly, are quite envious of this—is that we have demonstrated that you can have multiple identities: you can be proud of being an Ulsterman and a Brit; you can be proud of being a Hindu and a Scot; you can be proud of being both Welsh and British. We have solved one of the problems that the rest of the world is grappling with, and that is why we should keep our United Kingdom together.

> Yes, Britain is a Christian country. I believe that the fact that we have an established faith and that we understand the place of faith in our national life makes us a more tolerant nation and better able to accommodate other faith groups in our country. That is why, as I said earlier, we should be proud that this is one of the most successful multi-ethnic, multi-faith, multi-religion democracies anywhere in the world. That is not in conflict with our status as a predominantly Christian country; that status is one of the reasons why we have done it.[46]

Former Prime Minister David Cameron notes above that the United Kingdom is a Christian country at its core. He also notes that, as a result of Christian tenets, that the country does accommodate a wide range of groups because, he intimates, causes tolerance of others because Jesus calls his followers to love others.[47]

Although some might view this position as vacating Christian principles over governance, there is another component of the argument. Perhaps heterogeneous countries like the United Kingdom and Canada that provide substantial autonomy have best figured out ways to create functioning states that provide protections for Christians, but simultaneously provides substantial mechanisms to avoid civil war and rebellion within the territory. This is a useful development because, at some point, human beings have to live together, whether Christian or not—otherwise

---

46. Cameron, *"Prime Minister's Question Time."*

47. Cameron, "Prime Minister's Question Time."

the point made earlier that thousands of new regions might suddenly rebel and seek new states—comes to pass and world becomes much more violent and complicated. If existing countries can continue peacefully through power-sharing mechanisms, then it is a promising development. The Bible, of course, does not promise Christians any form of protection of comfort or prosperity, other than that God will be with the believer. Peace and prosperity should not be expected, but Christians can play an active role in creating peaceful institutions and countries, especially where opportunities are readily available.

Good governance is a key facet of the discussion here because many countries and empires, historically, have been torn apart through suboptimal governance. In his book on the history and eventual downfall of the Ottoman Empire, the American historian (who taught in Turkey), Sean McMeekin, starts with a quote from Isaiah 8:9 in the King James Version.[48]

> "Associate yourselves, O ye people, and ye shall be broken in pieces; and give ear, all ye of far countries: gird yourselves, and ye shall be broken in pieces; gird yourselves, and ye shall be broken in pieces."

By way of context, the NASB reading of Isaiah 8:9 is as follows:

> "Be broken, O peoples, and be shattered; And give ear, all remote places of the earth. Gird yourselves, yet be shattered; Gird yourselves, yet be shattered."

The NIV version presents another different reading:

> "Raise the war cry, you nations, and be shattered! Listen, all you distant lands.
>
> Prepare for battle, and be shattered! Prepare for battle, and be shattered!"

Regardless of the different translations of Scripture, the central idea here from McMeekin is that the Ottoman Empire fell, and that, biblically, countries and empires can splinter and fall at the whim of God, if God so allows such events to transpire. To repeat, the idea is not that secessionism in biblical, only that mighty kingdoms can fall, and sometimes quickly. What might seem unimaginable at one cut point in time can occur within the span of a few years. In fact, the whole backdrop of the Old Testament showcases the rise and fall of many great empires. The Egyptians, Israelites, Assyrians, and Babylonians all eventually fall throughout the Old Testament. A Christian leader, who focuses

---

48. McMeekin, *The Ottoman Endgame*, 1.

on good governance, will best find ways to avoid the downfall of his/her kingdom. There is no guarantee here, but governing for the good of all people is the admonition for leadership in the Romans 13 model.

What other options exist?

There is an old adage that states, "If your only tool is a hammer, every problem becomes a nail." Secession and rebellion are discussed at length in this book because both exist in numerous situations throughout the world. However, there are a range of other options. In a study of nationalism, it is useful to note that cultures often do not stop and start, even at national boundaries.

As noted in chapter 2, there are regions where significant cultural overlap exists, between countries. The historian, Colin Woodard, for example, argues that eleven "nations" exist within North America. Some of these nations, such as El Norte, overlap the north of Mexico (most of Nuevo León, Sonora, Baja California, Chihuahua, Tamaulipas, and Coahuila) and the southwest of the United States (sections of southern California, southern Arizona, New Mexico, west Texas, and southern Colorado).[49] Many people residing within these states share what Woodard argues is a *norteño* culture.[50] Another "nation" within Woodard's analysis is The Midlands, which encompasses sections of the Midwest in the United States, as well as parts of Canada in southern Ontario.[51] To cite another part of the world, in Central Asia, forced movements of people under some of the most recalcitrant dictators of the Soviet Union, has created a patchwork of different ethnic groups across national boundaries. Tajiks, Kyrgyz, Turkmen, Kazakhs, and Uzbeks, reside across many other countries within the region, also extending into Russia, Afghanistan, and China. To further complicate matters, ethnic Russians also make up significant minority populations in Central Asia, encompassing arguably the largest ethnic group outside of their host state.[52] In Central Africa, numerous mutually unintelligible languages are spoken, often bisecting national boundaries. These examples showcase the possibility of a person holding citizenship in one country, and also maintaining significant familial and cultural linkages with a neighboring country. Where the gospel has been newly translated into this language, Christians that traverse these different national settings are instrumental in making disciples.

49. Woodard, *American Nations*, 10.

50. Martinez, *Troublesome Border*, 107–108.

51. Woodard, *American Nations*, 6–7.

52. King, *Extreme Politics*, 142.

Politically, in situations where there is significant overlap between ethnic or linguistic kin, across national boundaries, autonomy is a useful instrument to maintain peace within a society. Ethnic kin networks will likely remain strong given that family members will want to visit each other with regularity. By providing autonomy, these existing familial networks can continue, with the requisite submission to authorities.

Is Irredentism acceptable?

Irredentism can be defined as: "concerning demands by any ethnic group for acquisition of territory claimed to be part of a historic homeland or populated by ethnic kin."[53] The original usage of the term irredentism refers to the italia irredenta—a nationalist movement within Italy that gained traction in the nineteenth century by promoting the inclusion of primarily Italian-speaking or ethnically Italian areas outside Italy into the country. Ultimately, Italy was built by combining politically Italian-speaking regions that were increasingly unified in the aftermath of the Austro-Sardinian war in 1859. This movement, known as Risorgimento, continued to move forward to the unification of Italy in 1861.[54] (Even then, the region of Veneto was added in 1866 after the Prussian-Austrian War, and Rome in 1871 completing the irredentist claim over Italy.)[55] Irredentism thus refers to any movement that attempts to unify territory, or to re-unify historic territory that was dissolved at an earlier point in history.

In some ways, the idea of irredentism is the reverse of secession—a country wants to regain specific "lost" territory, or territories. A recent, illegal example of this was Russia's 2014 annexation of Crimea. The country of Ukraine, under international law, legally owns Crimea even though the status of the region was transferred from Russia to Ukraine under the Soviet Union in 1954. As evidenced by the example of Russia, and the preceding discussion on secessionism in this chapter, there is nothing explicitly biblical about irredentism, either. In quick summation, the Bible does not provide evidence of support for irredentism, perhaps with the exception of Israel in the Old Testament with regards to conquering the Promised Land in the Book of Joshua. Even contemporary irredentist claims on behalf of Israel over the Palestinian territories and other surrounding countries must be take very cautiously given the possibility of initiating a wide, and vicious war.

---

53. Nolan, *The Greenwood Encyclopedia of International Relations*, Irredentism.

54. Evans, *Pursuit of Power*, 292.

55. Evans, *Pursuit of Power*, 254–257.

A connected and more nuanced component of the irredentism discussion is what to do with a situation of one nation, two states—a situation wherein a relatively homogenous nation is divided into two different states. For example, during the Cold War, there were two Germanys, two Yemens, and two Vietnams, which were all reunited around 1990 (Vietnam was reunited in 1975). However, one part of the world remains divided in its Cold War-like state: the Korean Peninsula. North Korea and South Korea remain divided along the arbitrary 38th parallel.

A useful contemporary example of whether irredentism to assess whether or not it is acceptable biblically is to examine a specific case of the Korean peninsula. Historically, this is a territory with a homogenous ethnic population who speaks that same language, fitting the definition of a nation in chapter 1. Given the growth of Christianity in South Korea, how should South Korean Christians respond to the North? What if the North attempts to go to war with the South? How should South Koreans respond if the North Korean government suddenly collapses?

To provide a quick, modern history, the Korean Peninsula was invaded by the Japanese Empire in 1905, and fully annexed in 1910.[56] The Korean people lived under Japanese occupation until the end of World War II in 1945. At the end of World War II, Korea was divided, much like Germany and Austria in Europe, into zones; the North under the Soviet Union, and the South under the United States. In 1948, the Democratic People's Republic of Korea (DPRK, also North Korea) was founded under Kim Il-Sung. Seeking to unify the Korean Peninsula under his dictatorship, Kim Il-Sung ordered the invasion of South Korea in June 1950, triggering the Korean War and drawing in great powers like the USA and China.[57] The conflict was long and bloody, and lasted until July 1953. Although the Korean War is often overlooked by many people given that the conflict occurred so soon after World War II, the conflict in Korea still resulted in an estimated 2–3 million dead.

The net result of the war was a stalemate, cementing the border between the two Koreas on the 38th parallel. In the early 1950s, the Koreas were among the least wealthy countries on the planet; given significant Soviet subsidies, North Korea was actually wealthier than South Korea, and had been provided advantages during Japanese occupation.[58] In 2020, the situation is vastly different: South Korea is a developed world country that is democratic, free, largely capitalist, and a pillar of hope to societies seeking to improve their

56. Cha, *The Impossible State.*
57. Marshall, *Prisoners of Geography*, 213.
58. Cha, *The Impossible State*, 23.

situations.[59] North Korea, by stark contrast, remains one of the poorest countries in the world with very little freedom of any kind—the country is one of the worst examples of totalitarianism in the world.[60]

South Korean Christians, perhaps more so than any other group, have worked to reach out to the North Korean people. Yet, there are fears as to how North Korea will act. Should South Koreans read Scripture as akin to the Old Testament warnings about the threats of invasion from the Assyrians and Babylonians?[61] It is highly unlikely that Kim Jong-un would attempt an all-out military attack on the South, but predicting the future is a perilous task.

There are pragmatic responses as well. Given their longstanding desire to, in the name of Christ, help North Korean defectors, South Korean Christians should continue to fill this vital role in this specific situation. There is nothing overtly biblical about helping ethnic kin over others, but the South Korean church has taken it upon itself to help the poor, the sick, the hungry, and the needy from North Korea—all situations wherein Christ himself helped and served the people of the day. It makes the most sense, pragmatically, because North Koreans and South Koreans share, most importantly, a common language as a means of communicating. In this regard, the South Korean church, and, in a connected sense, the South Korean government should respond to the collapse/end of the Kim dynasty in North Korea, if this event ever happens. Going back to the discussion of Romans 13 in previous chapters, the South Korean Constitution, for example, in Article III, claims that the South Korean government in the rightful government of the whole Korean peninsula—the people of North Korea are, then, automatically citizens of South Korea.[62]

Moreover, the South Korean church is more astutely aware of the rise of Christianity on the Korean peninsula that had its major roots in an 1882 "treaty of amity and commerce with the United States, which paved the way for missionaries to come to the peninsula"[63] and a 1907 conference in Pyongyang, as well as being well positioned to understand the North Korean "religion" of Juche—that is, self-reliance, and deification of the Kim family. Pyongyang, tragically, was once known as the "Jerusalem of the east" for its churches and adherence to Christianity.[64]

59. Grudem, *Politics according to the Bible*, 46

60. Freedom House.

61. Jenkins, *The New Faces of Christianity*, 63.

62. Demick, *Nothing to Envy*, 245

63. Cha, *The Impossible State*, 66–67.

64. Demick, *Nothing to Envy*, 45; Kim, "*Jerusalem of the East*."

Tangentially, since the growth of Christianity in China has also increased, how should Chinese Christians respond? In some ways, it seems natural that South Koreans would most quickly and helpfully act to help with a post-Kim dynasty North Korea, but China is the region's most powerful country now, and has significant rapport with thousands of North Koreans who have, at one point or another, crossed the border into China.[65] Chinese Christians, in the event that the South Korean government does not or cannot help North Korea, could step in to fill the void. This is not to encourage the Chinese Communist Party government, but to recommend filling the gap if there is a shortfall. Chinese Christians should supplement the work of South Korean believers, especially in areas where there has been success. Significant trade relations between China and South Korea are evidence of cooperation between the two countries, despite prickly geopolitical concerns.[66] Therefore, cooperation would be the most useful way of helping North Korea in the event of a regime change. The Chinese Communist Party has a political desire to stay close to North Korea, which is a negative scenario given that North Koreans will likely remain in authoritarianism, and be pushed towards atheism. Moving away from the evils of a communist system would be the ideal; however, allowing for some middle ground of using Chinese Christians to play a role in helping North Korea move forward has its uses. Bibles, presumably by the thousands, for example, have crossed into North Korea through China.[67]

Secession as a biblical option
for conflict resolution?

At this point, the chapter transitions from examining whether or not Christians should purport secessionism in their everyday circumstances to look at the concept of how secession can be used by Christians in positions of power either in powerful countries, or in international organizations such as the UN. The call in Matthew 5:9 is "blessed are the peacemakers for they shall be called sons of God."

With large-scale civil wars raging in Iraq and Syria throughout the 2010s, and significant conflicts erupting in Libya and Yemen as well in the latter part of that decade, the modern Middle East is potentially more volatile than it has been in centuries. Sparked by successful revolutions in Tunisia, Egypt, Libya, and Yemen, starting in December 2010 through 2011, the

65. Demick, *Nothing to Envy*, 198–210.

66. Jacques, *When China Rules the World*, 366.

67. Demick, *Nothing to Envy*, 214.

so-called "Arab Spring" has devolved into wars, which threaten to further spread across the region.[68] In Iraq, Syria, Yemen, and Libya, major fissures between groups have opened up partly along historic sectarian lines, long dormant in the wake of authoritarian rule, but exposed when a longstanding dictator was toppled or challenged.

Elsewhere in the world, similar fissures have emerged as secessionists have increased in their agitation. In recent decades, the people of Quebec in Canada, and Scotland in the United Kingdom have voted in formal independence referendums, albeit without success. In Quebec, in 1980 and 1995, both referendums were unsuccessful, although, the latter obtained 49.4 percent support for Quebec sovereignty. In Scotland, in 2014, 44.7 percent of voters supported the independence referendum.[69] Secessionism remains an important subject, but rarely do these movements achieve independence.[70] In these rare cases where independence is granted, they have become full-fledged independent states replete with membership in major international organizations like the UN.

In contrast to the above picture of regions gaining independence, retaining the status quo—territorial integrity—has been one of the hallmarks of the post-1945 world order. The international community only reluctantly accepts secession, but is this the most optimal way forward? After World War II, which began, in large measure, as a response to Germany, Japan, and Italy annexing territory, the post-war consensus was to detract from this idea. The UN Charter signed in 1945 as well as the 1975 Helsinki conference compounded the idea that the borders of national states should be respected, and that national sovereignty should be upheld. This consensus has been paramount for stability for the last 75 years with the exception of Russia's aforementioned annexation of Crimea in 2014. (Russia has also engaged in a covert military operation in Donbas in eastern Ukraine, specifically in the regions of Donetsk and Luhansk).[71] Otherwise, only Saddam Hussein's Iraq, which invaded Kuwait in 1990 has acted counter to this convention—and they were swiftly defeated in the 1991 Gulf War resulting in Kuwait's territorial integrity being restored.[72] Israel's victory in the 1967 War is another example; although this case is certainly more complex, since Israel returned the Sinai Peninsula to Egypt. The Golan Heights, annexed from Syria, and the nebulous status of the Palestinian

68. Anderson, "*Demystifying the Arab Spring*"

69. Duerr, *Secessionism and the European Union*, 77.

70. Dion, "*Why is secession difficult in well-established democracies?*"

71. Plokhy, *The Gates of Europe*, 343–4.

72. Duerr, "*War.*"

territories, remain a point of contention under international law.[73] Some scholars, like the British writer Tim Marshall, argue that China annexed Tibet in 1951 as part of spreading the control of the Chinese Communist Party.[74] This point is contested since Tibet long belonged to a Chinese empire, but Tibetans did declare independence in 1913 where it maintained significant autonomy until 1951.

It is important to briefly pause here and note the distinction between decolonization and secession.[75] After all, even in the twentieth century, many territories gained sovereign status. Many colonies began obtaining independence from the late 1940s through to the mid-1970s as colonial powers finally withdrew from territories across Africa, Asia, the Pacific, and the Caribbean. Cases of secession (as opposed to decolonization) have occurred, but are quite limited, in tandem with the idea that national sovereignty should be upheld. On rare occasions, the status quo has been disturbed in a major break. For example, three countries in Eastern Europe—the Soviet Union, Czechoslovakia, and Yugoslavia—all splintered in the aftermath of the fall of communism between 1991 and 1995 into 22 independent states.[76] (Montenegro's successful and peaceful referendum on independence now constitutes a 23rd case.)[77] Otherwise, the successful secessions around the world have been piecemeal solutions to longstanding conflicts: Eritrea gained independence from Ethiopia in 1993, East Timor from Indonesia in 2002, Montenegro from Yugoslavia (The Union of Serbia and Montenegro) in 2006, and South Sudan from Sudan in 2011. All other cases fall under a broad heading of decolonization, albeit with some complications.

An Argument on Secession and Scripture

Secessionism as a vehicle?

The argument outlined here is that secession is a biblical option for post-conflict resolution, and could be utilized—in a very limited capacity—to better defuse the most entrenched wars of today before they spread further. Secession could also be used as a mechanism to stop war in situations where

73. Shlaim, *War and Peace in the Middle East*, 42–43.

74. Marshall, *Prisoners of Geography*, 46.

75. The UN engaged in a significant push to decolonize parts of the world, and to provide independence for new member states (Fasulo, *An Insider's Guide to the UN*, 91–2).

76. Bunce, *Subversive Institutions*.

77. Darmanovic, *"Montenegro: A miracle in the Balkans?"* 152.

conflict remains intractable, provided that international actors have the will to become temporarily involved. From 1945–2000, over 25 million people were killed as a result of civil wars, most in cases where conflicts continued for an extended period of time.[78] The length of civil wars has also increased dramatically. From 1900–1944, the average civil war lasted for approximately 18 months, this average length tripled in civil wars in the second half of the twentieth century.[79] At the very least, secession should be considered as one option for post-conflict resolution.

Jesus notes at the beginning of the Sermon on the Mount in Matthew 5:9 that "blessed are the peacemakers, for they will be called sons of God." Jesus uses interesting language here. He does not say peacekeepers will be blessed, nor does He say that peacebuilders will be blessed. Instead, He uses very specific terminology—peacemakers—intimating that someone has to actively create peace, rather than to keep the existing peace (as a peace-keeper), or work towards peacebuilding. The connotation involves actively participating to stop a conflict while it is ongoing.

Rather than going to war, and potentially ruining the country with thousands of casualties and an obliterated economy, the two (or more) sides can opt to divide the territory, and govern two (or more) separate states. In effect, this replicates the decision made in 1 Kings 12 to divide Rehoboam's kingdom into Israel and Judah. Although, most outside observers, in recent decades, are loathe to become involved in the (re) drawing of national boundaries given the aforementioned international norm of respecting national sovereignty, the alternative may be worse. When thousands of people die, many thousands more flee across national borders to seek refuge elsewhere. Perhaps granting greater provision for secession would better conclude these conflicts before displaced persons leave en masse for other, safer countries.

Partition of states usually occurs with the blessing of powerful outside actors, anyway, especially large, great powers like the United States. For example, the European Union gave its blessing to Montenegro in 2006, as did Australia in the aforementioned case of East Timor in 2002. Sometimes partition occurs, as it did in 1971, with the support of India in the secession of East Pakistan—now called Bangladesh—from West Pakistan (now simply Pakistan). The tool of secession can also be useful if a large federation is not working for all parties. As another example, the division of the Federation of the West Indies (1958–1962) was an appropriate mechanism for all former members when Jamaica wanted to withdraw

78. Hironaka, *Neverending Wars*, 2.

79. Hironaka, *Neverending Wars*, 1.

from the federation in 1962. Likewise, the United Arab Republic, which lasted from 1958 to 1961, was peacefully dissolved after a few years into the previous countries, Egypt and Syria, once again.

Even the option of secession can help to increase peace. Where a referendum passes overwhelmingly, the option for independence can be obvious, at least as a measure of the people's will (assuming, of course, a free and fair referendum process). Less obvious, however, is the use of a referendum, which serves as a safety valve for people to voice their opinion on a matter of national belonging, and a bellwether on a Romans 13 governance model for the good of people. As noted in the earlier examples, referendums in Scotland and Quebec provided everyday citizens the opportunity to vote for independence, even if their regions ultimately opted to remain part of the United Kingdom and Canada respectively. The people of both regions have been better accommodated as a result. And, people within both societies share a sense that they have had their political voice heard. Not all will agree with the outcome, but at least they had their opportunity to politically and peaceful try to achieve their objectives.

The argument in this chapter, then, is that secession should only be granted where five main tenets are supported: 1) existing institutional lines for partition, 2) likely conditions for a democratic system to be tried, 3) provisions for the protection of minority groups within governing documents, 4) a likelihood that civil war abates, and 5) some international support. This will further limit the cases wherein secession can be used as an option for peacemaking[80] or post-conflict situations.

Ultimately, secession should still be difficult, but it could be used with more regularity. Ideally, there should be an existing region that is recognized, replete with democratic and free market systems that should be implemented as the best mechanism to gain wealth and achieve longstanding stability.[81] The new government should work to ensure that minority rights are upheld, peace should prevail since a major reason why war has been removed, and the international community should work to enable peaceful relations to continue.

Secession should remain a difficult process wherein political parties should represent separatist aspirations and ensure that democratic rules

---

80. Peacemaking connotes an active form of making peace, rather than peacekeeping after a conflict. Attorney, Ken Sande, argues that there are six biblical responses to make peace rather than enter conflict: overlook an offense, reconciliation, negotiation, mediation, arbitration, and accountability. These strategies are designed for resolving interpersonal conflict, but are applicable to international relations (Sande, *The Peace Maker*, 25–27).

81. Grudem and Asmus, *The Poverty of Nations*.

are followed through stringent institutions in democratic states. But, in cases of authoritarianism where these democratic possibilities do not exist, partition is a better strategy than ongoing war. Secession should not be the sole option when war breaks out; otherwise, the negative incentive increases to start a war in order to create an independent state from a remote territory that is governed reasonably fairly in its everyday circumstances. It is not biblical to create conditions that will heighten tensions and intensify the likelihood of conflagration.

Using Secession for a Romans 13 "Good"

Since many post-colonial countries were created by European powers in the sixteenth through the nineteenth centuries using very arbitrary lines based on European standards often lumping disparate ethnic, linguistic, and religious groups into one state, it is not surprising that conflict has arisen along some of these fault lines in the modern era. Recall, for example, the longstanding conflict in Sudan. Perhaps what is surprising is why more conflicts have not occurred along these fissures. By providing a mechanism to undo some of these lines, stability can return, and economic development can better flourish.

Also recall the case of East Timor in Southeast Asia, wherein a line crudely bifurcates a relatively small island. Or, utilizing another example, such as Somaliland (historically known as British Somaliland) in the north of Somalia, secession could be used as a means of developing peace in a war-torn region. The territory of Somaliland is essentially a de facto state, but it is inherently pegged to the concerns of Mogadishu. Since Somaliland is not an independent country, it is more difficult for the region to obtain foreign direct investment because most outside observers only see the failed state of Somalia. The government of Somaliland does not have the latitude to sign international agreements or work with other countries to better trade networks.[82] A change here could improve the region as a whole, and diminish instability in Somalia. It would also allow Somaliland to sign international agreements, and to develop more sophisticated trading patterns to grow the economy.

Perhaps more pressing, secession could be used as a peacemaking or post-conflict option in both Syria and Iraq. Conflict in these two countries seems intractable, has claimed the lives of hundreds of thousands, and led to the displacement of millions. As the American sociologist Ann Hironaka has shown in her book Neverending Wars (2005), civil wars in the post-World

82. Kaplan, "*The Remarkable Story of Somaliland*," 143

War II era last much longer, but are also fought with greater casualties as an outcome.[83] With entrenched civil wars in Syria and Iraq, an available option is secession for various regions of these countries, which would allow for better, more localized rule. Iraqi Kurdistan should be granted the ability to hold a binding referendum on independence—this would serve to bolster nascent democratic institutions in the country, and potentially liberate the world's largest ethnic group without a state. The central government in Iraq is heavily opposed to such an independence referendum, but, like Somaliland, Iraqi Kurdistan operates with a large amount of autonomy. In tandem with this point, Iraqi Kurds have created their own form of defense in order to make it difficult for a dictator to terrorize their population, someone akin the Saddam Hussein in the 1980s.

Independence for Iraqi Kurdistan would be contingent upon gaining permission from Turkey in order to work towards peace in the broader Middle East region. Most outside observers may argue that Ankara will never agree to a Kurdish state. But, incentives could be provided to Turkey as a means of solving a major historical grievance, and source of friction within Turkey and Iraq.

Solving this problem would settle the longstanding dispute over the Treaty of Sévres in 1920, and its succeeding agreement, the Treaty of Lausanne in 1923; in essence, Sévres promised the Kurds a state in exchange for assistance in World War I, great powers reneged upon the Sévres agreement culminating in some of the problems of the contemporary Middle East.[84] Put simply, the Kurds are the largest ethnic group in the world without a state. As already demonstrated earlier, ethnic groups without states are often the victims of genocide. Many Christians and other minorities live in this region and have suffered immensely under dictators like Saddam Hussein and recalcitrant terrorist organizations like ISIS.[85]

Concomitantly, the Partition of Sunni and Shia areas of Iraq should also be considered if Iraq does not stabilize in the near future. Both groups have sought to dominate the other in recent years, with the net result of oscillating power between the two sects and always a significant loss of life. In recent years, for example, under former prime minister, Nouri al-Maliki, Shia dominance over Sunni in Iraq has in large measure contributed to the rise of ISIS. Giving Sunni-regions of Iraq an opportunity to gain independence could undercut the conditions for the rise of recalcitrant groups like al-Qaeda and ISIS, since disenfranchised Sunni Muslims see no other

83. Hironaka, *Neverending Wars.*
84. Shlaim, *War and Peace in the Middle East*, 13–14.
85. Belz, *They say we are infidels*, 255–267.

alternative than to join a radical group in order to fight against Shia rule, and to connect Muslims around the world.[86]

Syria is perhaps even more complex than Iraq, but leeway could be provided for in developing independent Alawite, Sunni, Druze, and Kurdish areas. In theory, one or more regions could simply secede from Syria, which might serve to pacify the rest of the society; it is not necessarily to suggest that Syria needs to be divided into four, only that partitioning one (or two) parts could better lead to peace. It could also solve the current impasse between American and Russian foreign policy positions in Syria; Washington insists that Syria can only move forward without Assad, Moscow is equally adamant that Assad must remain.

Of course, neither Iraq nor Syria is a majority Christian territory. But, the principles outlined here could provide a pathway forward to peace, if the five-pronged argument is followed. The modern Middle East will not magically transform into an oasis of peace and prosperity, but a new option could be tried to shift the status quo that has been plagued with violence since the 1980s. Alongside the largescale loss of life, millions of people have been forced to flee from their homes, endure horrific political and sexual violence, and catastrophic loss of income. A different option is unlikely to provide a panacea, but is at the very least unlikely to make the geopolitical situation worse.

Tweaking international norms

As noted earlier, the post-World War II international norm that borders must not change is a cornerstone of the modern international system, except, as shown with numerous cases in this work that borders have actually changed pretty regularly since 1945. The premise that borders must not change is actually a misnomer and exists because it is coupled with the idea of protecting national sovereignty. Decoupling these concepts is useful because secession has been shown to be a useful post-conflict option; likewise, it could also be utilized for the purposes of peacemaking. Annexing countries, or regions of countries, should remain illegal, and as a contravention of international law. Not much will ultimately change in the international community; however, there will be more flexibility towards using secession as an option to resolve protracted and longstanding civil wars. This excludes any attempt to revive an identity including reviving dead languages, inventing traditions, and purporting pristine purities.[87] Advocating secessionist claims on ancient

---

86. Chua, *Political Tribes*, 114.

87. Gellner, *Nations and Nationalism*, 56.

myths and symbols that have recently been revived presents a danger to the stability of the country, and the wider region.[88] Only modern secessionist movements with known languages, cultures, and grievances, are eligible for statehood under this model. Countries could continue to solve the problem on their own, but the loss of life—people made in God's image—has been staggering, so other options, like secession, should be presented in some, narrowly bounded situations.

This position does require action by the international community. Since its foundation in 1945, the UN Security Council has been divided on many of the most prominent conflicts around the world. The Permanent Five members of the UNSC typically view the world differently. This intransigence will likely continue given that the USA, UK, and France tend to form one bloc in opposition to China and Russia in the other bloc. However, there may be opportunities to reach a solution on areas of shared concerns such as Iraq and Syria. China and Russia are reluctant to discuss secessionism for fear of their own partition, or concerns over sovereignty, but both have made recent exceptions. With Russia's intervention in forcefully separating Abkhazia and South Ossetia[89] in Georgia,[90] and their annexation of Crimea, it is clear that Moscow is not opposed to changing borders. Moreover, given China's lack of condemnation of the Russo-Georgia War and conflict in Ukraine, neither Beijing nor Moscow is explicitly opposed to change. Although both military actions violated international law, the intransigence over Iraq and Syria could be muted if the right deal was presented. More lives would be saved, and the great powers satisfied with the new balance of power in the region.

Another issue, historically, is that the idea of a small country cannot work. This is not an international norm, per se, but secession—and the creation of new, small states—is generally considered a faux pas. The premise, here, was that smaller countries would be invaded—and assimilated—by much larger states. Countries can suffer death.[91] After all, who remembers the Grand Duchy of Hesse? Or, the Cape of Good Hope? These entities still remain in the history books, but they functioned relatively well in their respective eras. Nothing precluded them from continuing, except by being absorbed

---

88. Kaufman, *Modern Hatreds*, 30.

89. There is a longer history here, especially pertaining to the early 1990s after the Soviet Union dissolved, with Georgia quashing guerilla warfare in both regions (Kaufman, *Modern Hatreds*, 85).

90. Russia's stated goal was to protect ethnic Abkhazians and Ossetians, many of whom were also Russian citizens from Georgia (King, *Extreme Politics*, 142; Giuliano, *Constructing Grievance*, 197).

91. Fazal, *State Death*.

by larger states. In the post-1945 world, however, the concept that national sovereignty matters means that smaller states cannot, by international law, be annexed. Small states can flourish, much like Norway after its secession from the Kingdom of Sweden in 1905.[92] Where government is localized, it often responds better to the needs of the average citizen. Just like comparing a small company with a large corporation, the average worker is more likely to have a voice when individuals are known by their leaders.

In international organizations, small states already play a considerable role in world affairs. With 193 member states of the UN, the organization is not going to be extraordinarily impacted by an additional dozen members. The UN leaders could also play a role in peacemaking by empowering an international institution to make peace in the midst of otherwise intractable conflicts, especially with the support of UNSC members.

Conclusion: Utilizing
the 1 Kings 12 model

The central argument in the latter half of this chapter is that although secession should be granted on a limited basis, the option of dividing countries as a means of peacemaking, or post-conflict resolution should have wider appeal. Critics will point to the possibility of this idea causing more wars because secessionists around the world will see it as a means of creating independent states. In effect, secessionist claims could beget more secessionism, which will ultimately lead to thousands of micro-states. These critiques are valid. However, the central premise in the argument here is that if secession is used only in intractable and overtly violent cases, very few people will want to go through the costs associated with only the possibility of a resultant independent state as the outcome. Secession should only be granted if the five conditions are met as outlined earlier in the chapter. Or, in cases where an independence referendum has been negotiated through democratic means. Only under those two scenarios should secessionism be promoted as an option for solving national and identity issues.

This proposal will mean, for example, that Syrian dictator, Bashar al-Assad—a modern day Rehoboam—will have some incentives to better treat his people, and listen to their demands rather than violently oppressing them as a means of maintaining his power. Otherwise, his calculation will ultimately lead to the partition of Syria, and his sphere of governance. The same conclusion could help alter the future of Iraq, which has, in essence, been embroiled in some form of overt or covert conflict since the Gulf War

---

92. Duerr, *Secessionism and the European Union*, 152.

in 1991. If similar conflicts continue in Yemen and Libya, the international community will have further crises with which to deal because of an inability to find workable solutions—the concerns of today: the bloodshed in the Middle East, the resultant migrant crisis in Europe and elsewhere, and the instability caused by these events on the international system, might seem mild if these conflicts are allowed to fester.

Secession should be considered to be part of a broader range of policy tools when seeking to help cases of intractable civil war, or situations where a shaky ceasefire exists. By allowing for secession, with the five caveats noted earlier in this article, severe conflicts could be terminated. The peacemaking or post-conflict solution could better resolve interminable situations, and present a biblical example to diffusing wars.

Although secession should be considered, it is not automatically the correct decision. In this chapter, the example of Libya has been purported. Historically, three major regions exist into which Libya could plausibly be divided today—Tripolitania, Cyrenaica, and Fezzan.[93] It is, however, worth remembering that Libya encompasses 140 different tribes,[94] such that it is simultaneously hard to restore the country under one government but also difficult to divide it into three pieces. Various peacemaking options should be negotiated, with secession as one of the possible outcomes.[95]

---

93. Marshall, *Prisoners of Geography*, 122–123.

94. Chua, *Political Tribes*, 34.

95. Duerr, "A proposal for the future of U.S. counterinsurgency," 111.

Chapter 6

Transnationalism

> For our citizenship is in heaven, from which also we eagerly
> wait for a Savior, the Lord Jesus Christ; who will transform
> the body of our humble state into conformity with the body
> of His glory, by the exertion of the power that He has even to
> subject all things to Himself.

—Philippians 3:20–21

THE ABOVE VERSES IN the book of Philippians point to coterminous citizenship for all followers of Christ. On the one hand, each Christian has a citizenship in heaven. On the other hand, we all have bodies, which live in the world and are subject to the rulers of this world as outlined in chapter 2 (Romans 13:1–7). Previous chapters in this book have already established the argument that most followers of Christ need to play some role in their respective countries. It obviously depends on circumstance, but each follower of Christ is called to make disciples (Matthew 28:19) and to be subject to rulers where applicable. There is an earthly place for each Christian, which can change, but generally requires living Christianly in a country and having an influence—whether modest in the case of most, or significant in the case of Christian political or economic leaders—on the government of that national state.

This chapter examines the second sentence of the first paragraph— that Christians have a heavenly citizenship. But, not only a heavenly citizenship in the future when the Christ follower gets to heaven, a real and also veritable linkage with other believers in the resurrection of Jesus

Christ, on earth, at the present time. In some ways, the intellectual back-drop of this point is to build upon the concept of Saint Augustine's City of God,[1] wherein there is a human city and a city of God.[2] It is a paradox in a way to hold multiple allegiances at the same time, but, Scripture also presents a paradox: to live on earth to influence the world for Christ, whilst knowing at any point the world means little, and the Christ-follower upon death will be united with Jesus.

This chapter first lays out the biblical basis for transnationalism through the Book of Acts, and then for greater linkages and solidarity with Christians across the world in both the New and the Old Testaments. It then discusses transnationalism in light of evangelism, as well as the case for transnationalism rather than globalism. Finally, this chapter concludes with an examination of transnationalism and its impact on various aspects of public policy.

Transnationalism and the Book of Acts

The Book of Acts is stunning in its telling of the expansion of the Christian faith. Almost flippantly, Luke, the author of Acts, notes the rapidity with which the gospel spread, not only as a message, but the number of people who accepted Christ. What is also noteworthy, however, is that people from all over the world at that time hear the message, and then proclaim faith in Christ. For example, from the establishment of the church in Acts 1, to the Day of Pentecost in Acts 2, the swiftness with which the gospel of Jesus Christ travels is breathtaking.[3]

In Acts 1:8, the Christians were centered in Jerusalem, and then told to go out into nearby Judea and Samaria, and then to the remotest parts of the world. In addition to these regions, listed within Acts are "Syria, Cyprus, many cities in Asia Minor, Macedonia, Greece, and finally Rome."[4] In Acts 2, notably, the whole situation changes when, in the aftermath of the death and resurrection of Christ, the presence of the Holy Spirit begins.[5] Acts 2:1:12 reads:

> "1 When the day of Pentecost had come, they were all together in one place. 2 And suddenly there came from heaven a noise

1. Augustine, *City of God*.
2. Carson and Moo, *An Introduction to the New Testament*, 38.
3. Escobar, *The New Global Mission*, 120.
4. Carson and Moo, *An Introduction to the New Testament*, 285.
5. Willimon, *Acts*.

like a violent rushing wind, and it filled the whole house where they were sitting. 3 And there appeared to them tongues as of fire distributing themselves, and they rested on each one of them. 4 And they were all filled with the Holy Spirit and began to speak with other tongues, as the Spirit was giving them utterance. 5 Now there were Jews living in Jerusalem, devout men from every nation under heaven. 6 And when this sound occurred, the crowd came together, and were bewildered because each one of them was hearing them speak in his own language. 7 They were amazed and astonished, saying, "Why, are not all these who are speaking Galileans? 8 And how is it that we each hear them in our own language to which we were born? 9 Parthians and Medes and Elamites, and residents of Mesopotamia, Judea and Cappadocia, Pontus and Asia, 10 Phrygia and Pamphylia, Egypt and the districts of Libya around Cyrene, and visitors from Rome, both Jews and proselytes, 11 Cretans and Arabs—we hear them in our own tongues speaking of the mighty deeds of God." 12 And they all continued in amazement and great perplexity, saying to one another, "What does this mean?"

In the early verses of Acts 2, the Holy Spirit begins a monumental work in the lives of early Christians. There is a connection here with transnationalism. In particular, the early Christians came from across the Roman Empire—the new faith was already transnational given that the backdrop of Christ's ministry was designed to reach all people.[6] Acts 2:9–11 is particularly interesting in that people from across the eastern and southern parts of the Roman Empire are in Jerusalem and come to faith. Verses 9 through 11 read like a geography quiz of different sections of the Empire. Yet, all of these Christians are together in Jerusalem, so, in a sense, Christianity is born as a transnational faith. Later, Acts 2:36–41 continues this update on the work of the Holy Spirit:

"36 Therefore let all the house of Israel know for certain that God has made Him both Lord and Christ—this Jesus whom you crucified." 37 Now when they heard this, they were pierced to the heart, and said to Peter and the rest of the apostles, "Brethren, what shall we do?" 38 Peter said to them, "Repent, and each of you be baptized in the name of Jesus Christ for the forgiveness of your sins; and you will receive the gift of the Holy Spirit. 39 For the promise is for you and your children and for all who are far off, as many as the Lord our God will call to Himself." 40 And with many other words he solemnly testified and kept on exhorting them, saying,

6. Willimon, *Acts*.

"Be saved from this perverse generation!" 41 So then, those who
had received his word were baptized; and that day there were
added about three thousand souls."

In the latter part of Acts 2, the work of the Holy Spirit begins in earnest as the
disciples grasp what Christ's ministry on earth was actually about—a spiritual,
rather than a political revolution. And while the message starts in Jerusalem,
this is just the beginning. The number of Christians begins to grow not only
in Jerusalem, but then out into the wider world. For example, the concluding
part of the discussion when Peter proclaims Christ is the Messiah in Acts
2:41, the people accepted his message and "about three thousand were added
to their number that day." Luke continues in Acts 2:42:

> "42 They were continually devoting themselves to the apos-
> tles' teaching and to fellowship, to the breaking of bread and
> to prayer. 43 Everyone kept feeling a sense of awe; and many
> wonders and signs were taking place through the apostles. 44
> And all those who had believed were together and had all things
> in common; 45 and they began selling their property and pos-
> sessions and were sharing them with all, as anyone might have
> need. 46 Day by day continuing with one mind in the temple,
> and breaking bread from house to house, they were taking their
> meals together with gladness and sincerity of heart, 47 praising
> God and having favor with all the people. And the Lord was
> adding to their number day by day those who were being saved."

To repeat, in Acts 2:47, Luke quickly notes that "the Lord was adding to their
number day by day those who were being saved." The number of people coming to faith was extremely fast and the people becoming Christians were from
disparate parts of the Roman Empire—a territory that spanned dozens of
modern day countries. The national origin had no bearing on whether or not
they could accept Christ. This is evident throughout the Book of Acts, in a
range of different passages, both central to the storyline, and in passing.

In Acts 4:4, the gospel is disseminated again, and about five thousand
men came to know Christ. Even though this took place in Jerusalem, people
from across the empire would come to the city. In Acts 4:36–37, the reader is
introduced to Joseph (Barnabas), a Levite of Cyprian birth who gave money
to the apostles. He buys a plot of land, then sells it, and gives all the profits to
the apostles. His background and national origin is almost an added piece of
information, but it clearly connotes that national identity is in no way a hindrance to the spread of the gospel. In Acts 5:16, the text notes that as people
were being healed, and then coming to faith, that people from beyond Jerusalem, albeit within the vicinity of the city, were coming to hear the message.

Israel is specifically references in verses 31 and 35. Thus far, even though many different people have accepted the Christian faith, the gospel has still been told in a limited geographic vicinity around Jerusalem.

Acts 6 starts by describing a dispute between Hellenistic (Greek) Jews and native Hebrews on account of the treatment of widows (Acts 6:1). Once again, the theme is that the gospel is beginning to spread throughout Jerusalem to the point that culture begins to impact relationships between Greeks and Hebrews. The exhortation from Luke is for unity. Regardless of the national and linguistic differences of the Christians, the transnational character of the faith should be the uniting factor, to overcome worldly differences that have been learned through culture and language.

As a mechanism of bridging the divide between Hellenistic Jews and Hebrews, seven men are chosen to lead the church (Acts 6:3) and to undertake ministries inside the church. Acts 6:5 then describes these seven men who were chosen to go out and share the gospel. One man, Nicolas, a proselyte from Antioch is specifically referenced as someone distinct in the group, an almost offhanded reference to his usefulness in witnessing to people in, and near, Antioch. Acts 6:7 still references Jerusalem as the number of people coming to faith in Christ continues to grow. Despite this, Acts 6:8–9 references one of the apostles, Stephen, facing arguments from men from Cyrene, Alexandria, Cilicia, and Asia—again, diverse regions in the eastern and southern parts of the Roman Empire. The apostle, Stephen, in chapter 7, then defends himself in front of the council wherein he describes Abraham's life in Genesis noting his movement from Mesopotamia to Haran, in the land of the Chaldeans. Stephen references the story of the people of Israel in Acts 7:6 that they would become aliens in Egypt for 400 years. The early part of Acts 7 recounts the history of Jacob and Joseph in Egypt in Genesis 37–50 noting the extensive travel between (what becomes) Israel and Egypt.

In Acts 8, there are several important narratives. First, Saul is introduced. He is described as the ultimate persecutor of Christians, especially in Jerusalem, but also in outlying Judea and Samaria (Acts 8:1). Given Saul's persecution, believers in Christ begin to flee to other parts of the empire (Acts 8:4) and inadvertently, the gospel spreads because Christians have moved (through fear of persecution) to other regions. Second, the apostle Philip is noted in particular because he begins sharing the gospel in Samaria (Acts 8:5). Philip begins to share with the crowd, and even a magician named Simon comes to faith in Christ (Acts 8:13). Finally, in Acts 8:23, the reader is introduced to an Ethiopian eunuch from the government of Queen

Candace and met by Philip,[7] who shares the meaning of a prophetic portion of Scripture foretelling the arrival of Jesus Christ in Isaiah 53. The eunuch comes to faith after an explanation from Philip, and then is baptized. Little is mentioned in Scripture about this encounter, but national origin and ethnic background are obviously of no hindrance to the gospel being disseminated.[8] It is also likely that the Ethiopian is the first gentile convert.[9]

Next, in Acts 10, the apostles meet with Cornelius, a Roman centurion (Acts 10:1), who, like many others already, becomes a believer in—and follower of—Jesus Christ.[10] One has to imagine extra-biblically as to the impact that Cornelius had on his fellow soldiers and their families across the Roman Empire. The apostle Peter is used to share the gospel with Cornelius. But, in doing so, Peter has to travel to Caesarea—in essence, where the gospel begins to be shared in cities and regions of the Roman Empire outside the direct vicinity of Jerusalem. Cornelius meets Peter in Acts 10:25 and immediately becomes a follower of Christ. From this point forward, the faith becomes truly transnational.

In Acts 11:19–21, the text notes how the apostle Stephen faced persecution in Phoenicia, Cyprus, and Antioch, but how others had come to faith, especially in significant numbers. This idea is built upon in Acts 13:4 where the apostle Paul (known as Saul in Acts 9—the zealous persecutor of Christians who miraculously comes to faith) undertakes his first missionary journey leaving from Seleucia near Antioch on the Mediterranean coast to Salamis and Paphos on the island of Cyprus. From here, the gospel is disseminated widely. In total, Paul undertakes three missionary journeys (The first in Acts 13:1–14:28, the second in Acts 15:36–18:22, and the third in Acts 18:23–21:16, as well as a journey to Rome (Acts 21:17–28:31).

Transnationalism throughout the Bible

Scripture consists of 66 books written by 39 or 40 different authors (depending on who penned Hebrews) via the inspiration of the Holy Spirit. It is a document that spans time and geographic location. Yet, there is a stunning unity to the Bible. These next sections explore the theme of transnationalism. Given the aforementioned geographic dispersion of Christians throughout the world, it makes sense that the New Testament would speak of a transnational faith. The next section begins in the New Testament. But, it is important to

7. Carson and Moo. *An Introduction to the New Testament*, 287.

8. Escobar, *The New Global Mission*, 123.

9. Jenkins, *The New Faces of Christianity*, 49.

10. Holmes, *Just War*.

reconcile that the Old Testament also discusses numerous themes of transnationalism as well. In that section, four different examples are provided beyond what has been discussed earlier in this book. Therefore, once the discussion of the New Testament concludes, the Old Testament is also investigated to see how the theme of transnationalism is described.

Transnationalism in the New Testament

As noted in chapter 2, Christians live under an earthly government described in Romans 13:1–7. Followers of Christ should be obedient to government structures. Of course, Christians should exercise their own voice to change, alter, and persuade government policy—this is obviously much easier in a mature, democratic system, or where a Christian happens to have influence in an authoritarian state. There are numerous sections of the New Testament that speak to the unity of believers wherein Christians can help one another regardless of circumstances.

The main point here is that the state, under which the Christian lives, has sovereignty. However, there is a tension—the life of a Christian is juxtaposed on living in a location, whilst also loving other Christians regardless of where they live in the world. For example, another theme of the New Testament in particular is the idea that Christians are set apart from the world, and do share transnational linkages. The book of 1 Peter is very specific in this regard. 1 Peter 2:9–10 reads:

> "9 But you are a chosen race, a royal priesthood, a holy nation, a people for God's own possession, so that you may proclaim the excellencies of Him who has called you out of darkness into His marvelous light; 10 for you once were not a people, but now you are the people of God; you had not received mercy, but now you have received mercy."

Perhaps the most interesting component of 1 Peter 2:9–10 is the idea that believers constitute their own nation under God. Not only are Christians a nation, but believers in Christ also constitute a chosen race. The term "race" is very interesting because it implies a oneness to all followers of Christ beyond skin color. Built in to this wording is also the admonition that racism of any kind is unbiblical.[11] Transnationalism, it seems, is built into the fabric of Christianity. Even with the tension of an individual believer living in a particular country, Christians are linked through their

---

11. Ham and Ware, *One Nation, One Blood.*

common faith in Christ. Throughout the New Testament, several pertinent examples of this idea arise in the text.

Later in 2 Peter, the author, Simon Peter refers to his time on earth as fleeting. In 2 Peter 1:13–14, specifically he refers to his earthly dwelling, his body, as limited. Ultimately, that he will soon die and be with the Lord. In this respect, there is a temporal component to life, especially national life. Human beings will spend a time on earth, but then eternity in heaven. In that regard, especially for people getting older, national identity means less and less for the follower of Christ. Christians should be careful to characterize any people as "enemies" in light of eternal ramifications. Geopolitical situations can change, and all people are made in the image of God. As an example, American missionaries prayed with members of the Soviet KGB as the USSR was in turmoil in the late-1980s and early 1990s before its ultimate dissolution.[12] None of this should dismiss national identity, or make any assumptions on the length of someone's life, but to realize that all humans will eventually die, such that Christians avoid living their whole lives with "enemies."

Throughout Paul's epistles, the theme remains the same as in 1 and 2 Peter. This section of the chapter discusses the letters to the Ephesians, Philippians, Colossians, and Galatians. Even though all of these cities are located in different parts of the empire, there is a striking unity that Paul describes when discussing how Christians should interact with one another. Ephesus, a port city in modern-day Turkey; Philippi, a port city in modern-day Greece; Colossae, an interior city within modern-day Turkey; and Galatia, a larger region near Colossae.

In Ephesians 1–3, the apostle Paul outlines how the Law of Moses changed with the life, ministry, death, and resurrection of Jesus Christ as it pertains to all believers. In many respects, this whole section of Scripture points to the idea of oneness in the lord Jesus Christ, over and above all other forms of identification. Ephesians 2:19 exhorts: "So then you are no longer strangers and aliens, but you are fellow citizens with the saints, and are of God's household." The idea here is that all believers are connected through Christ, and cannot be viewed as strangers and aliens, even if these Christians are refugees, asylum seekers, or tourists in another country. In context, this means that all Christians share the same heavenly citizenship, and even if their earthly citizenships may differ, they share the same cause and belief in Christ. The passage does not definitively tackle immigration into a country; although, Christians in all capable countries should

12. Yancey, *Praying with the KGB*, 29–37.

consider what they can do for less fortunate people—this idea is discussed in more detail in chapter 3.

The passage continues by discussing Christ as the cornerstone of the church. In Ephesians 3:6, "to be specific, that the Gentiles are fellow heirs and fellow members of the body, and fellow partakers of the promise in Christ Jesus through the gospel." Gentiles and Jews are unified in Christ.[13] Paul continues in Ephesians 3:8, "To me, the very least of all saints, this grace was given, to preach to the Gentiles the unfathomable riches of Christ." In essence, Paul is laying out the need to preach the gospel to all people, and when they come to know Christ as their personal savior, there is no distinction between believers, no hierarchy, and no special place for only certain types of people. No nationality or ethnic background is given prominence over any other. There is a level of unity and equality, even on earth, amongst all followers of Christ.

Even though Ephesians 4–6 is markedly different from Ephesians 1–3 in that the letters switches to a different topic, Ephesians 4:4–5 lays out a similar message: "there is one body and one spirit, just as you were called in one hope of your calling; one Lord, one faith, one baptism, one God and Father of all who is over all and through all and in all."

In Philippians 4:21–22, the apostle Paul exhorts believers to "Greet every saint in Christ Jesus. The brethren who are with me greet you. All the saints greet you, especially those of Caesar's household." This verse is very interesting in the sense that Paul has seemingly won converts throughout the city of Rome, and even in the house of Caesar. Throughout the Roman Empire, the political backdrop of the New Testament, numerous provinces existed. Despite unity in the Empire, there were major distinctions between people across the massive empire that, at its height, spanned from modern day England and Wales in the northwest to Israel and Kuwait in the southeast, Portugal and northern Algeria in the southwest to parts of Ukraine and Russia around the Black Sea. A massive empire was very heterogeneous ethnically, nationally, and socially. Roman citizenship was highly prized, as was residence in Rome. Yet, even people in Caesar's household have come to know Christ and send their greetings to other believers across of all of these societal distinctions. They are on equal footing with other Christians living elsewhere.

In Colossians 1:16, the apostle Paul writes, "For by Him all things were created, both in the heavens and on earth, visible and invisible, whether thrones or dominions or rulers or authorities—all things have been created through Him and for Him." While the things of this world may seem

---

13. Carson and Moo, *An Introduction to the New Testament*, 481.

permanent in our lifetimes, the Lord is sovereign. To the Christians written about in the New Testament, the Roman Empire must have seemed like an eternal, powerful entity that would rule forever. Today, the remnants of the Roman Empire are interesting for tourists to view in Rome, but no tangible earthly power resides there anymore. For example, the Arch of Constantine, erected in 315 commemorating victory in the 312 Battle of Milvian Bridge is a magnificent sight in the city of Rome. After its construction in the fourth century, it presented a message as to the absolute power and might of the Roman Empire; today, it is a nice sight for tourists to observe in between stops for cappuccino and gelato. Even the Colosseum, which must have seemed like the center of the universe during the time of Christ and Paul's missionary journeys, is a mere relic of a bygone era. The splendor of the Colosseum remains on the outside, but the inside reflects that of a museum and a history lesson rather than a center of life and society.

God raises up kingdoms and leaders, and He also brings them down. The lesson for Christians is to avoid becoming too connected to a leader, or a country. Overt faith in the institutions of the world is contrary to the biblical-lens through which the Lord looks at people. Each person is located in a particular place at a particular time, therefore, he/she should serve as a good citizen of the country so that more will come to know Christ. But, at the same time, the person must also remain heavenly minded in that overt linkages exist between members of the global community of Christ followers.

In Galatians 1, the apostle Paul also notes how he used to persecute the church of God (Galatians 1:13). His reason for these actions revolved around his steadfastness for Judaism, but also notably, he was "extremely zealous for his ancestral traditions" (Galatians 1:14). The danger for the Christ follower is to do the same thing—to be zealous for our own ancestral traditions, rather than for the gospel of Jesus Christ. Each person has a distinct family history, and should pay quiet homage to those that came before him. In some cases, a person can trace her ancestry back in the same country for centuries; in other cases, a person can trace his ancestry to numerous different countries, with recent movements into the new country in which his family now resides. Looking upon one's relatives with admiration is useful, but ancestral traditions should be viewed secondarily when compared to the Christian's life and work on earth.

In sum, the theme of transnationalism—in this case, the linking of Christians across national boundaries—reverberates throughout the New Testament. Although a range of different sections of Scripture have been discussed here, particularly Paul's letters, there is a wider theme throughout the New Testament, which points to the importance of transnationalism because the gospel must be shared with all people across the world. This is a basic discipline of the Christian—an admonition, which will be shown directly later in this chapter.

Transnationalism in the Old Testament

Critics will note that the case for transnationalism has been built thus far entirely on the New Testament. Much of the Old Testament centers on the Jewish, Hebrew, and Israelite people. Thus, in the Old Testament, Scripture seems to point towards a homogenous nation-state wherein all non-Jewish people are killed, as in the case of conquering Canaan. Yet, there are exceptions to every situation, as noted earlier in various chapters of this book. Rahab is spared given her allegiance to the Israelites in the book of Joshua. She is even included in Hebrews 11 alongside other pillars of the faith, despite often being referenced to as the harlot. The harrowing story of David and Bathsheba in 2 Samuel is juxtaposed on Bathsheba's husband, noted in Scripture as Uriah the Hittite, being away fighting David's wars when David sinfully sees Bathsheba bathing on a rooftop only to summon her for sexual purposes. An examination of the entirety of David's sinfulness is not possible here, only to note that Bathsheba's husband, a Hittite, was important in his army.

Not only are there numerous examples in the New Testament, but a range of sections of Scripture in the Old Testament point towards Jesus, and his established, transnational kingdom amongst all people. Examine, for example, the Book of Jonah—specifically chapter 3.

> "1 Now the word of the Lord came to Jonah the second time, saying, 2 "Arise, go to Nineveh the great city and proclaim to it the proclamation which I am going to tell you." 3 So Jonah arose and went to Nineveh according to the word of the Lord. Now Nineveh was an exceedingly great city, a three days' walk. 4 Then Jonah began to go through the city one day's walk; and he cried out and said, "Yet forty days and Nineveh will be overthrown." 5 Then the people of Nineveh believed in God; and they called a fast and put on sackcloth from the greatest to the least of them. 6 When the word reached the king of Nineveh, he arose from his throne, laid aside his robe from him, covered himself with sackcloth and sat on the ashes. 7 He issued a proclamation and it said, "In Nineveh by the decree of the king and his nobles: Do not let man, beast, herd, or flock taste a thing. Do not let them eat or drink water. 8 But both man and beast must be covered with sackcloth; and let men call on God earnestly that each may turn from his wicked way and from the violence which is in his

hands. 9 Who knows, God may turn and relent and withdraw His burning anger so that we will not perish." 10 When God saw their deeds, that they turned from their wicked way, then God relented concerning the calamity which He had declared He would bring upon them. And He did not do it."

At the time of the writing of the Book of Jonah, the Assyrian empire was a dominant force in world politics.[14] Nineveh was its capital; one of the most powerful cities in the entire world. The Kingdom of Israel was no longer at the zenith of its power as it was under Saul, David, and especially Solomon. In Jonah 1 and 2, Jonah tries to flee from God, and the city of Nineveh with his message.[15] When he delivers the message in Jonah 3 above, Jonah is not happy that God shows his mercy to Nineveh when, in his eyes, the city should be brought to destruction. This is the key lesson of the passage: repentance. Yet, in fitting with the discussion of this chapter, a foreign city in the capital of the occupiers, repents and asks God for forgiveness. This is stunning in that God forgives the people of Nineveh—the capital of the Assyrian Empire, which would soon conquer Israel[16]—and allows them to continue, albeit with a profession for changing their ways.

What is most interesting in this section of Scripture is that Nineveh is the Washington D.C., or Beijing of its time—the center of the most (or one of the most) powerful countries/empires in the world. Yet, when the King of the Assyrians in Nineveh pleads with God for the sinful ways of his people, the city is spared. The people commit themselves to Yahweh as the almighty God who must be respected, revered, and praised. The King, located in Nineveh, not only recognizes the gravity of the situation, but acts in such a way to spare his people.

Transnationalism is also important from a tangential point through Scripture: that God is sovereign. While many countries have ancient histories, and others seem extremely powerful, the lens of history shows that countries and empires rise and fall. For example, how often do people discuss the Assyrians today? In 2 Samuel, and some other sections of Scripture, Assyria was a predominant empire that conquered the people of Israel. However, this empire and its leadership ultimately submit itself to God.

In the second Old Testament example, in Micah 4, the prophet notes:

"1 And it will come about in the last days that the mountain of the house of the Lord will be established as the chief of the mountains. It will be raised above the hills, and the peoples will stream

14. Hill and Walton, *A Survey of the Old Testament*, 496.
15. Hill and Walton, *A Survey of the Old Testament*, 501.
16. Hill and Walton, *A Survey of the Old Testament*, 496–7.

to it. 2 Many nations will come and say, "Come and let us go up
to the mountain of the Lord and to the house of the God of Jacob,
that He may teach us about His ways and that we may walk in His
paths." For from Zion will go forth the law, even the word of the
Lord from Jerusalem. 3 And He will judge between many peoples
and render decisions for mighty, distant nations. Then they will
hammer their swords into plowshares and their spears into pruning hooks; Nation will not lift up sword against nation, and never
again will they train for war. 4 Each of them will sit under his vine
and under his fig tree, with no one to make them afraid, for the
mouth of the Lord of hosts has spoken. 5 Though all the peoples
walk each in the name of his god, as for us, we will walk in the
name of the Lord our God forever and ever."

Although the rest of Micah 4 proceeds to discuss Israel, especially in the
last days, verses 1–5 are very interesting as they pertain to the idea of
transnationalism. In verse 2, for example, the prophecy is that many nations of people will go to the Lord, and ask for instruction in His ways. In
many regards, this prophecy has come true in that a growing number of
countries are becoming increasingly Christian, and want instruction in
the ways of God. Verse 3 is equally interesting in this regard: the Lord will
judge between many peoples, and will settle their disputes. In essence, a
time of peace is coming—nationalism means very little when people subject themselves to God.

The UN has attempted to take up the mantle of Micah 4:3, "Then they
will hammer their swords into plowshares and their spears into pruning
hooks; Nation will not lift up sword against nation, and never again will they
train for war." On the grounds of the UN complex on the bank of the East
River in New York, there is a grassy area with numerous monuments sporadi-
cally laid out. One particular sculpture depicts a man molding his sword into
a ploughshare, a reference to Micah 4:3, gifted to the UN from Russia.[17] In the
Hague, a city in the Netherlands, is the International Court of Justice (ICJ),
the formal legal arm of the UN that arbitrates between member states. As-
cending the central staircase of the ICJ (known as the Peace Palace) building,
one immediately sees a statue of Jesus Christ reportedly made out of melted
armaments resultant from a peace treaty that staved off a war.

To be clear, the UN is not the vehicle through which peace will be
established on earth. In a fallen world, only the return of Jesus will create
a lasting peace. However, the UN should be acknowledged for its attempt
to create a more peaceful environment, and for some successes in stopping

---

17. American pastor David Jeremiah argues that this passage is misapplied in favor
of globalism under the UN (Jeremiah, *The Coming Economic Armageddon*, 38).

war in various parts of the world. The UN is far from perfect, but using Micah 4:3, the goal is that countries should never again train for war. If nothing else, the UN provides a place wherein countries can discuss their problems, rather than quickly resort to war.

A third example of transnationalism, in the Old Testament, in Malachi 2:10, the prophet asks the following questions: "10 "Do we not all have one father? Has not one God created us? Why do we deal treacherously each against his brother so as to profane the covenant of our fathers?" The context here is Israel, but it is also relevant to all followers of Christ in that the same God is over all Christians regardless of where they live. At minimum, there is a connection between all Christians who live under and serve one God. As human beings, divisions and tensions exist, but there is a transnational unity in knowing and serving Jesus Christ.

Moving to the fourth example, tangentially, throughout the Bible, the "gentiles" is a term used to describe non-Jewish people. The term is pejorative in some cases when referring to pagan practices. However, the term is also used with openness when the gospel is delivered to the gentiles. In effect, all non-Jewish people are gentiles, which means that if the gospel is open to all gentiles, it is open to all people of the world regardless of their national, or any other identity.[18]

In Genesis 12:2–3, God in talking with Abram (later Abraham) gives him the following promise: "2 And I will make you a great nation, and I will bless you, and make your name great; and so you shall be a blessing; 3 And I will bless those who bless you, and the one who curses you I will curse. And in you all the families of the earth will be blessed." This particular section of Scripture is noteworthy because God illustrates, even in Genesis, that all the people on earth will be blessed through Abraham via this covenant.[19] In many regards, this is a foreshadowing of the arrival of Jesus, and then the spread of the gospel to the entire world through the Abrahamic line. Ephesians 3:6 then expounds upon this idea: "to be specific, that the Gentiles are fellow heirs and fellow members of the body, and fellow partakers of the promise in Christ Jesus through the gospel." The blessing of Abraham to the entire world came to the gentiles through Jesus Christ, which shows that God had a plan for the gentile population even from the beginning. Transnationalism is a component part of the Bible—one glaringly obvious in the New Testament, but ultimately rooted in the Old Testament. Taken as a complete thread, the gospel of Christ is evident in the Old Testament, as much as it is in the New Testament.

18. Escobar, *The New Global Mission*, 158.
19. Hill and Walton, *A Survey of the Old Testament*, 67.

And, even though nationalism seems like a predominant theme in the Old Testament, with God the Father, the Son, and the Holy Spirit as the linking point, transnationalism is also apparent.

Evangelism and Transnationalism

> "16 But the eleven disciples proceeded to Galilee, to the mountain which Jesus had designated. 17 When they saw Him, they worshiped Him; but some were doubtful. 18 And Jesus came up and spoke to them, saying, "All authority has been given to Me in heaven and on earth. 19 Go therefore and make disciples of all the nations, baptizing them in the name of the Father and the Son and the Holy Spirit, 20 teaching them to observe all that I commanded you; and lo, I am with you always, even to the end of the age.""

One of the central commands for followers of Christ is to share the gospel, and to make disciples of all nations, as noted in the above section of Scripture in Matthew 28:16–20. The obvious point here is that people across the world must be given an opportunity to hear about salvation. What is not so obvious, though, especially for people without significant experience with evangelism is the transnational nature of sharing the gospel. Often missionaries, from numerous different countries, work together to share the gospel in a specific region or country, and begin to train local pastors and teachers to lead churches once enough local nationals have become followers of Christ, and have matured in their walks with Christ. Transnationalism, therefore, is intimately interconnected with the idea of evangelism. In order for people to be discipled, they must become followers of Christ. In investigating the sheer number of people around the world, in the billions, who have not heard about Jesus Christ, let alone accepted him as Lord and savior, transnational linkages are important for the future of the church. This future of all people is especially pertinent in a vision of heaven that is provided in Revelation 7:9–10:

> "9 After these things I looked, and behold, a great multitude which no one could count, from every nation and all tribes and peoples and tongues, standing before the throne and before the Lamb, clothed in white robes, and palm branches were in their hands; 10 and they cry out with a loud voice, saying, "Salvation to our God who sits on the throne, and to the Lamb.""

The idea here is explicit: people from every nation, tribe, people, and language will be standing before the throne of God. In order for this to occur, the obvious statement is that Christ followers have to work together to share the gospel, and to make disciples across the entire world. One country may have significant resources to shape where and how the gospel is disseminated, but, ultimately, it takes interaction and coordination between people of many different countries to be successful.

Transnationalism, not globalism

In chapter 1, the typology in Table 1.1 noted six different major types of national identity. These points were arranged on a continuum from no real sense of national identity (globalism) to hyper-national identity. From left to right, the categories were listed as follows: globalism (or post-nationalism), regionalism, patriotism, nationalism, colonialism, and hypernationalism (or ultranationalism). The argument made in chapter 1 was that it is better for the average follower of Christ to fall between patriotism and nationalism. However, in light of this discussion on transnationalism, some additional information will better draw out the argument.

The question of internationalism versus nationalism in evangelical Christian circles is one that is debated periodically. "Christian Internationalism" does not necessarily equate to globalism, but shares some common features of the argument. There are components of this debate, which serve as a very important rejoinder to the argument laid out in this book that the ideal position for a Christian on a continuum of national identity is in favor of patriotism and/or nationalism, as opposed to any other selection.

This debate on Christian Internationalism is particularly pertinent in the United States when it comes to Christianity and the culture; often discussed are how American Christians react to material possessions, responsible consumerism, and the roots of poverty.[20] What are the boundaries of the American political system and culture as they pertain to following Christ? Another related topic is war, most recently debating the Iraq War, and why some American Christians mourn the loss of other Americans, but never the deaths of Iraqis.[21] Without polling, this point is a difficult one to measure, but there is an important point concerning mourning the deaths of one set of people over others. In this sense, the accusation is that some American Christians are prone to "myopic" views of the world. A central reason in this line of thinking is that people become attached to nationalism

20. Claiborne, *The Irresistible Revolution.*
21. Claiborne, *The Irresistible Revolution.*

is that they desire community, which can be found in loving others and in living in community as Christians.[22]

In the Christian Internationalism versus patriotism debate, the internationalist viewpoint is that national loyalty is inherently antithetical to Christ's teachings.[23] Moreover, nationalism can result in the deification of the country even if Christ and nation are intertwined.[24] If nationalism becomes an idol in which a Christian relies, instead of God, then this ideology has to be properly bounded in how it applies to the life of the follower of Christ. Some authors argue that the internationalist view is that Christians must rediscover the principles that drove the early church and bring about the kingdom of God through looking at the world wherein all people are made in God's image, and are worthy of equal respect. This view is sometimes extended to patriotism and political participation such that the argument is to warn Christians about overt participation or hope in politics and should not identify with one national identity.[25]

There are useful admonitions in the Christian Internationalism view such that Christ is not a white-American Christian since some Christians intertwine the Bible with favorability with their country. These points need to be strongly contested. However, the Christian Internationalism view has some shortcomings in that leaders are raised up by God. Additionally, without some proactive policy on the world stage by followers of Christ, there is a vacuum that is left to people who do not read the Bible. Some of these people are capable of some very good actions, but people in leadership are often inclined to take from others. The same logic applies to Christian police officers. Without Bible-believing members of law enforcement, the security of the society is prone to questions of honesty.

Sections of the arguments regarding "Christian Internationalism" must check the extent of the argument for Christian nationalism and patriotism, for which this book advocates. In his book *Chosen Nation*, Braden P. Anderson opens the discussion with a description of a painting by the artist John McNaughton titled, *One Nation under God*.[26] Herein, Anderson notes that Jesus is depicted as a Caucasian-American in the painting replete with bible verses and the US Constitution. "Behind Christ stands an array of figures from American history, and behind them, the United States Capitol and Supreme Court buildings, as well as the US flag, occupying the highest point

---

22. Claiborne, *The Irresistible Revolution*.

23. Claiborne and Haw, *Jesus for President*; Anderson, *Chosen Nation*, 150.

24. Koyzis, *Political Visions & Illusions*, 97.

25. Claiborne and Haw, *Jesus for President*.

26. Anderson, *Chosen Nation*, xi.

in the painting, save the Statue of Freedom atop the Capitol dome."[27] This overview of a painting captures nicely the critique leveled by "Christian Internationalists" against the intertwined nature of how some Christians view Jesus as favoring the United States. In this light, the Christian internationalist view of national identity is antithetical to Christ's teachings.[28]

Although some of the points should be taken very seriously, the danger in the "Christian Internationalism" argument is that it extends towards globalism (also sometimes called post-nationalism) which, falls outside of the boundaries, I argue, of where a Christian can fall along the nationalism continuum in chapter 1. As noted in an earlier chapter, if some authors explicitly portend towards transnationalism (rather than globalism), there are still many benefits of his argument, albeit properly bound in very specific circumstances. However, as also argued in chapter 2, the Christ follower should maintain a coterminous relationship with God and with a country given the ability to influence the world for Christ through the country if the vehicle is applicable. This argument is unpacked more fully in the next section, but is worth mentioning here given the dangers of relying too heavily on globalism. Transnationalism, after all, is juxtaposed on having a national identity (or two) *and* an identity in Christ with a heavenly citizenship. With a rejection of some elements of national identity, globalism could become the mainstay for the Christian. In the scenario of globalism, vehicles such as the UN are ultimately responsible for being peacemakers, rather than Christians, who, in the Sermon on the Mount, are exhorted to be blessed for being peacemakers (Matthew 5:9). This is because the Christian, for some authors, has given up her responsibility within her country to lobby for the government to not only "to do justice, to love kindness, and to walk humbly with your God" (Micah 6:8), but to also "to governors as sent by him for the punishment of evildoers and the praise of those who do right" (1 Peter 2:14). With globalism, the latter is given up (using political leaders to punish wrongdoers) while attempting to better complete the former (implementing justice, kindness, and humility). Christian transnationalism, in contrast to globalism however, can accomplish both.

In many regards, internationalism and globalism have some level of overlap. There is an overarching point that fits well with the argument outlined in this book—that some elements of globalism can be useful for the missionary who serves in multiple different country, or the Christian who is advanced in age living in light of impending eternity rather than decades left on earth. However, there are real benefits of patriotism and nationalism

---

27. Anderson, *Chosen Nation*, xii.

28. Claiborne, *The Irresistible Revolution*.

as it extends to supporting ideas to prevent genocide for example. By withdrawing from a national context, the country does not have the ability to speak morality into the international arena.

One author who views this tension between nationalism and transnationalism well is Scottish theologian Doug Gay.[29] He recognizes the current direction of theological treatises that appear to be turning more and more against any concept of nationalism and seek rather to embrace some sort of internationalism or anarchism. Written surrounding the issue of the secession of Scotland, Gay argues that while nationalism can lead to war, colonization, ethnocentrism, and racism, nationalism in and of itself is not inherently racism or imperialist.[30] He asserts that nationalism is, simply put, a desire for self-determination and is key to preventing various forms of imperial aggression. While using Christian theology to justify fair and peaceful nationalism, Gay refutes ideas of "Christian Nationalism" supported by historical voices like the Dutch theologian and politician, Abraham Kuyper.[31] Kuyper's "Christian Nationalism" though explicitly rejects elements of colonialism, preferring instead the idea of trusteeship.[32] For Gay, trusteeship is still problematic because it asserts one set of people over another; yet there are softer edges to Kuyper's proposition as leader of a Western European country at the height of colonial activity around the world. This idea of Christian nationalism in light of a discussion of transnationalism is worth discussing in greater detail in the next section.

Under what circumstances is "Christian Nationalism" useful?

In general, "Christian Nationalism" does more harm than good to the gospel of Jesus Christ. It is a policy alternative to be avoided since it attempts to spread Christianity by the sword, a practice that runs counter to the teachings of Christ, for example, to turn the other cheek (Matthew 5:39). Recalling the definition of nationalism in chapter 2, there is a militaristic component to nationalistic policy. In part, the definition centers on the issue of self-defense, wherein most national constitutions have some level of provision for protecting the population from outside military force.

This work also advocates for the use of military force, where possible, to stop ethnic cleansing and genocide since all people are made in God's image. This is not a simple principle in practice because utilizing military resources

---

29. Gay, *Honey from the Lion.*

30. Gay, *Honey from the Lion.*

31. Gay, *Honey from the Lion.*

32. Joustra, *"Abraham Kuyper's Overseas Manifesto"*

to stop genocide in one part of the world may result in a third global conflagration—a World War III. Thus, the intent to save some will result in the deaths of millions. There are very few easy decisions for world leaders, which serves as another reason to pray for leadership (1 Timothy 2:2).

There is another situation wherein Christian nationalism has its uses. Take, for example, any given society. Without Christian influence, many activities and practices that run counter to any moral teaching may run rampant since there are no checks on behavior. Some Christians may argue that since their kingdom is not of this world, they should separate themselves in order to protect the community. This separation undercuts Christ's admonition to make disciples of all nations in Matthew 28. Thus, there should be some level of Christian witness in the public sphere.

The same logic holds for the international community. Where there are rules and law in the international sphere, norms are created against unbiblical practices like genocide and ethnic conflict. Since human beings are sinful, there is no way to stop all evil practices, but developments in international law can lead to justice.[33] Many Christians and others have built a robust framework of protection since the end of World War II in 1945. However, there are dangers in 2020 such that world order is fraying. To paraphrase the American geo-strategist, Robert Kagan, the jungle is growing back.[34]

When the "jungle grows back" it invites recalcitrant actions by some countries like annexing territory, or allowing the use of chemical or nuclear weapons. The political scientist, John Mearsheimer, also argues that where numerous great powers compete against each other, there are explicit dangers to the security of the world when the system loses its balance of power.[35] In 2020, therefore, some form of Christian nationalism has its uses in that it can uphold the international system built by Christians and others to safeguard certain rights and liberties for all human beings in the world laid out in the UN Charter. Undergirding support for human rights protections is international law and organizations, but also the reserve power of NATO countries. Additionally, a rules-based international order helps different countries understand what is acceptable and what is not when dealing with human beings. In some senses, a form of Christian nationalism preserves this order. Losing it could be very detrimental to the state of world affairs, and the relative peace that has been enjoyed since 1945 measured in terms of reduced numbers of wars and battle deaths.[36]

33. Duerr, "*Evil Empire and Axis of Evil*," 232.

34. Kagan, *The Jungle Grows Back*.

35. Mearsheimer, *The Tragedy of Great Power Politics*.

36. Goldstein, *Winning the War on War*.

Impact on Policy?

Thus far, the discussion of transnationalism has been very ethereal—broadly philosophical in some areas, and engaging in a discussion of international balance of power politics in others. But what impact does this discussion have on policy within countries? If Christians have a transnational relationship with other Christians across the world, how should the average follower of Christ act? The question is a difficult one because it has a different interpretation depending on where one is stationed in the world. However, the answer has a number of broad similarities and differences across the world, regardless of location. A Christian has a much better chance of lobbying his or her government in a country with a large majority Christian population, vis-à-vis a country with a very small Christian minority; the Christian population of Iraq, for example, has according to the historian Sean McMeekin, "mostly tried to keep their heads down and avoid the crossfire" between larger sects within the country.[37] Much depends on one's view of government: should the government be responsible for helping other Christians across the world? It depends on the trajectory of the people in the country, so as to ascertain the political strength of the Christian population, and, as a more baseline question: whether there are any Christians or not.

Outside of the government, every Christian should, within reason, do his/her best to support the global church, especially where there is a great need—whether it be from persecution, economic hardship, or supporting orphans and widows.[38] But, the Christian can also work under, within reason, the government, if it is mobilized to do things advocated in Scripture. Christians should seriously examine the commandment to not murder (Exodus 20:13). Obviously, a rudimentary definition of murder involves the meditated killing of one human being by another. But, what are the implications if one person witnesses the meditated killing of another but does nothing to stop the murder? It depends on the circumstances; in some cases, the person would be culpable for not stopping the murder; in other cases, say, a pregnant mother, she would probably be morally excused for not stopping the murder provided that she called the proper authorities. What about this scenario at the international level? Are Christians in Belgium responsible for not intervening to stop the aforementioned genocide in Rwanda in 1994 (noted in chapter 1)? Belgium is a small country that did provide troops to the UN Assistance Mission for Rwanda (UNAMIR),[39] but what about a

---

37. McMeekin, *The Ottoman Endgame*, 493.

38. Moreau, Corwin, and McGee, *Introducing World Missions*, 14.

39. Dallaire, *Shake Hands with the Devil*, xiv.

hegemonic superpower with a large number of Christians, like the United States? Are American Christians culpable for not preventing the slaughter of ethnic Tutsis and moderate Hutus in Rwanda? The question is a difficult one to answer, but it is hard to implicate people on the other side of the world. However, at a minimum, transnationalism is a better response than globalism because it notes that importance of personal responsibility under a national government, rather than a reliance on a relatively weak international organization like the UN, which tried to stifle the conflict in Rwanda. Where there is rampant bloodshed, Christians should work to stop the suffering of people in different parts of the world.[40]

Switching to another angle in the discussion, globalization has a lot of common ground with the subject of transnationalism. With regard to globalization, Christianity has been prepared for the twenty-first century, even in the first.[41] A global, transnational church is one that responds well to globalization. The gospel has already penetrated the hearts of hundreds of millions of people throughout the world across myriad different ethnic, historical, linguistic, and social backgrounds.

Often the layperson will assume a level of homogeneity within countries or entire regions of the world. The terms, this "Islamic country," or that "communist country" are often used to describe a given polity. Yet, countries can change. And, states are typically quite heterogeneous.[42] With the exception of very few countries in the world, most have significant ethnic diversity, as well as identity or linguistic diversity. There are no Muslim countries, only Muslim-majority countries. Christians should be attuned to this nuance. The ability to help share the burdens of persecution with fellow believers in Iran, North Korea, or South Sudan is something that many believers argue is commanded biblically.[43] The same logic of transnationalism as noted earlier in the Rwandan genocide example is applicable here.

A discussion of transnationalism, especially after the examination of the Book of Acts in the opening section of this chapter, is apt because it demonstrates the fluidity of change in a society. After the timeline denoted in Acts (especially Acts 8), whole countries soon became predominantly Christian. Ethiopia, as an example, became one of the first predominantly Christian countries in the world.

In many respects, the world is easier to discuss when large groups are discussed. The American political scientist, Samuel Huntington describes

---

40. Hertzke, *Freeing God's Children.*

41. Jenkins, *The Next Christendom.*

42. Ker-Lindsay, *The Foreign Policy of Counter Secession,* 5.

43. Hertzke, *Freeing God's Children,* 41–72.

the concept of a "clash of civilizations" as a major point of conflict in the post-Cold War era.[44] In observing nine civilizations in the world, several are centered on a particular religious grouping: Islamic, Buddhist, Orthodox, and Hindu civilizations exist.[45] The terminology is only useful to talk in generality. But where Huntington has been critiqued, among other places, is his overgeneralization of a single, monolithic civilization. Predominantly Islamic, or predominantly Catholic, is a better way to phrase references to various countries across the world.

For example, to go back to the discussion of Acts, there was a time when countries like Libya and Turkey were predominantly Christian. But, societies change. Both Libya and Turkey are predominantly Muslim today. To cite another example, South Korea now has a large Christian population in excess of one-third of the population, which was merely a fraction of one percent in 1900. Likewise, Nigeria was largely animist in its beliefs in 1900; today, it is almost 50 percent Christian.[46] Concomitantly, Nigeria's population has also increased dramatically as the percentage of Christians has also grown—a trend that is also evident in several countries throughout Sub-Saharan Africa.[47] Forecasting ahead, Nigeria will probably look quite differently in 2100 as well, with projections that Nigeria will overtake numerous countries to plausibly become the second most populous country in the world.

There are also dangers of assuming an explicitly Christian (Protestant) country; although as the late-political scientist Samuel Huntington has argued, there may be a cultural Christian core.[48] In the United States, for example, there is an ongoing debate as to whether or not the country is a "Christian nation." Wayne Grudem makes the following argument here in his book, *Politics according to the Bible*. He asks nine different, more specific iterations of the question: Is the United States a Christian nation? For the first five questions, he answers in the affirmative. These include: "1) is Christian teaching the primary religious system that influenced the founding of the United States, 2) Were the majority of the Founding Fathers of the United States Christians who generally believed in the truth of the Bible, 3) Is Christianity (of various sorts) the largest religion in the United States, 4) Did Christian beliefs provide the intellectual background

44. Huntington, "*The Clash of Civilizations?*"; Huntington, *The Clash of Civilizations and the Remaking of World Order*.

45. Huntington, *The Clash of Civilizations and the Remaking of World Order*, 26–27

46. Jenkins, *The New Faces of Christianity*.

47. Jenkins, *The Next Christendom*, 83.

48. Huntington, *Who are We?* 59–80.

that led to many of the cultural values still held by Americans today, and 5) was there a Supreme Court decision at one time that affirmed that the United States is a Christian nation."[49] However, Grudem goes on to argue that a negative answer is the best fit for the next four questions: "1) Are a majority of people in the United States Bible-believing, evangelical, born-again Christians, 2) is belief in Christian values the dominant perspective promoted by the United States government, the media, and universities in the United States today, 3) does the United States government promote Christianity as the national religion, and 4) does a person have to profess Christian faith in order to become a US citizen or to have equal rights under the law of the United States."[50] Clearly, this is a complicated subject, but there are pitfalls in terms of identifying one particular country as Christian, rather than noting the transnational nature of Christianity, and the linkages that exist between individual believers across countries, rather than just a majority of people in one country.[51]

In tandem with Grudem's discussion, it is worth pausing to investigate the global implications for saying that the United States is a Christian nation. After all, if the United States is a Christian nation, is it responsible for Hollywood? Is Hollywood, Christian? The answer is complex than one might imagine. Many good, wholesome (and sometimes explicitly Christian) movies come from Hollywood, but so do many movies that could not in any form be considered Christian. The resultant outlook for the rest of the world is to associate parts of Hollywood with Christianity—a point that would probably embarrass most Christians in the United States. Another example is the city of Beirut, the capital city of Lebanon in the Middle East. The country of Lebanon is one of the most heterogeneous states in the world. It even fought a fissiparous conflict from 1975 to 1991.[52] At issue is the role of the Christian—specifically Maronite Catholic—population. While many take the faith seriously, the indication in other parts of Lebanon is that Christianity is intertwined with alcoholism, drug use, sexual promiscuity, and other sins that run counter to Christ. In the "Christian" sector of Beirut, there is significant political and social freedom, but alcohol, drugs, and illicit sexual encounters have been allowed in this part of the city, whereas these activities are banned in other sectors of the city. To more fully discuss this topic, the Maronite Christians of Lebanon have historically been the most successful group economically within the country, so the ability to sell goods is a

---

49. Grudem, *Politics according to the Bible*, 64–65

50. Grudem, *Politics according to the Bible*, 65

51. Clouse, *War*, 85.

52. Najem, *Lebanon*, chapter 2.

factor in enriching some "Christians" within Lebanon.[53] All of this is perhaps not optimal, but expected in a fallen world (Genesis 3) that purports various constitutional freedoms. The only shortcoming is the use of the word, "Christian" to describe the sector of the city.

The reverse situation also has some challenges. For example, the old Chinese axiom, "one more Christian, one less Chinese" is an affront to Chinese followers of Christ. In some respects, this idea has dissipated in China. Indeed, given the popular conceptualization of Chinese statehood as synonymous with Han Chinese ethnicity,[54] there is nothing that prohibits Chinese Christians from fully engaging in the society of China bearing in mind the Ten Commandments to not put any other gods before the Lord, nor to make false idols (Exodus 20). Engaging with the Chinese Communist Party (CCP) is another matter and has significant drawbacks,[55] notably since the CPP has enacted major clampdowns against Christian activities. This policy has gone through some vicissitudes, though, where the CCP allowed for some level of autonomy at times within some provinces, but at other points initiated draconian measures that led to the desecration of churches and the imprisonment of believers.[56] As an example, the journalist David Aikman, provided a nuanced timeline of policy changes in China. His 2003 book, *Jesus in Beijing*, highlights the rapid growth of Christianity within China, noting historic high and low points. The book even dedicates a chapter to named Christians in various vocations from art to literature to academia.[57] Unfortunately, many of the Christians listed in the book were then arrested by the authorities.

Although Christians are a minority in China, an estimated 50–100 million Chinese Christians now reside, and make-up a sizeable portion of the society (according to Aikman, in 2002, there were close to 80 million Christians in China).[58] Some projections even argue that Chinese Christians will number approximately 250 million in the forthcoming years, perhaps as early as 2025.[59] China is not a Christian nation, but the influence of Christians on China is growing, and, if current trends of evangelism hold, will continue to grow in the future. At what point

53. Chua, *World on Fire*, 214.

54. Jacques, *When China Rules the World*, 297.

55. Yun and Hattaway, *The Heavenly Man*, 53.

56. Aikman, *Jesus in Beijing*, 227–244.

57. Aikman, *Jesus in Beijing*, 245–262.

58. Aikman, *Jesus in Beijing*, 7.

59. Chan, *Understanding World Christianity: China*, 188.

should Chinese Christians seek to influence the CCP and initiate wider scale changes within the society?

Therefore, in light of these situations, a Christian sense of transnationalism is important. Christians can seek to influence their own specific governments, while maintaining linkages with one another across the world. The situation is obviously different depending on the size of the Christian population. In some countries like Nigeria, Christians have significant voice; in others, like Pakistan, Christians are a very small minority who usually do not have the ability to overtly influence the actions of Pakistan on the world stage.

Conclusions

Transnationalism plays a key role in a number of different Christian disciplines, namely evangelism and discipleship. Christianity is a global faith and national distinctions are of little, substantive importance. In Acts and Revelation, for example, people from across the world become followers of Christ. Linkages are formed between these people in order to continue making more disciples. Moreover, the whole backdrop of the New Testament is written with the Roman Empire as the global superpower of the day. This has implications because people could move across the empire to trade or visit family without major, overt challenges—of course, this depends on the person with regards to wealth and status within the empire, as well as the ability to maintain security, and pay taxes or fees for the ability to travel.

Perhaps the most interesting section of Scripture on the future of the church is at the end of John 17—in John 17:20–26. Here Jesus personally prays for all future believers. The personal call here is for unity in the church. Yet, the implicit point here is that in churches full of followers of Christ, significant diversity—including diversity of national origin—will exist. Unity must be maintained as best as possible in order for the church to present itself as a representation of Christ to the world. John 17:20–26 reads:

> "20 "I do not ask on behalf of these alone, but for those also who believe in Me through their word; 21 that they may all be one; even as You, Father, are in Me and I in You, that they also may be in Us, so that the world may believe that You sent Me. 22 The glory which You have given Me I have given to them, that they may be one, just as We are one; 23 I in them and You in Me, that they may be perfected in unity, so that the world may know that You sent Me, and loved them, even as You have loved Me. 24 Father, I desire that they also, whom You have

given Me, be with Me where I am, so that they may see My
glory which You have given Me, for You loved Me before the
foundation of the world. 25 "O righteous Father, although the
world has not known You, yet I have known You; and these
have known that You sent Me; 26 and I have made Your name
known to them, and will make it known, so that the love with
which You loved Me may be in them, and I in them."

At this point, it would be tempting to argue that transnationalism is the best
way forward for the believer in Christ. The unity of all believers in John 17 is a
major admonition, but it must be massaged with the idea that Christians can
have an impact on their respective national states and governments. Ignor-
ing the ability to make an impact in one's national state is to ignore Romans
13:1–7 as well as 1 Peter 2:13–14 and 1 Timothy 2:1–2. An appropriate balance should be found. After all, to reiterate the argument in chapter 2, where
a vacuum of power exists in the world, whether domestically or internationally, the Christ follower is inadvertently saying that he/she does not object to
the misuse of power. Where Christians fail to act, non-Christians will act. In
democratic societies this action is often benign given appropriate checks and
balances on power. But, not always, as evidenced by major changes to culture
through legislation; Christians do not necessarily always have to win because
a democracy includes many non-Christians who may purport different views,
but it is important to stand for biblically based values. Furthermore, after the
Christian has communicated a biblical position, the next step is to merely
allow the Holy Spirit to work in the ways that He sees fit.

Especially in the international arena, it is paramount that Christians
stand for a range of different biblical virtues. For example, Christians in the
United States have the power to mobilize the country's tremendous resources for a range of different projects. Followers of Christ in Nigeria have the
ability to influence West Africa as the premier regional power—tangentially
Christians in Nigeria also have the opportunity to counteract the heinous
terroristic actions of Boko Haram (also known as the Islamic State West
African Province—ISWAP). Brazilian Christians can impact politics and
global affairs throughout the world as a growing power with strong linkages
to many parts of the Global South. Christians in South Korea can evangelize
people in North Korea given their shared cultural, linguistic, and ethnic ties
in ways that people from no other country can reach them.

Chapter 7

Conclusion: A Theology of Nationalism

All nations whom You have made shall
come and worship before You, O Lord,

And they shall glorify Your name.

—PSALM 86:9

IN THE ABOVE VERSE, written by King David, the prophecy here is that all
people will one-day worship God. More specifically, all people, from all
countries, will one day worship before the Lord. It is similar to Revelation
7:9 where people of every tribe, tongue, and nation will likewise worship
before the Lamb. Sections of Scripture consistently point followers of Christ
to eternity. Thus, for a Christian wrestling with issues of national identity,
the end goal—heaven—should remain at the forefront of one's mind.

Chapter 7 concludes the book with a discussion of sixteen central points
that are applicable to the lives of followers of Christ. In part, this section re-
caps the different types of nationalism, and describes how Christians should
act upon each subtype of nationalism. Obviously, scenarios and circumstances differ based on the country in question, but all questions come back
to their anchor in the Bible. Patriotism is often preferred to nationalism, but,
depending on the situation, this dichotomy could be reversed. Secession and
Supranationalism are two very different situations, and both are best avoided,
or engaged with some strict limitations. However, what can the believer do if
they find themselves in this position by birth, or marriage, or circumstances
beyond their immediate control? Life is hard to predict. Very few people,

scholars and laypersons alike, saw the fall of the Berlin Wall in 1989 and the dissolution of the Soviet Union in 1991, or 9/11, 2001, or the Covid-19 pandemic outbreak in early 2020. Thus, the principles of Scripture should be used in differing times, situations, and circumstances.

After this discussion of sixteen conclusions, the concluding chapter will then add to the debate over how best to govern people utilizing a biblical lens. The section on unitary and federal states provides some application of how to develop patriotism over nationalism such that no one country becomes too nationalistic to the point of colonialism or hypernationalism— the continuum outlined in chapter 1. Finally, this chapter concludes with a discussion of transnationalism versus globalism. The general move towards greater interdependence leading to globalism has gained momentum since the end of World War II, and really accelerated in the 1980s with the signing of numerous free trade agreements and the further development of the EU, Mercosur, the African Union, and USMCA/NAFTA in particular. In a limited sense, all of these agreements provide important additions to national economies, but the danger is one of outright globalism. Instead, for the follower of Christ, limited Supranationalism alongside transnationalism is the best path forward for Christians.

Sixteen Conclusions

What conclusions can concretely be imparted about the Bible and issues of nationalism and patriotism? In total, in my view, there are sixteen key conclusions stemming from the first six chapters of this book as applied from Scripture to the Christian living in the twenty-first century. Scripture is sufficient, and needs no updating. But, for Christians living in radically different circumstances from the first century church, some application has practical implications for how followers of Christ live today. Each of the sixteen points is discussed elsewhere in the book, but the conclusion provides a place where all of these points can be recapped, and discussed concisely.

First, God is sovereign. He has a plan a purpose for each human being, which typically includes residence in a particular place at a particular time. While every human being can set goals and dreams for their individual life, which may include moving to a more peaceful and prosperous country, Christians should listen to the leading of the Holy Spirit in that work might need to be accomplished in their current situation. God positions people in certain circumstances that only He knows. Perhaps evangelism best takes place amongst one's own people, even in the midst of difficult circumstances.

Second, God has depicted the signposts of the world; in essence, He has demarcated people into different territories. Ever since Genesis 11 when the Tower of Babel was brought down, and the languages were scattered, people have lived in different circumstances. And, in many countries, people reside in different countries based on having a mutually unintelligible language from one's neighbors. Much of Europe is structured in this way. People in Hungary speak Hungarian, people in Slovakia speak Slovak, people in the Czech Republic speak Czech.[1] The lines get murkier in other places; for example, in Nigeria, the official language is English, but Hausa, Igbo, and Yoruba are also widely spoken. Beyond this, there are 19 other widely spoken languages in the country, and this number does not include smaller languages and dialects. Even in a country with relative linguistic homogeneity like the United States, English is the language of government, but Spanish, and many other languages are also utilized depending on one's location. The idea of linguistic demarcation is fluid, as evidenced by the preceding two examples, in that people have always traveled, and that people need to travel to move the gospel from one part of the world to another. It is a step too far to say that God specifically created countries, but God has certainly allowed countries to be used and mobilized. At times in Scripture, the world had vast empires, and at other times, there were clear delineations of countries.

Third, every Christian has a coterminous sense of citizenship—(s) he is at the same time a citizen of a country (or countries) on earth, but also has a heavenly allegiance through faith in Jesus Christ. Virtually every person has an earthly citizenship (technically, some people are in the precarious situation of having no citizenship) to which they belong and call home. No Christian should ever forget their final destination. While life may seem long, upwards of 120 years for a rare few, eternity is much longer. Revelation 7:9–10 says,

> "9 After these things I looked, and behold, a great multitude which no one could count, from every nation and all tribes and peoples and tongues, standing before the throne and before the Lamb, clothed in white robes, and palm branches were in their hands; 10 and they cry out with a loud voice, saying, "Salvation to our God who sits on the throne, and to the Lamb."

The language in the text, at least in this instance, does not segregate Christians based on their earthly allegiances. People from every nation, tribe, and tongue are all present worshipping God as noted in the introduction to this chapter.

---

1. Duerr, *Secessionism and the European Union*.

Fourth, patriotism is the most optimal form of national attachment, and, as argued in this book, if the Christian places first allegiance to God, he or she is free to celebrate his or her unique culture and history. It is also imperative on the Christian to fully investigate his/her background and to provide a full picture—overt attachment to one nationality or ethnic group can proliferate where certain aspects of one's genealogical histories are ignored. Ancestral lineage can become an idol in life that obfuscates their relationship with God. Patriotism is also acceptable biblically only if it is devoid of jingoism and hatred towards other countries and groups—peoples that God lovingly created in His image. A definition of patriotism also requires the society to be "color-blind." Immigrants should be able to move to the country and gain membership if they adopt core constitutional principles. This is not to argue that a government must accept immigrants, or refugees, or asylum seekers, but agreed upon by the people, immigrants must be able to adopt the national identity in a relatively seamless manner and simultaneously contribute to the society.

Fifth, nationalism, in very limited situations, may be an acceptable extension of patriotism. Where military mobilization is deemed beneficial, again, under very limited circumstances, nationalism may be biblically viable. Notably, nationalism is a suitable policy option when one is attacked by an aggressor. Or, if a country chooses to intervene on behalf of a group that has been attacked such that ethnic cleansing and genocide have taken place. Preferably, intervention would take place whilst people are in the midst of being killed, not after all the people have been mercilessly slaughtered. It is too early to preemptively defend people on the basis that they might be killed because this stance can be taken too readily by world leaders as an excuse to biblically justify aggressive military actions.[2] The existence of nuclear weapons changes this calculation to some degree in that a nuclear detonation could eviscerate the entire population of a city instantly, but, since no nuclear weapon has been used since 1945, the assumption should be that no state will use nuclear weapons—if and when another nuclear weapon is every used, this calculation changes immediately.

Sixth, a civic structure of the state is more biblically representative than ethnic nationalism. Although dominant ethnic and linguistic groups tend to, as one would expect, dominate many countries of the world, there are very few archetypal nation-states with a highly homogenous population. In many cases in excess of 75 percent of the population is homogenous ethnically and linguistically, it is important to undercut tension within a country by creating an ethnically inclusive state. The United

---

2. Holmes, "*Response to Preventive War.*"

States Constitution, for example, pays heed only to citizenship, not ethnic background. Even though the United States has been far from perfect, the Constitution glues people towards unity as Americans, rather than as an ethnic group. In this sense, civic nationalism—perhaps better described in light of the definitions in this book as civic patriotism—is more useful because it undercuts the potential for ethnic strife and secessionism. And, since all human beings are created in the image of God, government can better protect all of His image bearers.

Seventh, Christians should raise the concept of transnationalism over globalism. Although some recent Christian critiques of US foreign policy, regarding the Iraq War in particular, are well conceived, the resultant argument towards globalism is faulty (see chapter 6). Instead, transnational linkages between Christians is a more important outcomes because it links believers in Christ across national boundaries. The warning against calling Jesus a White-American is an important realization, but the reaction to this point is not to proffer globalism as a response. Globalism connotes an abrogation of the gospel to secular or non-Christian tenets, whereas transnationalism connects Christians to one another on earth. This unity of Christians will be imperfect, because it is comprised of sinful human beings, but this should not abridge an attempt at connecting people who follow Scripture.

Eighth, where legal, people can certainly access multiple citizenships. If the laws of a given country allow for dual citizenship, then Christians can obtain paperwork that acknowledges affiliation in two or more countries. This is a relatively rare circumstance, but people also move, sometimes to different countries—where the two governments allow for dual citizenship, this could be a benefit for the gospel.[3] By happenstance of birth to parents with different citizenships, a person may be connected to two or more countries. Like the apostle, Paul, Christians should use whatever earthly blessings they have been provided for the advancement of the gospel. If a person happens to possess two or more citizenships, then, as a follower of Christ, he or she should utilize the opportunity of multiple citizenships for the gospel. Or, if a follower of Christ happens to speak multiple languages, or happens to belong to numerous different ethnic groups, then this situation should be used to disseminate the gospel in a culturally sensitive and sophisticated way. God can use anyone to share the gospel, but as many contemporary missions' agencies have recently noted, using nationals to share the gospel is the most effective tool to the growth of vibrant churches in new communities.

Ninth, Christians should obey their governments—this is an admonition under Romans 13:1–7. This may even involve membership in a

---

3. Sider and Knippers, *Toward an Evangelical Public Policy*, 151.

supranational organization if the leaders of the state have viewed it appropriate to join a larger bloc. Christians can advance the position of joining with other countries for specific goals, such as trade, but also understand that this concept is very limited in Scripture. 1 Kings 3 and 5 provide examples, but not requirements. Pooling resources and sovereignty do not have any specific admonitions in Scripture. Nevertheless, where organization exist, and work for the good of the people, there is no need to arbitrarily destroy a supranational group, especially if a Matthew 5:9 model of being a peacemaker is applied.

Tenth, where Supranationalism is utilized, it should be limited. The model of 1 Kings 5 is useful in order for states to engage in trade with other states. The warning of this model is 1 Kings 9, which takes place 20 years after the initial deal by King Solomon of Israel and King Hiram of Tyre in 1 Kings 5. Supranational organizations also have a limited life cycle. As the former British Prime Minister, Lord Palmerston once noted, "Britain has permanent interests, not permanent friends." The idea here is that sinful human beings will fluctuate in their relationships—the same applies to countries. No one country will ever likely maintain a friendship for all time with another country. Countries should seek to be peaceable, but under the realization that circumstances can change. For this core reason, Supranationalism should be questioned regularly where it no longer fits the good governance of the people.

Eleventh, there are very limited areas where governance across borders should be applied. But, governance should be applied nonetheless. If the UN remains an agent of global governance,[4] rather than global government, then it can serve a useful Matthew 5:9 purpose to actively bring peace to conflict zones that have experienced the worst parts of the human experience. Likewise, under the Genesis 1:28 creation mandate, a larger, supranational bloc can help to preserve the environment for future generations. Human beings should remain the center of God's creation, and take dominion over the earth in order to flourish.[5] But, humans should also respect what God has created and not seek to destroy without regard to future generations. These two, sometimes opposing views, need to be balanced so as to allow humans to explore and flourish, whilst also protecting the environment for future generations.

Twelfth, in a related point, international and supranational organizations should do more to protect human rights across the world. Christians, and many other minority groups, are persecuted heavily in parts of the world

---

4. Slaughter, *A New World Order*.

5. Grudem and Asmus, *The Poverty of Nations*.

despite these same countries signing on to the Charter of the United Nations. More must be done to stop the killing of Christians, and, should these nefarious activities continue under a group like the UN, then serious censure should be discussed including a withdrawal of funding.

Thirteenth, secession from an existing state should be a very rare event, and under very specific and limited circumstances;[6] however, Christians and others should be able to protect their family members from genocide or ethnic cleansing. Advocating for war is a subject that is beyond the scope of this book, but should only be engaged in by Christians, again, in very limited and specific circumstances. Moreover, if an existing union is not working, a referendum is an acceptable way to peacefully resolve issues between groups. The Scottish independence referendum of September 2014 provides an apt example of peacefully deciding questions of secession.[7] In response to the desire for the Scottish National Party (and other supporters) to promote the independence of Scotland, the British government (and other supporters) engaged in a campaign to argue for the existence of the United Kingdom of Great Britain and Northern Ireland, including Scotland as a part of the territory. Countries are not bound to offer an independence referendum, but holding a plebiscite is a useful vehicle to vent pressure from an agitated secessionist group, especially one that has a movement based on democratic norms.

Fourteenth, the international community should support the secession of a given territory in the event of ethnic cleansing or genocide (in the event, under point number five, if no country comes to the aid of the persecuted group). Secession is a rare event in world politics, and is generally viewed as legitimate only when looking back in time.[8] If Christians are to love their neighbors, then they should agree that not killing them is an appropriate response. Equally, Christians should stand by idly when people are mercilessly slaughtered by their own governments. Stopping genocide is a difficult act, especially when the government in power presents national sovereignty arguments. Yet, national sovereignty is violated, under the UN's "Responsibility to Protect" mandate in cases of ethnic cleansing. Christians should be at the forefront of protecting the weak and powerless.

Fifteenth, there is no clear biblical case for colonialism. Of course, in the twenty-first century, critiquing colonialism is akin to bashing a defenseless piñata, but the point is worth making for future generations—the history of colonialism is replete with racism, oppression, and exploitation. Even though

6. Buchanan, "Secession"; Buchheit, *Secession*.

7. Duerr, *Secessionism and the European Union*, 77.

8. Buchheit, *Secession*.

Genesis 1:26 grants human beings dominion, or rule, over the earth, there is no implication that human beings have an intrinsic right to take over the territory of other human beings. Missionaries, who in some circumstances, accompanied colonial powers (for example, the Catholic Church and Spanish missionaries to Latin America), did so as part of a mandate to share the gospel. Scripture, however, pushes back against the sentiment to share the gospel via any violent or coercive means. Jesus, in Matthew 26:52–53 warns against advancing the gospel by coercion: "52 Then Jesus said to him, "Put your sword back into its place; for all those who take up the sword shall perish by the sword. 53 Or do you think that I cannot appeal to My Father, and He will at once put at My disposal more than twelve legions of angels?" Although colonialism seems like a form of governance from a bygone era, it is difficult to predict how future generations will want to govern. If Christians find themselves in a colonial world again at some point in the future, since slavery is referenced in the Bible and at all intervening points in history since then, followers of Christ should take no part in colonialism. Nevertheless, in order to meet the needs of people, conversionary missionaries historically played an important role in colonial societies. The political scientist, Robert Woodberry, persuasively shows that the existence of protestant conversionary missionaries is highly statistically correlated with virtuous societal improvements such as literacy, mass printing, education, and newspapers among others.[9] In this case, then, Christians can help people, advocate for people against colonial structures, and make the best of a bad situation bestowed upon them.[10] In some cases, literacy and infrastructure were positive elements of colonialism,[11] noting the disclaimer that colonial governments were always prone to violence and subjugation.

Sixteenth, there is very little evidence for the advancement of hypernationalism in Scripture. Only in very specific cases, pertaining to ancient Israel, is it ever palatable to take territory by nationalistic force. In Joshua, for example, the Israelites are instructed to take the land promised to them by God. The Battle of Jericho was more about displaying the supernatural power of God, than of bloody conquest. No world leader has a mandate from God to violently overtake numerous countries as a means of accumulating power. In fact, the reverse is true. Christians are positioned well to stand against maniacal leaders who seek world domination; followers of Christ, in this sense, can stand up for the weak and afflicted.

9. Woodberry, "The Missionary Roots of Liberal Democracy," 244.

10. Escobar, The New Global Mission, 50.

11. Grudem and Asmus, The Poverty of Nations, 86.

Optimal Governance at the National Level:
Federalism or Unitarism?

As noted in chapter one, most of the 193 countries of the world—replete with UN recognition—are heterogeneous.[12] That is, there is a lot of diversity within virtually every country with ethnic, linguistic, cultural, and/or identity-based differences. Yet, human beings live best when peaceable; human flourishing is most likely when people are at peace. What, then, is the most optimal form of government?

A majority of the countries in the world have a strong, centralized government unit commonly known as a unitary state. In this view, national unity remains paramount, and the stability of the government is not in question. The challenge with the unitary state is that it reduces diversity, and attempts to place people within a narrowly bounded national identity. This view can also be challenged on the grounds that stability seems certain until one or more groups angrily rebel against an overbearing central government that has choked the life out of their culture, language, or identity. Centralized, unitary states can work well, but usually in circumstances when the population is sufficiently homogenous, which, as noted in the above chapter, is actually quite rare in contemporary geopolitics.

The structure of the Kingdom of Israel provides an interesting overview of how a modern heterogeneous state might be organized. Of the twelve tribes of Israel, they were each provided some level of autonomy, and expected to raise men and revenue for the army. In a sense, governance was devolved down to a more local level. It would seem then, especially in light of heterogeneous populations that a federal state might work better. Scripture provides an overview of this type of governance structure in Genesis 49. The groundwork is laid in Genesis 49:1–2, which reads as follows: "1 Then Jacob summoned his sons and said, "Assemble yourselves that I may tell you what will befall you in the days to come. 2 "Gather together and hear, O sons of Jacob; and listen to Israel your father."

At the beginning of Genesis 49, Jacob (also a representation of Israel) lays out the charge to each of his 12 sons, who become the 12 regions, or geographically located tribes, of Israel. Reuben is given the first instructions in Genesis 49:3–4; Simeon and Levi (Genesis 49:5–7); Judah (Genesis 49:8–12); Zebulun (Genesis 49:13); Issachar (Genesis 49:14–15); Dan (Genesis 49:16–18); Gad (Genesis 49:19); Asher (Genesis 49:20); Naphtali (Genesis 49:21); Joseph (Genesis 49:22–26); and Benjamin (Genesis 49:27). After Jacob has addressed each of his 12 sons, Scripture first describes the 12 tribes of Israel

---

12. Ker-Lindsay, *The Foreign Policy of Counter Secession*, 5.

in Genesis 49:28: "All these are the twelve tribes of Israel, and this is what their father said to them when he blessed them. He blessed them, every one with the blessing appropriate to him."

This is not to argue that all unitary states should adopt a federal model immediately. The circumstances must be appropriate to devolve power down to various subnational units. However, in countries where there are difficulties governing a heterogeneous population, a sensible form of federalism can be useful. Of course, devolving power has to be done carefully, otherwise it can exacerbate tensions between groups, and ultimately lead to rebellion and/or secession.[13] Nevertheless, where clear distinctions exist, whether territorial, industrial, or geographic, sensible changes can be enacted to maintain a patriotic identity whilst simultaneously displaying the beauty of God's diverse creation.

Looking at the modern world, federal states abound across the globe. In North America and the Caribbean, federal states include: the United States, Canada, Mexico, and St. Kitts & Nevis; in South America: Brazil, Argentina, and Venezuela; in Europe: Germany, Austria, Belgium, Switzerland, Russia, and Bosnia-Herzegovina; in Africa: Nigeria, Sudan, Ethiopia, Somalia, South Sudan, and Comoros; in Asia: India, Pakistan, Malaysia, Nepal, Iraq, and the United Arab Emirates; in Oceania: Australia and Micronesia.[14] Federations are generally created in countries with larger land mass. These countries are more difficult to govern from a centralized core given the vastness of their territory. Moreover, these types of countries are most likely to have distinct regional differences given the changes to terrain and industry. Nevertheless, not all federations are in large countries. A federal solution is often imposed in countries with largescale cleavages in society as a means of preventing the outbreak of violence and accommodating entrenched differences.

Which structure is more peaceful? Which structure is more successful economically? From this list, many federations are very stable. Throughout the Western Hemisphere, federations help to provide stability for the region. Several federations are not peaceful; in fact, some countries like Iraq, South Sudan, and Somalia are in the midst of fissiparous ethnic conflicts.

Economically, some of the wealthiest countries in the world are also federations. Countries like the United States and Germany are ranked first and fourth in overall gross domestic product.[15] Other federations like Canada, Australia, Belgium, Switzerland, and Austria have very high per

---

13. Bird et al., "*Is Decentralization" Glue" or" Solvent" for National Unity?*"

14. ForumFed.

15. International Monetary Fund.

capita gross domestic product figures. But, several other countries on the list are relatively poor. In sum, the answers to both questions posed at the top of the paragraph have mixed results. Assessing these situation further, some of the most successful, large countries have adopted federalism with very good results. It is also plausible, but not yet verifiable, that other countries have exceeded expectations through the adoption of federalism. For example, might Nigeria have descended into a civil war without some overarching protections of devolved power? This is a difficult question to prove in any concrete sense.

The dichotomy between unitary and federal states also has some practical limitations. There are countries like the United Kingdom that, while technically a unitary state, have devolved some powers. Scotland, Wales, and Northern Ireland, all of which are known constituent countries of the UK, have some additional devolved powers even though London still maintains a very tight grasp on political decisions within the country. Spain, with 17 autonomous communities, is listed by many scholars as a unitary state, but has some trappings of a federal union. Ultimately, the key component here is that human beings can be governed well under a Genesis 49 model of devolution to various subnational units should the need arise.

There are a lot more unitary states that exist in the world. Examining the same questions as above—which structure is more peaceful? which structure is more successful economically?—is a difficult because the outputs differ. Optimally, countries exist where people are at peace, and they can flourish economically. But, life in a fallen world does not promise prosperity. In investigating unitary states, some have done very well in nurturing environments that have allowed the gospel to flourish, and for people to be discipled in God's word.

A final recommendation is that states adopt a federal structure where there are challenges to national unity. This transition should be done carefully to not encourage widespread secessionism. Nor should this transition take place if violence is the likely outcome. On the Sermon on the Mount, Jesus noted that peacemakers are blessed, and will be called sons of God (Matthew 5:9). Enacting a federal structure simply to make a change could cause violence in some cases, so any shift towards a Genesis 49 model of the 12 tribes should be implemented carefully.

Transnationalism? Or, Globalism?

The question of transnationalism and globalism was discussed briefly, earlier in this chapter among the sixteen conclusions. Given the geographic dispersion of the Christian faith across the world, it is a noteworthy point is to consider the rise of globalism, also referred to as post-nationalism and/or non-nationalism. All three of these positions have been purported so as to counter the rise of nationalism, and ultimately its leading to colonialism and hypernationalism. Globalism is not the same as internationalism, which connotes a level of interdependency and shared governance between countries.[16] Globalism refers, instead, to a global identity where borders are much more malleable based on trade. Post-nationalism and non-nationalism are very similar positions. At their core, these terms can be defined as to create a pre-Genesis 11 world again wherein borders do not exist. And, as such, national identity does not exist. A minority of people hold one of these positions on globalism, but this viewpoint could increase in popularity over time. As such, it is important to note that none of these positions has biblical support. Genesis 11 and the tearing down of the Tower of Babel are, in a sense, a decree of a new era wherein national lines have been set.

Internationalism, in a very limited sense, can be supported provided that trade falls under the 1 Kings 5 umbrella, and, if extended beyond two countries, governance over shared issues is the focus for the purposes of dominion, rather than global government. Christians must tread carefully when traversing this ground from national identity to internationalism.

Christians should not adopt holistic positions of globalism and/or internationalism. Globalism, at its furthest extent, reaches towards a one world government—either as unified under the Antichrist, or some form of united Roman Empire.[17] The idea, in theory, is useful for Christians because ultimately Jesus Christ will return and run the world in a one-world government. However, the idea is only viable in helping Christians thinking about that future time. Any other conceptualization of one-world government essentially re-creates a Genesis 11 scenario of human beings sinfully seeking to usurp power that rightfully belongs to God. Of course, as argued earlier, governance across borders, and even very limited global governance can be useful in terms of reducing the risk of war and providing stewardship for the planet. There are areas of policy such as waste in the oceans that require some level of cooperation across the world. But, otherwise, global governance should be strictly limited.

What is useful, however, is transnationalism. Followers of Jesus Christ are not located solely in one country; Christians live in every country on the planet. As a result, Christians should continue to seek transnational

16. Slaughter, *A New World Order*.

17. Lindsay, *The Late Great Planet Earth*, 86; Ankerberg et al., *One World*, 63–66; Swindoll, Walvoord, and Pentecost, *The Road to Armageddon*, 88–90; Jeremiah, *The Coming Economic Armageddon*, 46.

linkages with one another outside of governmental lines. Organizations like Compassion International,[18] for example, link Christians from some parts of the world to help provide tangible physical needs in another part of the world so that the gospel can be disseminated, and young Christians can be discipled in the faith.

Christians must walk a fine line when thinking about transnational identity and the gospel. Transnationalism is very useful because national borders have never limited discipleship and evangelism. However, transnationalism should not be conflated with globalism and/or internationalism and/or post-nationalism or non-nationalism. A sovereign God has placed each Christian within a national context with an ability to reach people in that country, and to serve a particular purpose on earth.

Final Points

After living one's life on earth, followers of Christ must look to what comes next. Human life is temporary, fleeting, and, in Scripture, akin to a vapor or a mist that will blow away quickly in the wind (James 4:14). Hebrews 11:13–16 allows the Christian to view what is ahead, and to think about eternity, rather than the brevity of life on earth:

> "13 All these died in faith, without receiving the promises, but having seen them and having welcomed them from a distance, and having confessed that they were strangers and exiles on the earth. 14 For those who say such things make it clear that they are seeking a country of their own. 15 And indeed if they had been thinking of that country from which they went out, they would have had opportunity to return. 16 But as it is, they desire a better country, that is, a heavenly one. Therefore God is not ashamed to be called their God; for He has prepared a city for them."

National identity is part of the contemporary human experience. If God is sovereign, then He has placed each Christian in a particular location for His specific purposes. National identity, though, is also coterminous with heavenly belonging. A Christian should hold national identity like a prized possession—since it is from God—but in light of the heavenly allegiance, the same Christian should hold this possession with a loose, rather than a firm hand. A good way to visualize this point is to think of holding a valuable, but also fragile material in one's hand. It is important to maintain a sturdy grip so as to not drop the item, but not so robust a

---

18. Compassion International.

grip that the item is prone to damage. One of the reasons for this position here is that Scripture teaches the importance of generations to God. Deuteronomy 7:9, for example, notes that God will keep his covenant to the one thousandth generation. Ultimately, what is important in life is obedience to God. One thousand generations will not likely last within the same country, culture, or ethnic background—God's kingdom encompasses all people across time. Since each person lives within a national context it is an act of obedience to honor one's rulers, but to simultaneously remember the timelessness of God's kingdom.

The Lord may call the Christian to the mission field, and a life away from his or her "homeland." God may also call a Christian to move to another country for work, or a Christian may be forced to flee from their home country due to war or pestilence. National identity should be corralled as a blessing from a sovereign God, but not grasped too tightly; heavenly identity should be at the forefront of the Christian's mind, but not at the expense of the physical and spiritual tasks here on earth.

Bibliography

Aikman, David. *A Man of Faith: The Spiritual Journey of George W. Bush.* Nashville, TN: Thomas Nelson, 2004.

———. *Jesus in Beijing: How Christianity is Transforming China and Changing the Global Balance of Power.* Washington D.C.: Regnery, 2012.

Akin, Daniel L. *1, 2, 3 John: An exegetical and theological exposition of Holy Scripture.* Vol. 38. Nashville, TN: B&H Publishing Group, 2001.

Anderson, Benedict. *Imagined Communities: Reflections on the Origin and Spread of Nationalism.* New York: Verso Books, 2006.

Anderson, Braden P. *Chosen Nation: Scripture, Theopolitics, and the Project of National Identity.* Eugene, OR: Wipf and Stock Publishers, 2012.

Anderson, David A. *Gracism: The Art of Inclusion.* Downers Grove, IL: InterVarsity, 2010.

Anderson, Lisa. "Demystifying the Arab Spring: Parsing the Differences between Tunisia, Egypt, and Libya." *Foreign Affairs.* 90 (2011): 2-7.

Ankerberg, John, et al. *One World: Biblical Prophecy and the New World Order.* Chicago: Moody, 1991.

Archer, Clive. *International Organizations.* 3rd ed. New York, NY: Routledge, 2001.

Augustine, (Saint). *The City of God.* Peabody, MA: Hendrickson, 2009.

Baker, Hunter. *The End of Secularism.* Wheaton, IL: Crossway, 2009.

Bale, Tim. *European Politics: A Comparative Introduction.* New York, NY: Palgrave Macmillan, 2013.

BBC News. "Mercosur suspends Venezuela over trade and human rights." http://www.bbc.com/news/world-latin-america-38181198

Barrett, David B., and Todd M. Johnson. *World Christian Trends, AD 30-AD 2200: Interpreting the Annual Christian Megacensus.* Pasadena, CA: William Carey Library, 2001.

Bartkus, Viva Ona. *The Dynamic of Secession.* Cambridge: Cambridge University Press, 1999.

Bellegarde-Smith, Patrick. *Haiti: The Breached Citadel.* Boulder, CO: Westview, 2004.

Belz, Mindy. *They Say We are Infidels: On the Run from ISIS with Persecuted Christians in the Middle East*. Carol Stream, IL: Tyndale Momentum, 2016.

Bird, Richard M., et al. "Is Decentralization" Glue" or" Solvent" for National Unity?" *Andrew Young School of Policy Studies*, International Studies Program Working Paper 10-03 (2010): 1-41.

Brady, Thomas A. "Phases and Strategies of the Schmalkaldic League: A Perspective after 450 years." *Archiv für Reformationsgeschichte* 74 (1983): 162-181.

Brown, Harold O.J. "The Crusade or Preventive War" in *War: Four Christian Views*, edited by Robert Clouse, 153-68, Winona Lake, IN: BMH, 1986.

Buchanan, Allen. "Secession: The Morality of Political Divorce, from Fort Sumter to Lithuania and Quebec." *Philosophical Review* 102 (1993):622-624.

Buchheit, Lee C. *Secession: The Legitimacy of Self-Determination*. New Haven, CT: Yale University Press, 1978.

Bunce, Valerie. *Subversive Institutions: The Design and the Destruction of Socialism and the State*. Cambridge: Cambridge University Press, 1999.

Byrd, James P. *Sacred Scripture, Sacred War: The Bible and the American Revolution*. New York: Oxford University Press, 2013.

Bush, George Walker. *Decision Points*. New York: Crown, 2010.

Cameron, David. "Prime Minister's Question time" December 16, 2015. http://www.publications.parliament.uk/pa/cm201516/cmhansrd/cm151216/debtext/151216-0001.htm#15121619000005

Carson, Donald A., and Douglas J. Moo. *An Introduction to the New Testament*. Grand Rapids, MI: Zondervan Academic, 2009.

Cha, Victor. *The Impossible State: North Korea, Past and Future*. New York: Random House, 2012.

Chan, Kim-Kwong. *Understanding World Christianity: China*. Minneapolis: Augsburg Fortress, 2019.

Chua, Amy. *World on Fire: How Exporting Free Market Democracy Breeds Ethnic Hatred and Global Instability*. New York: Anchor, 2004.

———. *Political Tribes: Group Instinct and the Fate of Nations*. New York: Penguin, 2018.

Claiborne, Shane. *The Irresistible Revolution: Living as an Ordinary Radical*. Grand Rapids, MI: Zondervan, 2006.

Claiborne, Shane, and Chris Haw. *Jesus for President*. Grand Rapids, MI: Zondervan, 2009.

Clouse, Robert G. *War: Four Christian Views*. Downers Grove, IL: InterVarsity, 1981.

Corsi, Jerome R. *The Late Great USA: The Coming Merger with Mexico and Canada*. New York: Wnd, 2007.

Coyle, James J. *Russia's Border Wars and Frozen Conflicts*. New York: Springer, 2017.

Dallaire, Roméo. *Shake Hands with the Devil: The Failure of Humanity in Rwanda*. Toronto: Vintage Canada, 2009.

Darmanovic, Srdjan. "Montenegro: A miracle in the Balkans?." *Journal of Democracy* 18 (2007): 152-159.

Demick, Barbara. *Nothing to Envy: Ordinary Lives in North Korea*. New York: Spiegel and Grau, 2010.

Department of Homeland Security. "2018 Yearbook of Immigration Statistics." https://www.dhs.gov/sites/default/files/publications/immigration-statistics/yearbook/2018/yearbook_immigration_statistics_2018.pdf

Dion, Stéphane. "Why is secession difficult in well-established democracies? Lessons from Quebec." *British Journal of Political Science* 26 (1996): 269-283.

Donovan, John C., et al. *People, Power, and Politics: An Introduction to Political Science.* 3rd ed. Lanham, MD: Rowman & Littlefield, 1993.

D'Souza, Joseph, and Benedict Rogers. *On the Side of the Angels: Justice, Human Rights, and Kingdom Mission.* Colorado Springs, CO: Authentic, 2007.

Duerr, Glen. "Traversing Borders: Supranationalism, Public Policy and the Framing of Undocumented Immigration in the United States and the United Kingdom," *CEU Political Science Journal: The Graduate Student Review*, 2 (2007): 175-191.

———. "Evil Empire and Axis of Evil: The Evocation of Evil in Political Rhetoric" in *A History of Evil in Popular Culture: What Hannibal Lecter, Stephen King, and Vampires Reveal about America*, Volume 2, edited by Sharon Packer and Judy Pennington, 231-241, Santa Barbara, CA: Praeger/ABC-CLIO, 2014.

———. "Identity, Tradition, Sovereignty: The Transnational Linkages of Radical Nationalist Political Parties in the European Union" in *Digital Media Strategies of the Far Right in Europe and the United States*, edited by Patricia Anne Simpson and Helga Druxes, 105-121, Lanham, MD: Lexington, 2015.

———. *Secessionism and the European Union: The Future of Flanders, Scotland, and Catalonia.* Lanham, MD: Lexington, 2015.

———. "A Proposal for the Future of US counterinsurgency: Military Peace with Economic Incentives and Political Devolution" in *The Future of US Warfare*, edited by Scott N. Romaniuk and Francis Grice, 99-113, Abingdon: Routledge, 2017.

———. "War" in *Violence in American Society: An Encyclopedia of Trends, Problems, and Perspectives, Volume II.*, edited by Chris Richardson, 549-572, Santa Barbara, CA: ABC-CLIO, 2020.

Duignan, Peter. *NATO: Its Past, Present, and Future.* Stanford, CA: Hoover, 2000.

Dunn, James. *East Timor: A Rough Passage to Independence.* Sydney: Longueville, 2003.

Durham, William H. *Scarcity and Survival in Central America: Ecological Origins of the Soccer War.* Stanford, CA: Stanford University Press, 1979.

Eidsmoe, John. *God and Caesar: Biblical Faith and Political Action.* Eugene, OR: Wipf and Stock, 1997.

Escobar, Samuel. *The New Global Mission: The Gospel from Everywhere to Everyone.* Downers Grove, IL: InterVarsity, 2003.

Evans, Richard J. *The Pursuit of Power: Europe 1815-1914.* New York: Penguin, 2016.

Fabey, Michael. *Crashback: The Power Clash between the US and China in the Pacific.* New York: Simon and Schuster, 2017.

Fasulo, Linda M. *An Insider's Guide to the UN.* New Haven, CT: Yale University Press, 2015.

Fazal, Tanisha M. *State Death: The Politics and Geography of Conquest, Occupation, and Annexation.* Princeton, NJ: Princeton University Press, 2011.

Feinberg, John. S. *No One Like Him: The Doctrine of God.* Wheaton, IL: Crossway, 2001.

ForumFed. http://www.forumfed.org/

Freedom House. *Freedom in the World 2019: The Annual Survey of Political Rights and Civil Liberties.* Lanham, MD: Rowman & Littlefield, 2019.

Fried, Johannes (trans. Peter Lewis). *Charlemagne.* Cambridge, MA: Harvard University Press, 2016.

FIFA. "Federation of International Football Associations" www.fifa.org

Garrard-Burnett, Virginia. *Terror in the Land of the Holy Spirit: Guatemala under General Efrain Rios Montt 1982-1983.* Vol. 7. Oxford: Oxford University Press, 2010.

Gatrell, Peter. *The Unsettling of Europe: How Migration Reshaped a Continent.* New York: Basic, 2019.

Gay, Doug. *Honey from the Lion: Christian Theology and the Ethics of Nationalism.* Norwich: SCM, 2013.

Gellner, Ernest. *Nations and Nationalism.* Ithaca, NY: Cornell University Press, 2008.

Gilbert, Mark. *European Integration: A Concise History.* Lanham, MD: Rowman & Littlefield Publishers, 2017.

Giuliano, Elise. *Constructing Grievance: Ethnic Nationalism in Russia's Republics.* Ithaca, NY: Cornell University Press, 2011.

Goldstein, Joshua S. *Winning the War on War: The Decline of Armed Conflict Worldwide.* New York: Penguin, 2011.

Griffiths, Ryan D. *Age of Secession: The International and Domestic Determinants of State Birth.* Cambridge: Cambridge University Press, 2016.

Grudem, Wayne A. *Systematic Theology: An Introduction to Biblical Doctrine.* Grand Rapids, MI: Zondervan Academic, 2009.

———. *Politics according to the Bible.* Grand Rapids, MI: Zondervan, 2010.

Grudem, Wayne, and Barry Asmus. *The Poverty of Nations: A Sustainable Solution.* Wheaton, IL: Crossway, 2013.

Gundry, Robert H. *A Survey of the New Testament*, 4th ed. Grand Rapids, MI: Zondervan, 2003.

Gurr, Ted. *Why Men Rebel?* Princeton, NJ: Princeton University Press, 1970.

Ham, Ken, and A. Charles Ware. *One Race, One Blood: A Biblical Answer to Racism.* Green Forest, AR: New Leaf Publishing Group, 2010.

Hazony, Yoram. *The Virtue of Nationalism.* New York: Basic, 2018.

Hechter, Michael. *Containing Nationalism.* Oxford: Oxford University Press, 2000.

Hertzke, Allen D. *Freeing God's Children: The Unlikely Alliance for Global Human Rights.* Lanham, MD: Rowman & Littlefield, 2004.

Hickey, Donald R. *The War of 1812: A Forgotten Conflict.* Champaign, IL: University of Illinois Press, 2012.

Hill, Andrew E., and John H. Walton. *A Survey of the Old Testament*, 2nd ed. Grand Rapids, MI: Zondervan, 2000.

Hironaka, Ann. *Neverending Wars: The International Community, Weak States, and the Perpetuation of Civil War.* Cambridge, MA: Harvard University Press, 2009.

Hobsbawm, Eric J. *Nations and Nationalism since 1780: Programme, Myth, Reality.* Cambridge: Cambridge University Press, 2012.

Holmes, Arthur. "Just War" in *War: Four Christian Views.*, edited by Robert Clouse, 117-35, Winona Lake, IN: BMH, 1986.

Huntington, Samuel P. "The Clash of Civilizations?" *Foreign Affairs* 72 (1993): 22-49.

———. *The Clash of Civilizations and the Remaking of World Order.* New York: Touchstone, 1996.

———. *Who are We?: The Challenges to America's National Identity.* New York: Simon and Schuster, 2004.

Ignatieff, Michael. *Blood and Belonging: Journeys into the New Nationalism.* New York: Penguin, 1993.

International Monetary Fund. www.imf.org

Jacques, Martin. *When China Rules the World: The End of the Western World and the Birth of a New Global Order*. New York: Penguin, 2009.

Jelen, Ted G. and Clyde Wilcox, eds. *Religion and Politics in Comparative Perspective: The One, the Few, and the Many*. Cambridge: Cambridge University Press, 2002.

Jenkins, Philip. *The Next Christendom: The Coming of Global Christianity*. New York: Oxford University Press, 2002.

———. *The New Faces of Christianity: Believing the Bible in the Global South*. New York: Oxford University Press, 2006.

———. *God's Continent: Christianity, Islam, and Europe's Religious Crisis*. New York: Oxford University Press, 2007.

Jeremiah, David. *What in the World is Going On?: 10 Prophetic Clues You Cannot Afford to Ignore*. Nashville, TN: Thomas Nelson, 2008.

———. *The Coming Economic Armageddon: What Bible Prophecy Warns about the New Global Economy*. New York: FaithWords, 2010.

———. *Agents of Babylon: What the Prophecies of Daniel Tell Us about the End of Days*. Carol Stream, IL: Tyndale, 2015.

———. *The Book of Signs: 31 Undeniable Prophecies of the Apocalypse*. Nashville, TN: Thomas Nelson, 2019.

Johnson-Sirleaf, Ellen, and Robin Miles. *This Child will be Great: Memoir of a Remarkable Life by Africa's First Woman President*. New York: Harper, 2009.

Jolliffe, Jill. *East Timor: Nationalism and Colonialism*. Brisbane: University of Queensland Press, 1978.

Joustra, Robert. J, "Abraham Kuyper among the Nations" *Politics & Religion*. 11 (2018): 146-168.

Joustra, Robert. J. "Abraham Kuyper's Overseas Manifesto" *Providence Magazine*. May 6, 2020. https://providencemag.com/2020/05/abraham-kuyper-overseas-manifesto-foreign-policy-calvinism-amsterdam-school/

Kagan, Robert. *Of Paradise and Power: America and Europe in the New World Order*. New York: Vintage, 2004.

———. *The Jungle Grows Back: America and our Imperiled World*. New York: Knopf, 2018.

Kaplan, Seth. "The Remarkable Story of Somaliland." *Journal of Democracy* 19 (2008): 143-157.

Kasparov, Garry. *Winter is Coming: Why Vladimir Putin and the Enemies of the Free World Must be Stopped*. New York: Public Affairs, 2015.

Kaufman, Stuart J. *Modern Hatreds: The Symbolic Politics of Ethnic War*. Ithaca, NY: Cornell University Press, 2001.

Keohane, Robert and Joseph Nye. *Transnational Relations and World Politics*. Cambridge, MA: Harvard University Press, 1971.

Ker-Lindsay, James. *The Foreign Policy of Counter Secession: Preventing the Recognition of Contested States*. Oxford: Oxford University Press, 2012.

Kim, Robert. "Jerusalem of the East: The American Christians of Pyongyang, 1895-1942" July 13, 2016. https://providencemag.com/2016/07/jerusalem-east-american-christians-pyongyang/.

King, Charles. *Extreme Politics: Nationalism, Violence, and the End of Eastern Europe*. Oxford: Oxford University Press, 2010.

Kuyper, Abraham. *Wisdom and wonder: Common Grace in Science and Art*. Grand Rapids, MI: Christian's Library, 2011.

Kuyper, Abraham, et al. *Our Program: A Christian Political Manifesto*. Bellingham, WA: Lexham, 2015.

Ladd, George Eldon. *A Theology of the New Testament*. Grand Rapids, MI: Eerdmans, 1993.

Lasserre, Jean. *War and the Gospel*. London: James Clarke & Co., 1962.

Letham, Robert. *The Holy Trinity: In Scripture, History, Theology, and Worship*. Phillipsburg, NJ: P&R, 2004.

MacArthur, John, and Richard Mayhue, eds. *Biblical Doctrine: A Systematic Summary of Bible Truth*. Wheaton, IL: Crossway, 2017.

MacGregor, Neil. *Germany: Memories of a Nation*. New York: Vintage, 2014.

Maier, Pauline. *American Scripture: Making the Declaration of Independence*. New York: Vintage, 2012.

Marsh, William M. *Martin Luther on Reading the Bible as Christian Scripture: The Messiah in Luther's Biblical Hermeneutic and Theology*. Eugene, OR: Wipf and Stock, 2017.

Marshall, Tim. *Prisoners of Geography: Ten Maps that Explain Everything about the World*. Vol. 1. New York: Simon and Schuster, 2016.

———. *A Flag Worth Dying for: The Power and Politics of National Symbols*. Vol. 2. New York: Simon and Schuster, 2017.

Martin, Glenn Richards. *Prevailing Worldviews of Western Society since 1500*. Marion, IN: Triangle, 2006.

Martinez, Oscar. *Troublesome Border*. Tucson: University of Arizona Press, 1988.

Massey, Mary Elizabeth. *Refugee Life in the Confederacy*. Baton Rouge: Louisiana State University Press, 1964.

Mazower, Mark. *Dark Continent: Europe's Twentieth Century*. New York: Vintage, 2009.

McCormick, John. *Understanding the European Union: A Concise Introduction*. New York: Palgrave, 2002.

McCullough, Matthew. *The Cross of War: Christian Nationalism and US Expansion in the Spanish-American War*. Madison, WI: University of Wisconsin Press, 2014.

McMeekin, Sean. *The Ottoman Endgame: War, Revolution, and the Making of the Modern Middle East, 1908-1923*. New York: Penguin, 2015.

Mearsheimer, John J. *The Tragedy of Great Power Politics*. New York: WW Norton & Company, 2001.

Mercosur. www.Mercosur.int

Metaxas, Eric. *Amazing Grace: William Wilberforce and the Heroic Campaign to End Slavery*. Grand Rapids: Zondervan, 2007.

———. *Bonhoeffer: Pastor, Martyr, Prophet, Spy*. Nashville: Thomas Nelson, 2011.

———. *Martin Luther: The Man Who Rediscovered God and Changed the World*. New York: Penguin, 2017.

———. *Seven Men: And the Secret of their Greatness*. Nashville: Thomas Nelson, 2013.

Moore, Rebecca. *NATO's New Mission: Projecting Stability in a Post-Cold War World*. Westport, CT: Praeger Security International, 2007.

Moravcsik, Andrew. "Europe, the Second Superpower." *Current History* 109 (2010): 91-98.

Moreau, A. Scott, Gary R. Corwin, and Gary B. McGee. *Introducing World Missions: A Biblical, Historical, and Practical Survey*. Grand Rapids, MI: Baker Academic, 2004.

Mutibwa, Phares Mukasa. *Uganda since Independence: A Story of Unfulfilled Hopes.* Trenton, NJ: Africa World, 1992.

Najem, Tom. *Lebanon: The Politics of a Penetrated Society.* New York: Routledge, 2012.

Neuhaus, Richard. "Our American Babylon" First Things (December 2005). https://www.firstthings.com/article/2005/12/our-american-babylon

Niebuhr, Reinhold. *Christian Realism and Political Problems.* New York: Scribner, 1953.

Nugent, Neill. *The Government and Politics of the European Union.* 6th ed. Durham, NC: Duke University Press, 2006.

Nolan, Cathal J. *The Greenwood Encyclopedia of International Relations.* Vol. M-R. Westport, CT: Greenwood Publishers, 2002.

Nugent, Neill. *The Government and Politics of the European Union.* 6th ed. Durham, NC: Duke University Press, 2006.

Parke, Caleb. "3 million evangelicals march in Brazil: 'Our country belongs to Jesus'" *Fox News.* June 28, 2019. https://www.foxnews.com/faith-values/brazil-evangelicals-jesus-march-millions

Pastor, Robert. *Toward a North American Community: Lessons from the Old World for the New.* Washington D.C.: Peterson Institute, 2001.

————. *The North American Idea: A Vision of a Continental Future.* Oxford: Oxford University Press, 2011.

Pew Forum. "Global Christianity – A Report on the Size and Distribution of the World's Christian Population." December 12, 2011. http://www.pewforum.org/2011/12/19/global-christianity-exec/

Pew Forum. "Arab Spring Adds to Global Restrictions on Religion." June 20, 2013. http://www.pewforum.org/2013/06/20/arab-spring-restrictions-on-religion-findings/#relharass

Pinker, Stephen. *The Better Angels of Our Nature: Why Violence has Declined.* New York: Viking, 2011.

Piper, John. *Let the Nations be Glad!: The Supremacy of God in Missions.* Grand Rapids, MI: Baker Academic, 2010.

Plokhy, Serhii. *The Gates of Europe: A History of Ukraine.* New York: Basic, 2015.

Population Reference Bureau. "International Data." https://www.prb.org/international/

Pray for ISIS. http://prayforisis.com/day-4-evil-plans-used-for-good/

Reid, Thomas R. *The United States of Europe: The New Superpower and the End of American Supremacy.* New York: Penguin, 2004.

Renan, Ernest. "Qu'est-ce qu'une nation?.What is a Nation?» In *Nationalism in Europe,* 54-66. New York: Routledge, 2002.

Rifkin, Jeremy. *The European Dream: How Europe's Vision of the Future is Quietly Eclipsing the American Dream.* New York: John Wiley & Sons, 2004.

Robinson, Geoffrey. *"If you Leave us Here, We Will Die": How Genocide was Stopped in East Timor.* Princeton, NJ: Princeton University Press, 2009.

Rostampour, Maryam, and Marziyeh Amirizadeh. *Captive in Iran: A Remarkable True Story of Hope and Triumph Amid the Horror of Tehran's Brutal Evin Prison.* Carol Stream, IL: Tyndale House, 2013.

Sande, Ken. *The Peace Maker.* Grand Rapids, MI: Baker, 2004.

Schaeffer, Francis. *The Mark of the Christian.* Downers Grove, IL: IVP, 2006.

Shlaim, Avi. *War and Peace in the Middle East: A Concise History.* New York: Penguin, 1995.

Sider, Ronald J., and Diane Knippers, eds. *Toward an Evangelical Public Policy: Political Strategies for the Health of the Nation.* Grand Rapids, MI: Baker, 2005.

Slaughter, Anne-Marie. *A New World Order.* Princeton, NJ: Princeton University Press, 2009.

Sloan, Stanley. *Defense of the West: NATO, the European Union and the Transatlantic Bargain.* Manchester: Manchester University Press, 2016.

Smith, Anthony. *National Identity.* Reno, NV: University of Nevada Press, 1991.

Smith, Mark Caleb, et al. *Rendering to God and Caesar: Critical Readings for American Government.* Salem, WI: Sheffield, 2015.

Steil, Benn. *The Marshall Plan: Dawn of the Cold War.* New York: Simon & Schuster Paperbacks, 2018.

Swindoll, Chuck, John Walvoord, and Dwight Pentecost. *The Road to Armageddon.* Nashville, TN: Word, 1999.

Tombs, Robert. *The English and their History.* London: Penguin UK, 2014.

Trenin, Dmitri. *What is Russia up to in the Middle East?* Medford, MA: Polity, 2017.

Turner, Henry Ashby. *Hitler's Thirty Days to Power: January 1933.* New York: Basic, 1996.

United Nations. *The United Nations Today.* New York: United Nations, 2008.

Verhofstadt, Guy. *Europe's Last Chance: Why the European States Must Form a More Perfect Union.* New York: Basic, 2016.

Willimon, William H. *Acts: Interpretation: A Bible Commentary for Teaching and Preaching.* Westminster: John Knox, 2010.

Weber, Nicholas Aloysius. "Schmalkaldic League" *Catholic Encyclopedia,* Volume 14.

Wilde, Robert. "The Schmalkaldic League: Reformation War" April 19, 2019. https://www.thoughtco.com/schmalkaldic-league-reformation-war-part-1-3861006

Wilson, Peter. *The Thirty Years War: Europe's Tragedy.* Cambridge, MA: Harvard University Press, 2009.

Wood, John R. "Secession: A Comparative Analytical Framework." *Canadian Journal of Political Science* 14, no. 01 (1981): 107-134.

Woodard, Colin. *American Nations: A History of the Eleven Rival Regional Cultures of North America.* New York: Penguin, 2011.

Woodberry, Robert D. "The Missionary Roots of Liberal Democracy." *American Political Science Review* 106 (2012): 244-274.

Yancey, Philip. *Praying with the KGB: A Startling Report from a Shattered Empire.* Portland, OR: Multnomah, 1992.

Young, Robert Andrew. *The Secession of Quebec and the Future of Canada.* Montreal: McGill-Queen's University Press, 1998.

Yun, Brother and Hattaway, Paul. *The Heavenly Man: The Remarkable True Story of Chinese Christian Brother Yun.* Grand Rapids, MI: Monarch, 2010.

Name Index

Subject Index

Scripture Index

Genesis

Exodus

Leviticus

Numbers

Deuteronomy

Joshua